From Essex to
EVERYWHERE
An Airline Pilot's Life

David Willmott

Published by David Willmott
48 Houlgate Way   AXBRIDGE   Somerset   BS26 2BY
Tel. 01934 732171

Printed by Biddles
Kings Lynn Norfolk UK
www.biddles.co.uk

Preface and Acknowledgments

THIS BOOK is primarily about my varied career in aviation, covering forty-eight years, thirty employers and around fifty different types of aircraft. I therefore apologise to any family and friends who may feel I've given them scant mention or have even left them out completely, but had I included everything I could possibly have written about I fear many readers would give up before reaching the end.

Inevitably, most of what follows will resonate with those who have a particular interest in aviation rather more than it will with those who don't, but I hope that, with the help of my wife, Larraine, I have managed to tell a story that will appeal in some way to almost everyone. To this end I have generally tried to avoid including the kind of highly technical detail that could *only* be meaningful to aviation people, whilst at the same time I have attempted to explain certain aeronautical facts and concepts in ways that I hope will make them comprehensible to all. For that reason, some of these explanations may seem rather unnecessary or over-simplified if you happen to know a bit about flying, but I hope this won't detract from your enjoyment.

Of course, I am extremely grateful to Larraine for all the work she has done to turn my original set of rather vague and disorganised notes into this book; fortunately, she is aviation-savvy herself, so when necessary she has subjected me (and Google) to some serious inter-rogation to make sure, as far as possible, that any factual details are correct; however, if you find anything that does not seem quite right then please put it down to my increasing age and the inevitable vagaries of memory when trying to recall events from years past.

Sadly, I never carried a camera with me during my career, so I am very grateful to **Tony Eastwood** of TAHS (The Aviation Hobby Shop), **Brian Pickering**, of Military Air Pictures (MAP) and **David Welch**, all of whom have agreed that I can use pictures they have supplied. Any photos shown without a credit are ones that have come into my possession from various sources that I cannot recall and therefore am unable to acknowledge but which are still greatly appreciated.

David Willmott

January 2015

This book is dedicated to all the friends, family and fellow fliers who have contributed to my wonderful store of memories.

Any profits I may happen to make from sales of this first and, in all likelihood, only edition of this book will be donated to the Air Pilots Benevolent Fund, a charity arm of the Honourable Company of Air Pilots, formerly known as GAPAN (The Guild of Air Pilots and Air Navigators).

David Willmott
January 2015

Some notes on language and punctuation

As you might expect, this book contains a great many alphanumeric references to aircraft types such as the DC6, the DC8, the MD83 and the Boeing 720B, and many of these references are in the plural. To avoid any confusion, apostrophes are used to indicate plurals of these alphanumeric designations, for example DC8's, MD83's and Boeing 720B's. The use of an apostrophe in such cases clearly separates the numbers and letters of the aircraft type designation from the following "s", and as I understand this use of the non-possessive apostrophe is an accepted convention I hope this will be helpful.

Whilst talking about plurals, it may also be worth mentioning that the word "aircraft" in this book can mean both the singular and the plural; in other words, I do not subscribe to the current trend of saying "aircrafts" when referring to more than one.

Finally, wherever I may have referred to a general "he" or "him" and not "he or she" or "him or her", this will reflect the fact that in the context to which I refer (for example, a particular company) there were *no* female flight deck crew members to take into consideration anyway, and it would therefore be misleading to imply otherwise. Towards the end of my career I did fly with some very good female co-pilots, but for most of it the flight deck was very much a masculine zone.

Prologue

I REACHED FORWARD and tapped the fuel gauges with my finger. This was not a modern "glass cockpit" aircraft, with highly sophisticated electronic displays presented on video screens, but one that relied entirely on electro-mechanical instruments, with needles that were often slow to react.

The co-pilot, with an anxious look on his face, was busy calculating, from the "fuel used" readouts, how much fuel we probably had left in the tanks, hoping his figures would more or less agree with the fuel gauge readings. We had already been airborne some four-and-a-half hours on the final leg of a nine-day delivery trip, bringing an old HS748 50-seater turboprop airliner from New Zealand to the UK. After an overnight stop in Corfu we had decided to take off well before dawn (0420 GMT, 0620 local time) with our fuel tanks completely full, giving the aircraft the ability to remain airborne for some seven hours or so, subject to suitable altitude clearances enabling the engines to work at their maximum efficiency. It was our intention to make a refuelling stop somewhere in the middle of France before carrying on to our ultimate destination of Southend Airport, in Essex, but the weather forecasts for such airfields as Lyons and Tours were not encouraging, with mist or low cloud just within our visibility limits for landing. We just hoped they would improve a bit during the morning.

Our aircraft, with only us two pilots and its owner on board, had climbed out of Corfu in the dark, dodging a few thunderstorms. We had then routed via Nice at an altitude of 16,000 feet, but as the sun came up we could see that the ground below was completely obscured. We listened out to the various French airfield weather reports and forecasts, and were concerned to hear that there was now a blanket of fog covering virtually the whole of France. However, luck had come to our aid in the form of a thirty-knot tailwind to speed us northwards, and this, along with the full tanks of fuel we'd been able to lift out of Corfu, had given us the option of continuing towards the Channel coast, where we could land, if needed, to pick up some more fuel at an airport such as Le Touquet or Calais.

Continued . . .

After nearly five hours of flying we contacted Le Touquet and were given the good news that the visibility there was improving. We had been rerouted several times by French air traffic control, and had therefore used a little more fuel than we might otherwise have done, but when we were about fifty miles south of Le Touquet we heard on the UK South aviation weather report that Southend, Stansted and Ostend (Belgium) were now all within our landing limits.

After a quick check on our fuel situation I decided we could continue to Southend, as we had enough fuel to hold for a while and then divert to Stansted if necessary. The cloud-base at Southend was 400ft with improving visibility of two miles underneath; that was OK for us, as we were allowed to descend to 200ft using the instrument landing system (ILS) before deciding whether we could see the runway well enough to make a safe landing. The only problem was that there was a light wind blowing from the north-east, which meant we would have to land with the wind behind us in order to use the ILS in the first place — as at most relatively small airports, the equipment at Southend was designed to handle approaches from only one direction, as landings would usually be made into the prevailing wind coming from the west. With the wind behind us the landing would be just a little bit trickier.

Fortunately, we were given clearance to approach without delay, so we gently descended through the thick layer of grey cloud, constantly checking our instruments to make sure we were coming in not only at the correct rate of descent but also lined up fairly accurately with the centre-line of the runway. The welcome sight of the bright runway lights greeted us as we emerged from the murk, but because of the tailwind our speed across the ground was rather faster than it would normally be just before landing, and I had to put the aircraft down quite firmly to avoid taking up rather more runway length than was comfortable. It wasn't the smoothest landing of my long career, but in circumstances that are less than ideal it is sometimes necessary to sacrifice a bit of finesse in order to keep everything safe and sensible.

We were on the ground at 1035 GMT, having been airborne for some six hours and fifteen minutes, and so it was that at the age of sixty-six, just a couple of months short of my sixty-seventh birthday, and having retired from commercial flying nearly two years previously, I completed the longest flight I had ever done on an HS748, an aircraft type designed for short hops of just an hour or two. I was pretty certain that I would never fly a 748 or anything else of similar size again, and it was therefore very appropriate that I was back at Southend Airport, where my career in aviation — a career that had had taken me from Essex to just about Everywhere — had begun so many years before.

Here is my story . . .

Chapter 1

MY PASSION FOR THINGS AERONAUTICAL was probably sparked during the summer of 1943. I was nine years old and living on a farm called Ivy Lodge near Barnstaple in Devon, though this was not my real home. I was an Essex boy from Westcliff-on-Sea, near Southend, but my father, a businessman, had sent my mother and me, along with my aunt and cousin, to the relative safety of North Devon soon after the outbreak of hostilities in 1939.

My memories of those years in Devon are still surprisingly vivid. I can remember all of us sitting clustered round the wireless, listening to speeches by Winston Churchill and all the latest war news. I also remember standing on a hilltop at night, watching in awed silence as the city of Plymouth burned in the distance, casting a vivid orange glow over the southern sky. It was all rather exciting for a child, of course, though I am sure my mother must have been going through agonies of anxiety whenever she heard of any bombing raids on London; my father was spending the war there, working to keep the family business running.

The family into which I had been born on 1 March, 1934, was what you could call "comfortably off" rather than seriously wealthy. At the age of three I had started at St John's Infant School in Westcliff-on-Sea – I wasn't a child prodigy, it was simply that they had rather good nursery facilities – and my parents had naturally anticipated that I would continue my junior education locally before, with any luck, finding myself a place at Westcliff High School. The war, of course, changed all that, with the result that my junior years were spent at various North Devon village schools and then at the Bluecoat School in Barnstaple. In 1944, I passed my Eleven-Plus exam and thus gained myself that place at Westcliff High School, though it was to be another year before the end of the war allowed my family to return home and me to embark on the next stage of my education.

However, that seminal moment in which a passion for aviation was planted in my youthful soul had come in 1943, when a couple of boys from London came to stay at Ivy Lodge for a summer holiday. They brought with them something that I had never seen before: a model aircraft kit, made by a company called Keil Kraft. Utterly enthralled, I watched them turn a seemingly meaningless jumble of balsa wood into a sleek model aircraft that not only looked beautiful but actually flew with grace and agility. I was smitten, and now I had something in life to aim for: I wanted to be an aeromodeller.

It took me a little while to realise my new ambition, but as things settled down again after the war I was able to start making steady progress towards my goal. During my early teens, I spent all my spare time (once homework was out of the way, of course) and most of my pocket money on building and flying various types of model aircraft. I joined the local model aircraft club and soon became its secretary. Essex in general – and the Southend area in particular – was the perfect environment for such activities. Sometimes my fellow club members and I flew our models from the local golf course, which in those days was not very active. Sometimes, we flew them at our local Southend (Rochford) Airport, particularly on summer mornings when we would rise at dawn to get in some action before the first airline movement was scheduled to depart. And on competition weekends we would often rush off to some disused RAF airfield in Essex or Suffolk – and there were plenty of them then, before many were swallowed up by the post-war building boom. I enjoyed some success in these competitions and even managed to set a few UK model-flying records, but my proudest moment was when I became only the third holder in the world of an FAI International "C" Certificate for duration flights using three different types of models: gliders, engine-powered (diesel or glow-plug), and rubber-powered (i.e. models powered by tautly wound rubber strips).

At sixteen I had to take my General School Certificate exams, which I managed to pass in seven subjects, and I decided, with family approval, to stay in the sixth form at school to study for "A" Levels. I had realised by then, of course, that making model aircraft was a great hobby but no great passport to a well-paid career, so I was faced with the dilemma we all go through as we make that transition from childhood to adulthood: what kind of job did I want to do? The answer seemed simple: as a successful aeromodeller, I clearly had a good grasp of what it takes to produce a successful aircraft (albeit a small-scale one), so it seemed obvious I should transfer my skills from models to full-sized aircraft and become an aircraft designer.

With this in mind, I applied to the Royal Aircraft Establishment at Farnborough to become a Student Apprentice, and if all went well this would lead, eventually, to a degree in aeronautical engineering and a long-term career as an aircraft design engineer. The RAE, recognising my obvious potential, accepted my application, so all I had to do was pass my scheduled "A" Levels, of which the most important would be Pure Mathematics. Everything looked set, just so long as nothing went wrong with my exams.

Unfortunately, however, I was already beginning to find Pure Maths a bit of a struggle, and I was beginning to have some doubts about making the grade. In fact, I even began to consider what I might do if I didn't end up as an aircraft designer after all. If I couldn't design them, I reasoned, perhaps I might enjoy flying them, though as I'd never been in an aircraft, not even as a passenger, I had no idea whether this was something at which I'd be reasonably proficient or not.

Then, during my final sixth-form year, I noticed an advertisement asking for young men who were due to do their National Service to apply for Fleet Air Arm pilot training. National Service was something that I knew I might have to do some day because at that time (the early 1950s), most young men were expected to complete two years of National Service in one of the armed forces. There were exceptions, of course – if I made it into the RAE, for example, my National Service would be deferred until I had completed my apprenticeship – but for most of the nation's young males, two years of compulsory military service were to be enjoyed or endured between leaving school and settling into the more mundane business of earning a living and finding a mate.

Anyway, I replied to the Fleet Air Arm advertisement and was subsequently invited for two days of medical checks, interviews and aptitude tests at RAF Hornchurch. Everything seemed to go well, and I began to think that it wouldn't, after all, be such a disaster if I did fail my Pure Maths. But suddenly my hopes of an exciting alternative career were dashed: the doctor who did my medical had found that I was short-sighted in one eye and thus unsuitable for pilot training. So that was that: even piloting, it seemed, was out of the question for me.

Everything, then, depended on those "A" Level results, but when they came through it was not good news. Yes, I'd passed Physics and Handicraft (which included things like metalwork and technical drawing that would be of use to an aircraft designer), but I had, as I'd feared, failed the Pure Maths exam, which seemed to have put paid to my RAE apprenticeship. However, the RAE were still rather keen to recruit me, and so they gave me a second chance. They told me they would hold a place open for me until I had completed my National Service – which I would now, of course, have to do at the usual time – and they suggested that I should opt to go into the Army where, in the Education Section, I would probably obtain a commission and would have an opportunity to study for and then retake my Pure Maths examination in the hope that I would achieve a pass.

The Army, however, had other ideas. When they looked at my record, with its heavy emphasis on aeromodelling and my expressed desire to pursue a career in aircraft design, they had little hesitation in pointing out the blindingly obvious: you don't want the Army, son, you want the RAF!

Thus it came to pass that in October, 1952, I arrived at RAF Padgate, near Liverpool, as an AC2 recruit and was assigned to a Nissen hut with a number of other raw recruits from various backgrounds. It was at this point that I discovered that I had thus far led a rather sheltered life. Conversation in the hut was richly punc-tuated with words that I had rarely heard, let alone used, and it certainly didn't involve much of the kind of subject matter I had been used to discussing with my aeromodelling friends. As we sat in the grimy hut, huddled around a heating stove that was proving less than equal to its task, I began to feel that I was about to enter the most miserable phase of my life so far. How, I began to wonder, was I going to survive two years of this hell. And with no immediate prospect of retaking my Pure Maths and getting into the RAE, what was I going to do with my life when I eventually returned to civvy street?

Then, very suddenly, the door opened, and a corporal came in. In a loud voice, he announced the purpose of his visit to our miserable quarters: he was looking for volunteers willing to be considered for aircrew training.

It was probably good that I was in such a low mood, for if I hadn't been feeling so desperate I might well have omitted to raise my hand. After all, I already knew there was little chance of my passing the medical test because of my dodgy eye but, feeling as I did, I was willing to grasp at any lifeline that might get me out of that awful hut, even temporarily. I lifted my hand and pointed it skywards. It was undoubtedly one of the best things I ever did.

Very shortly thereafter, I found myself being led over to the office of Squadron Leader JR Mason, the officer in charge of aircrew recruitment. During an impromptu interview, I attempted to convince him that I would make a good pilot, bearing in mind my long-standing acquaintance with matters aeronautical through my aero-modelling activities. He, however, could see another, more immediate way of putting my talents to good use.

Aircraft recognition was (and, I'm sure, still is) an important part of RAF training – pilots who fail to distinguish friendly aircraft from unfriendly ones are unlikely to come top of their squadron popularity poll – and, in those days much of this aircraft recognition training was carried out with the aid of accurate, hand-made scale models. It so happened that RAF Padgate was at that time in urgent need of models of the new V-bombers (the Victor, the Valiant and the Vulcan), and Squadron Leader Mason saw that I could provide the answer to this particular problem.

Thus it was that less than seventy-two hours after bidding my parents a fond farewell I was once again ringing the front doorbell of my home in Westcliff-on-Sea. In the interim, I had been made tempo-rarily rankless (there being no rank structure for model-makers), been given a 48-hour pass with a free rail warrant and been sent home to Westcliff to collect all the tools and materials I would need to complete the task assigned to me. My father, an army veteran of World War I, could hardly believe his eyes when he opened the door to find me standing there on the step. As he glanced nervously up and down the road I realised what he was thinking – I must, he reasoned, have gone AWOL, and the Military Police might well be hot on my trail. It took me a couple of minutes to calm him down and reassure him by explaining exactly what had actually happened during my unexpectedly short absence.

It was good to be home again, if only for one night, and it was certainly hard to tear myself away yet again the next morning, but on returning to Padgate I was pleased to discover that I had been assigned a fairly comfortable, single room with adjoining workshop facilities. Over the next few weeks, I completed production of the Vickers Valiant model and started on the Avro Vulcan, but while I was still working on this second project I was informed that Squadron Leader Mason had arranged a medical appointment for me with an army colonel at Chester Military Hospital.

On the assumption that I would soon be starting my flying training I was asked to seek out another recruit to complete the aircraft models, and I did manage to find an ideal candidate to take over my rather unusual role. But as I set off for my medical appointment in Chester, I was still very doubtful that he would actually take up his new post; if, as I expected, I failed the eyesight test again, I would be returning to the workbench myself, and even though that was certainly an attractive proposition I could hardly expect to spend the entire two years of my National Service commitment making model aeroplanes. What else, I wondered, might the RAF find for me to do?

I passed my basic medical examination at Chester without any trouble, but for that all-important eyesight test I had to travel down to RAF Hornchurch, where I was to be examined once again by the eye specialist who had previously failed me. I steeled myself for the bad news, and was therefore surprised and delighted when he gave me a clean bill of health. There was, though, a simple explanation for the improvement in my vision: my previous examination, for the Fleet Air Arm, had been done when I was still studying hard for my "A" Levels. My eyes had been under great strain from all those hours spent poring over books and working out fiendish maths problems, but now, with the pressure of exams removed, they had returned to normal and were well within the prescribed limits for aircrew. It seemed I was to become a flier after all.

By mid-November, 1952, I had been posted to No. 2 Grading Unit at RAF Kirton-in-Lindsey, in Lincolnshire. This unit was run by

Airwork, a civilian company to which the RAF had outsourced (to use a modern phrase) the task of sorting out new entrants according to their particular skills and talents. My particular intake included both long and short service trainees — the "long" ones were those who had signed up for a career in the RAF, the "short" ones were those doing National Service — who were aiming to qualify as pilots, navigators, air signallers or flight engineers, and the idea of the grading unit was to determine their aptitude so that they could be channelled into the appropriate training course. All of our group were given twelve hours of instruction on Tiger Moths by civilian instructors who were also officers in the RAF Volunteer Reserve, and of just over a hundred trainees only six were deemed sufficiently competent to be sent on their first solo flight, though there were several more who qualified for further pilot training even if they didn't actually fly solo. Fortunately, I was one of that lucky half-dozen who did.

A de Havilland Tiger Moth
Photo: MAP

As any pilot will tell you, flying an aircraft on your own for the first time is an experience that defies description. Even with all my background in aeromodelling, I had never been airborne at all until my first lesson in a Tiger Moth on 27 November, 1952, but less than three weeks later, on one bright, snowy December morning, I donned my usual RAF blue uniform, plus overalls, fur-lined long boots, three pairs of gloves (silk, kid leather and leather gauntlets) and leather helmet, then

In my flying gear: not very elegant, but absolutely essential for winter flying in an open cockpit.

wrapped my trusty old Westcliff High School scarf round my neck, and went out to prove myself as a potential pilot by flying an aircraft all on my own.

I felt what I'm sure every first-soloist feels: the exhilaration of leaving the ground (and so much sooner now that there is just one person on board instead of two); the delight of climbing into the clear, cool air; the shudder of realisation that now you have somehow managed to get the machine airborne you have to deal with the small matter of putting it back down again; the utter relief of feeling the wheels make contact with the ground and the even greater relief of bringing the aircraft safely to a halt. This last bit was extremely important in my case, as there are no brakes on a Tiger Moth — just a metal tail-skid — and the runway on which I was landing was composed of snow-covered grass. Somehow, though, I managed to keep everything under control and completed my first solo without mishap. It was the best Christmas present I'd ever had.

After a short break for the seasonal festivities, the successful Cadet Pilots from my group were transferred by rail and ferryboat to RAF Jurby on the northern side of the Isle of Man, where for the next twelve weeks we would undergo rigorous officer training. As well as the usual "square-bashing", we had to undergo outdoor initiative tests designed to evaluate our merits as leaders of men and potential future officers.

By great good fortune, my bed in our accommodation block was next to that of Cadet Pilot Reg Turner, a native of the Isle of Man. It seemed obvious that his local knowledge would give him something of an advantage in terms of these tests, and so it proved. On one test he and I were teamed up with more than twenty other cadets in a team called Red Squadron, and our mission required us to make our way on foot from a drop-off point on one side of Snaefell, the island's highest mountain, to a hut on the other side that was defended by another cadet group (Blue Squadron), which we were to "capture" within a maximum time-span of forty-eight hours.

The test was certainly no picnic; it was the middle of winter, and our survival skills would undoubtedly be put to the test. As someone who likes his comforts I did not relish the thought of wandering around on a mountain for two days in the depths of winter.

But I had reckoned without the Reg factor. As we climbed out of the vehicles at the drop-off point, I made as if to follow the other members of our group as they set off in the general direction of our objective. Suddenly, I felt a hand on my arm.

"Hang on a minute, Dave," said Reg. "Let them get ahead of us."

I have always liked to get on with things, so I was half-tempted to ignore Reg and follow the others, but something in his expression held me back, and as the others struck off across country, Reg and I stayed close to the road for what seemed like a couple of hours. Then suddenly a Morris Eight car hove into view, and Reg's face broke into a broad grin as it pulled up alongside us: it was his girlfriend, whose name, I regret to say, is lost in the depths of my overburdened memory.

We somehow managed to pile our kit and ourselves into the little car, and within half-an-hour we were sitting in a warm kitchen, drinking tea and looking forward to a relatively comfortable night in Reg's girlfriend's flat. We stayed there until the following afternoon, and then it was back into the little Morris once again to be dropped off within easy walking distance of the Blue Squadron base; in fact, Reg and I were ultimately among the very few members of Red Squadron to reach it without being intercepted by its defenders. It seems no-one in authority ever discovered our subterfuge, or if they did they must have considered it an excellent example of using initiative and available resources, because no mention was ever made of it to us.

Most of the cadets in our intake passed out from the Jurby course with the rank of Acting Pilot Officer at the end of March, 1953, and happily I was among them. In early April, I was posted to No. 5 Basic Flying Training School at RAF Desford, a small grass airfield near Leicester. The training school itself had been set up to cater for four courses of students at a time, with bungalow accommodation for four students per unit, but as the whole National Service system was being

In National Service "mess kit" of battledress and bow tie outside my bungalow at Desford

run down at that time we were actually the last course to be trained at Desford, so we were allocated one bungalow *each*, along with the officer's batman or batwoman who looked after it. We felt very privileged indeed to have someone to keep our accommodation neat and tidy, look after our uniforms and even clean our shoes, as such comfortable quarters and excellent care would be beyond the wildest dreams of most National Servicemen.

We were required to complete an intensive, 75-hour course on the wonderful Chipmunk aircraft, an experience I greatly enjoyed, and it was therefore quite easy for me to make my next important decision about the direction I would take in my future career: whether I could, should or would continue with my Pure Mathematics studies. If I did not, I would be saying a definite goodbye to any chance of a career in aeronautical engineering.

By now, though, I had discovered not only that I preferred the idea of *flying* aircraft rather than designing or building them but also that I had a reasonable aptitude as a pilot, while at the same time I knew that I would probably always struggle slightly with my maths, even if I did manage to get that elusive "A" Level. Farnborough and the RAE therefore faded into the realms of what might have been, while I threw myself with even greater enthusiasm into flying and the other assorted

The de Havilland Chipmunk
Photo: MAP

delights of life at Desford, including playing cricket for the local village team.

However, by the end of June, 1953, my training on "Chippies" had come to an end, Desford was closing down, and I found myself posted to RAF Pershore, in Worcester, where I was to undergo an Advanced Flight Training course on twin-engined Airspeed Oxfords.

Pershore was a more formal RAF station, and there were several other flying training courses running ahead of us. The aircraft themselves were approaching the end of their working lives, but they were good enough for our needs as we got to grips with the skills needed for flying something with two engines instead of just one. In fact, when I look at the Oxford now (there is one in the Imperial War Museum at Duxford), I am amazed to see just how *big* it is. It seems incredible that inexperienced pilots like us were sent off in such substantial machines — particularly as it was in an aircraft of this type that Amy Johnson had made her final, fatal flight in 1941 — but I think we were all much less risk-averse in those days.

Anyway, I soon learnt to fly the Oxford with reasonable proficiency, and I began looking forward to progressing onto something more exciting, but things did not work out as I'd hoped. The government suddenly decided that if it was going to spend lots of money training us young lads to fly aeroplanes it had better make absolutely sure that we were intending to put those skills at the

An Airspeed Oxford
Photo: MAP

disposal of the RAF for a decent period afterwards. Pressure was put on us to sign up for at least four years, and preferably eight. If we did, our flight training would continue as planned; if not, it would come to a premature end. It was as simple as that.

I did consider staying on in the RAF, and if I had been offered a commission on any large aircraft type I might well have signed on the dotted line. The RAF, however, had other ideas: they were adamant that if I wanted to stay on I would have to join a fighter squadron.

I didn't want to fly fighters, as I knew by this time that my ultimate aim in life was to be a civil airline pilot, so I politely informed the RAF that I did not wish to continue my career with them beyond my National Service commitment. As expected, I was taken off flight training, and instead I was posted to a Maintenance Unit at Foulsham in Norfolk, where the RAF managed to keep me busy for a few weeks, before being put to work as a general dogsbody in Air Traffic Control, first at RAF North Weald, in Essex, and later at RAF Waterbeach, near Cambridge. I was fortunate, though, that during these last few weeks of my National Service career I managed to get airborne a few times in a de Havilland Vampire T-11, courtesy of a sympathetic instructor. This was, of course, my first taste of jet-powered flight, but it was something I would not experience again for a very long time.

Chapter 2

HAVING BEEN RELEASED BY THE RAF, I returned to live with my parents at Westcliff-on-Sea and contemplated how I should achieve the next logical step in my flying career: getting my Commercial Pilot's Licence. On the strength of my sixth-form results, which were good enough to indicate that I was not a total dunce, I managed to obtain a grant from our local Education Committee that enabled me to study for my Commercial Pilot's Licence at the John Cass College in London (now part of London University). I was amazed to discover that every Friday afternoon one of the lecturers would lead our little group of trainee pilots round to the local Labour Exchange, where we would draw unemployment pay for the week, based on the premise that we were out-of-work commercial pilots. The fact that we were not yet completely qualified didn't seem to matter.

I had thus joined the hordes of daily train commuters travelling between Southend and Fenchurch Street, and it was during this period that I met not only many new friends but also the young lady – Pam – who was eventually to become my wife. No amount of commuting and studying, however, would get me the flight time I needed for my Commercial Licence, and although our family was far from poor it was clear that our budget would not stretch far enough to cover my needs.

Fortunately, though, my father had some good and generous friends, among them a Northern Ireland businessman who was willing and able to finance me through this vital stage of my developing career. With Southend Airport just down the road and with enough cash behind me to cover both my flight training, in an Auster aircraft, and my flight tests with the MCA (Ministry of Civil Aviation), I made rapid progress towards my goal, and on 19 May, 1955, I passed my Commercial Pilot's Licence flight test in an MCA Chipmunk. For better or worse, I was now a professional pilot.

My commercial licence was issued on 20 May, 1955, and on 5 July I operated my first commercial flight: on behalf of a company called BKS Aviation, I took one passenger from Southend to Leeds (Yeadon)

Auster G-AIGE, owned by Southend Municipal Flying School, on which I did my flight training for my Commercial licence; that's me beside the aircraft, trying (and failing) to look suitably suave.

in a single-engined Taylorcraft. In fact, we had to turn back soon after departure because we ran into thick cloud that neither I nor the aircraft was equipped to cope with, but after we'd waited on the ground for a couple of hours conditions had improved along our whole route, and at the second attempt we made it to Leeds with no further problems. As I landed back at Southend I could not help feeling immensely proud of myself, for at long last I was beginning to earn money as a "proper" commercial pilot, even though I was still confined to single-engined light aircraft operating in reasonably fair weather.

Not long after that first flight I received an enquiry from a man called Roy Stephens who had a charter company at Stapleford Tawney in Essex: would I be available to fly three important passengers from Gatwick to Le Mans for the famous 24-hour car race? I most certainly would be, I told him, and after a check flight in Stephens' Miles Messenger aircraft (G-AJWB) I was despatched to Gatwick to pick up my three VIP passengers. In those days, the main terminal at Gatwick was a round building known as the Beehive, which went out of use long ago but was preserved as an interesting historical relic (as have so many other things that featured in my aviation career).

The trip had been arranged at such short notice that I never even had time to obtain proper aeronautical charts for France, so I had to make do with the only cartographic aids I could get hold of: a good set of road maps. Fortunately, they proved equal to the task, and our trip to Le Mans was uneventful. Sadly, though, one could not say the same about the race itself, for this was the unfortunate year (1955) when a number of spectators were killed as a car left the track and ploughed into a grandstand. Luckily, neither I nor any of my passengers were in the wrong place at the wrong time.

In fact, as we all met up again for the return journey to England, I could see that my passengers had had a very enjoyable time at Le Mans. Just how enjoyable became clearer still when we dropped into Le Touquet for fuel; for safety reasons, I had to disembark my passengers while we filled up with gasoline, and in the process of

The Miles Messenger that I flew to Le Mans on my first overseas trip as a commercial pilot

stepping down from the aircraft wing onto the ground one of them managed to get his legs in a muddle and ended up collapsing in an ungainly heap on the tarmac. Unfortunately, this little incident was witnessed by the Airport Manager, who told me that in France it was not permissible to fly with drunken passengers. We were grounded.

Fortunately, my passengers took all this with good humour, especially as we all ended up in a very pleasant local hotel that had its own casino. The three of them had a good night at the tables, the proceeds of which, if I remember rightly, covered the cost of our enforced night-stop. The final leg home to Gatwick the next day was pleasant and uneventful, and thus my first international charter was successfully completed, albeit a little later than planned.

I then spent a few days flying Army Co-operation flights in Miles Messengers from Stapleford. These flights were to help train ground radar operators, so all I had to do was to fly a prescribed route while the operators on the ground tried to keep track of me; such jobs as these were obviously useful in helping me build up experience, but I was, of course, constantly looking out for a permanent flying job with a proper aviation company.

I was therefore delighted to be offered employment with East Anglian Flying Services, of Ipswich, which later became better known as Channel Airways. The aircraft I was to fly was the Auster, the type on which I had already flown many hours in order to build up enough flight time to qualify for my Commercial Licence. Thus on 25 June, 1955, I travelled up to Ipswich by train, took a taxi to the airport, and there made my first acquaintance with Auster G-AGXP, which was to form the foundation of my regular flying career.

X-Ray Papa and I were to be based at Portsmouth, doing pleasure flight for holiday-makers, so my first task was to fly it down there. The trip itself was uneventful, but on arrival I felt honoured to be met by the Chairman of the company, Squadron Leader Jack Jones, who gave me a quick introductory tour of the company's new base he'd set up at the airfield; it consisted of a small caravan, in which was accommodated a young lady who looked after the office work and administration. The company had also rented a kiosk on Southsea beach to house the sales and marketing side of its operation, in the shape of another young lady, whose job it was to sell tickets to holiday-makers.

That left just one part of the service that had to be covered – transporting said holiday-makers from beach to airport – and I soon discovered that this part of the venture was to be entrusted to me. I was provided with an early-model Volkswagen minibus in which to collect the passengers and drive them to the airport; there I installed them, three at time, in the Auster and gave them either a short sightseeing flight over Portsmouth or, if they were willing to pay a bit more, a longer flight over Southampton to have a look at whichever ocean liners might happen to be in port that day.

Although I was now in regular employment, albeit seasonal, my relatively humble position did not warrant the extravagance of a uniform, nor even so much as a set of epaulets. It was therefore quite common for passengers boarding our minibus at Southsea to assume that I was nothing more than a driver employed solely to convey them to the airport and back, and I'm sure that at least some of them harboured expectations that their flight would be piloted by a reassuringly mature veteran of World War II, who could regale them with exciting tales of dogfights with Messerschmitts or bombing raids on German cities. Indeed, I would often see in their faces a flicker of surprise when they discovered that I was to be their pilot as well as their driver, but none of them changed their minds about getting airborne with me, and they all came back safe, I'm pleased to say.

I had a lot of fun during that summer of 1955. My salary was just £10 a week, but out of that I was able to cover my bed-and-breakfast cost of £2.10s (£2.50 for those of you who never experienced the joys of pounds, shillings and pence), and I was able to run a Riley Treen sports car. I averaged about seven or eight flights a day, including occasional charter flights to such exotic destinations as the Isle of Wight or Shoreham-by-Sea, along with a few flights to Southend for regular aircraft maintenance.

I also achieved the important step of progressing onto a twin-engined commercial aircraft after passing the technical exam and flight test to enable me to fly the de Havilland Rapide, which was introduced in response to a need for something that could carry more

This de Havilland Rapide was the first civilian multi-engine aircraft I flew
Photo: MAP

passengers than the dear old Auster. My training on Oxfords during my National Service days came in very handy, as I found the Rapide quite easy to fly, even though it was rather unusual in having just one pilot's seat up the front, not the two that are found on almost every other aircraft of a similar size and kind. This meant that the instructor on any Rapide training flight had to sit *behind* the trainee, with no immediate access to the controls, so if the trainee did something wrong the only thing the instructor could do was to shout at him in the hope he'd sort things out. Probably because of my Oxford experience, very little shouting (if any) was required in my own case.

I was kept very busy at Portsmouth, but I did manage to fit in a bit of studying, with the result that during that summer I negotiated another major hurdle in any pilot's career: gaining my Instrument Rating. When you first learn to fly an aircraft, it's not entirely different from learning to drive a car, in that you rely a great deal on looking out of the window as a means of ensuring basic truths such as whether you are going in a straight line or turning, whether you are seeing the things you expect to see along your route, and whether there are any obstacles or hazards that you need to worry about. Of course, you do need to refer to the aircraft's instruments for some things – your speed, for example, and confirmation of the compass direction in which you are steering the aircraft – but VFR (Visual Flight Rules) flying is concerned very much with using what's known as "Mark One Eyeball" to orient yourself and the aircraft in relation to the earth beneath you and the skies around and above.

Of course, one's ability to fly visually can only be exercised in what is called VMC – Visual Meteorological Conditions — for even the keenest-eyed human has yet to develop the ability to see through thick clouds, fog and darkness. So as aviation, both military and civil, developed in the twentieth century, mankind had to find ways of enabling pilots to find their way around even when bad weather or darkness meant they could see nothing beyond the cockpit window.

Thus came into being the networks of radio beacons and landing aids that gave pilots the ability not only to know where they were at any point along their route with reasonable accuracy but also to make (in most cases) a safe approach and landing at their chosen destination, even when the weather conditions would have rendered such an attempt foolhardy if relying on eyesight and familiarity alone.

Learning to fly on instruments, therefore, is a vital part of the flying education of anyone who wishes to become a professional pilot, a skill that has to be learned and honed by dint of considerable effort and repeated practice. Modern airliners have integrated electronic instruments that can be displayed together on one screen to give an instant picture of where the aircraft is, where it's going and what it's doing, but in smaller and older aircraft pilots have to repeatedly scan a number of different analogue-type instruments and assimilate the information from each one in order to build up a coherent picture of what is going on at a particular moment.

The amount of mental processing involved is considerable, just as it would be if you were trying to draw a picture of a vase of flowers from a written description instead of just looking at the vase itself. A great deal of theoretical knowledge has to be absorbed, and flying skills have to be polished to a degree of accuracy and consistency that is far higher than that required for simple visual flight. Passing the Instrument Rating test thus really does mark a pilot's transition into the realms of the true professional.

It actually took me a couple of attempts to gain a full pass in my Instrument Rating test, but in those days it was quite common to put in for the test as a means of gaining a bit of extra instrument flying practice. The test fee was £5, which was actually much cheaper, hour-for-hour, than the cost of hiring a twin-engined aircraft to practise on, so failures on these test flights were fairly common, and candidates whose flying was of a reasonable standard but not quite good enough for a full pass could easily come back again a few days later and have another go. Only if the examiner stipulated that they must undergo further flight training before a retest would they need to go to the expense of having further tuition but, fortunately for me, my initial effort was good enough to avoid this eventuality. My second attempt, as I have said, was successful.

The stamping of the Instrument Rating onto my Commercial Pilot's Licence at the Ministry of Aviation's office in the Strand, London, marked the *real* beginning of my career as an airline pilot. I had just 390 hours in my logbook, but with that precious instrument rating I was now in a position to seek out a more interesting and demanding job than doing pleasure flights over the south coast of England. I felt sure I would soon be flying to wild, exciting and exotic places. The world was my oyster, or so I thought.

I wrote letters of application to many airlines and was agreeably surprised to receive an invitation for interview with Air Charter Ltd of London, which was owned by Freddie (later *Sir* Freddie) Laker. At their headquarters in Wigmore Street I was interviewed by the Chief Pilot, Norman Jennings, a tall, imposing gentleman with a pointed ginger beard, who, I believe, had had prior careers as both a policeman and a butler. It seemed he found me just about acceptable, although he commented on my low experience, especially in terms of night-flying, but despite this my appointment was confirmed immediately after the interview. I was to be a Second Officer, on the princely salary of some £850 per year.

I had made the breakthrough! Now I was not just a pilot, I was an *airline* pilot, and it was with barely concealed excitement that I reported to the premises of Messrs Miller, Rayner & Heysham, at Liverpool Street Station, London, to be measured for my first airline uniform. When I collected it some days later I looked proudly at myself in the mirror, and as my eyes looked down at the single gold ring on each black sleeve I really thought that the most difficult part of my career was over. Here I was, just twenty-one years old, and an airline pilot already.

The rest, I thought, should be fairly straightforward. How wrong I was!

My first airline uniform:
Air Charter Ltd

Chapter 3

IT SEEMS AMAZING NOW, but in those days (the 1950s) there were no formal technical training courses for new pilots, as it was felt that any young flyer worth his salt should be able to mug it all up on his own from the manuals. My first major task as an Air Charter pilot was therefore to acquaint myself with a reasonable amount of technical knowledge about the aircraft on which I'd be flying: the Bristol 170, otherwise known as the Bristol Freighter (or sometimes "Bristol Frightener"), in order to pass the technical exam set by the Air Registration Board (ARB).

Now, trying to learn to fly an aircraft by looking at the manual is a bit like trying to learn to swim by reading a book and never going near the water, so even though I applied myself as best I could to the complexities of the aircraft manual I felt less than confident about my chances of passing the very demanding ARB examination. However, there were, as you might expect, certain ways in which one could improve one's chances, one of which was to fit into one's study schedule a visit or two to a delightful elderly gentleman called "Pop" Speller at his home in North Harrow.

There were many wonderful things about visiting Pop. First of all, there was the chance to sit down and chat to Pop himself, and to hear his many reminiscences about the old days of aviation; then there was the chance of seeing, if only for a fleeting moment, one or both of Pop's very attractive daughters, who were, I am sure, the subject of many a young pilot's fantasies. But the most important thing was that Pop's son just happened to be a test pilot for the Air Registration Board, as a result of which Pop was able to provide, on payment of a small sum (and quite legitimately, I hasten to add), copies of previous examination papers to give us aspiring airline pilots some idea of the kind of questions we would ultimately be faced with.

I eventually managed to pass both the ARB exam and a written test on the aircraft's performance, and towards the end of October, 1955, I commenced flying as a supernumerary pilot on the Channel Air Bridge operation out of Southend. This was essentially a car ferry operation: three cars would be carried in the bulbous nose of the aircraft and up to twenty passengers in the noisy rear cabin, flying between Southend and Calais, Ostend or Rotterdam. It might seem strange that people wanted to fly their cars across to Europe, but in those days RORO (roll-on/roll-off) ferry services were in their infancy, and there was not a great deal of difference between the air and sea fares. Of course, flying was much quicker than surface travel, so the idea of putting one's car on an aeroplane to get to the Continent was not so outlandish as it seems today. Calais, for example, was just twenty-eight minutes' flying time from Southend, so the holiday could start a lot quicker than it would after a lengthy sea crossing,

The Bristol 170 (Bristol Freighter)
Photo: TAHS

particularly for anyone living north of the Thames.

Having passed my exams, the only thing I needed to do in order to gain my co-pilot rating was somehow to complete six landings from the right-hand (co-pilot's) seat. Until then I had to fly as a non-essential third pilot, waiting for an empty sector with no cargo or passengers on board so that I could sit in the right-hand seat and attempt to land the aircraft with as little drama as possible. Fortunately, these empty flights came up with reasonable frequency, so that even with my minimal experience and no formal flight training I did somehow manage to pull off six landings to the necessary standard (i.e. without damaging the aircraft, myself or anyone else), and by 6 November, 1955, I was legally qualified to operate as a Bristol Freighter co-pilot on commercial operations.

However, before I'd had a chance to consolidate this on-the-job training Air Charter decided to send me to work in Berlin for a while, so one day in November, 1955, I found myself at Heathrow amongst the passengers boarding a BEA (British European Airways) Airspeed Ambassador aircraft (a type also known as the Elizabethan), in company with an Air Charter Flight Engineer called Jim Hawkins. This was the largest aircraft I had ever been on — in fact, it was my first time in a "proper" airliner — and I was suitably impressed. It was quiet, comfortable and pressurized, a delightful change from the dear old Bristol Freighter on which I had so recently become a legally qualified pilot.

On arrival in Berlin, Jim and I were accommodated at the Schöneberger Hof, a decidedly second-class hotel mainly used by lower-paid staff such as ground mechanics. As a Flight Engineer Jim was also expected to stay at this particular establishment, and as I was travelling with him I found myself there as well. In fact, Jim was quite happy as he had stayed there many times before and had struck up a good friendship with the family who ran the place, but for me it was a new experience and, as it turned out, not a very happy one.

This was the first night I had spent in any major city outside Britain, so I was feeling quite excited at the thought that I would be waking up somewhere new and different. However, when I did awake very early the next morning I found I was no longer alone: a large rat was sitting on my stomach, and my sudden yells of horror brought a couple of staff members rushing to my bedroom door. I expected them to be as shocked as I was, but I soon realised that they found it rather odd that I should be so concerned. After all, the rat hadn't bitten me, so what was I worried about?

Of course, I complained to my employers, and as a result I was told that henceforth I would be staying in the Tusculum Hotel on the Kurfürstendam, where all the company's pilots were normally accommodated at that time. This was an improvement, but later on we would stay in even better quarters at the US Air Force officers' mess at Tempelhof Airport, where no sensible rat would dare show its face.

Anyway, after that first rather disturbing night-stop in Berlin I reported for duty with Jim at Tempelhof Airport, where we met Captain Alan Firman. From Tempelhof we were to fly two return cargo flights to Hanover and one return trip to Hamburg, and not only was this to be the first time I'd ever set foot on a four-engined aircraft – in this case an Avro Tudor IV Super Trader – but it was also my first flight as a crew member on such a beast, and I'd had absolutely *no* prior instruction! Yes, in those days, there really was no legal requirement for co-pilots on cargo flights to have type-ratings, so presumably someone in authority had decided that if a cargo aircraft were to get into trouble it wouldn't matter very much.

Anyway, as I settled myself into the co-pilot's seat I looked urgently around the cockpit in an effort to familiarise myself with the layout. Having four engines instead of two meant there were a lot more dials than I was used to, but I was mainly concerned with locating the control levers for the two most important pieces of equipment that I'd been told I would be expected to operate: the undercarriage and the flaps. By the time we taxied out for take-off I was reasonably confident that I would be able to perform my meagre duties to an acceptable standard.

As we rose from the runway minutes later, I was ready to respond the moment I heard the captain utter the words "Gear up". As he said them I immediately reached forward to yank the gear lever smartly upwards but was amazed to find that my first effort was to no avail. The lever failed to move an inch, and our undercarriage remained stubbornly in the down position.

Now, as you may be aware, in a heavily laden aircraft that has just become airborne it is fairly important to get the wheels up as smartly as possible, since they create considerable drag and can have a significant and often distressing effect on an aircraft's flying qualities if left dangling for too long after take-off. It was thus with an increasing sense of urgency that I struggled vainly for what seemed like an eternity in my efforts to persuade the recalcitrant handle to move upwards. Sweat was breaking out on my forehead; surely this was the kind of simple task that a well-trained monkey could do, so why was I having such trouble?

The mystery was solved with the help of both the captain and the flight engineer, who, in rather urgent tones, revealed the innermost secrets of the Tudor's undercarriage lever. It seemed that Avro, the aircraft's builders, were concerned that said lever might be too easily operated inadvertently, and with this in mind they had designed it so that in order to move it up or down one had to simultaneously press in two buttons situated on either side of the lever, then pull the lever out, move it up or down and then push it back in again. It was a manoeuvre that required not only a reasonable level of manual

G-AGRY, one of Air Charter's Avro Tudors; the car is Freddie Laker's Bentley.
Photo: MAP

dexterity but also, I reckon, a fair bit of practice. How welcome a bit of training would have been *before* setting off on my first four-engined commercial flight!

At least I did get plenty of practice that day, and by the end of it I was beginning to feel that I was making a reasonable contribution to the general conduct of an operation that was later to become known in aviation circles as the "little Berlin airlift". I was, of course, too young to have been involved in the main Berlin Airlift of the late 1940s, during which steady streams of aircraft had carried food and other vital goods to the blockaded Berliners, but in 1952 another flare-up in the Cold War created the need for a smaller but rather similar operation going in the opposite direction that lasted for many years therafter. The Russian and East German authorities had decided not to allow manufactured goods produced in Berlin to be transported out of the city by road or rail, so various UK airlines, including Skyways, Air

Charter and Transair, were brought in to carry them to Hamburg and Hanover. Most crews would do three return flights a day along the two air corridors to Hamburg and Hanover, returning empty to Berlin after each one.

The Tudor, one of those aircraft which had been developed from the basic design of the Lancaster bomber, was originally planned to be Britain's competitor to the American Douglas DC4 and Lockheed Constellation. It was pressurised and had a circular section fuselage – as distinct from the square section of the Avro York, another Lancaster derivative – and it was powered by the latest Rolls Royce Merlin 723 engines with two-stage superchargers, enabling the aircraft to cruise at the (then) relatively high altitude of 15,000 to 20,000 feet. To provide warmth when flying at altitude, Tudors were equipped with Janitrol heaters, devices which burnt aviation gasoline from the aircraft's tanks and passed heated air to the cockpit and cabin through the pressurisation and air-conditioning system. Unfortunately, this arrangement may well have caused the Tudor's ultimate demise as a passenger aircraft, because the loss of two Tudors – *Star Ariel* and *Star Tiger* – in two separate accidents in the so-called Bermuda Triangle had led to their permanent grounding by the Ministry of Civil Aviation.

The exact causes of the two accidents were never determined, but Freddie Laker, a qualified engineer, was convinced that they were due either to structural failure related to pressurisation – something that was later and more famously to affect the ill-fated Comet 1 – or by catastrophic problems associated with the Janitrol heating system. He put his views forward to the Ministry, and was able to persuade them that the aircraft could be safely operated on cargo services provided the pressurisation and heating systems were removed. Freddie thus acquired the whole seventeen-strong Tudor IV fleet for about £10,000 each, renamed them 'Super Traders" and put them to work once again on various cargo operations.

Anyway, the very next day after my first Tudor trip, on 11 October, 1955, I was confronted by another change of aircraft type. This time I was to fly as co-pilot on the other four-engined aircraft derived from the Lancaster that I've mentioned above: the Avro York. I was destined to fly the York for the next few weeks, mainly with a very helpful Training Captain called Mike Graty, and most of our arrivals, especially at Tempelhof through low cloud-bases, were made using GCA (Ground Controlled Approach) procedures. With the benefit of very precise radar, the ground controllers, who were US military personnel, would give us headings and heights to fly, using very clear, direct and positive commands; for instance, if you were told for a second time that you were high on the required glide-path, the very next communication was likely to be a firm "push your aircraft down". In the York, both pilots wore throat-mikes that were held on a fairly tight band around the pilot's neck; these were absolutely essential, as the two inboard Merlin engines were located not far from the front of the aircraft, which made for a very noisy flight deck indeed.

During a GCA, the controller would be talking constantly, so the best way a captain could communicate with his crew to call for a change in power setting or aircraft configuration was in a strange, high-pitched squeal that could be heard over the voice of the controller.

I mention this because after a few weeks of flying with Captain Graty I was then crewed with a rather impatient and bad-tempered Dutch captain. On our first GCA approach to Tempelhof, instead of calling for a power change in the usual manner he simply pointed at the engine gauges, perhaps because he felt it was rather below his dignity to use the necessary high-pitched tones in order to communicate. After checking the other instruments and listening to the con-

An Air Charter Avro York at Tempelhof Airport, Berlin

troller I decided that we were both high and fast, so I started pulling the throttles back. Almost immediately, however, the captain reached out and hit me hard on my left arm, and as I withdrew my now painful limb he took over the throttles himself, applying a considerable power increase but then reducing it seconds later. To this day I do not understand his thinking, nor do I have any idea of why he thought I could somehow read his mind in order to work out his intentions, but at least this was the only time I was ever physically assaulted in an aircraft cockpit.

I returned from Berlin in mid-December, 1955, and then did a few Bristol 170 flights from Southend. However, my next assignment was to be somewhere much more exotic than Berlin, for in early January I found myself aboard an Air Charter York en route from Stansted to Accra, capital of what was then the Gold Coast but is now Ghana. I was about to have my first experience of Africa.

The aircraft I would be flying in West Africa was a smaller version of the Bristol 170 Freighter, known as the Bristol Wayfarer, and this type of aircraft had been used by WAAC (West African Airways Corporation), a subsidiary of BOAC. Unfortunately, in late 1955 a WAAC Wayfarer had had its wings torn off in severe turbulence of the kind sometimes encountered in West Africa, and the (mostly) British expatriate pilots employed by WAAC decided not to fly them again. The aircraft were therefore withdrawn from service.

However, the British Army in West Africa decided that a military role for the Wayfarer could be found — at this time, of course, Gambia, Sierra Leone, the Gold Coast and Nigeria were still British colonies requiring British protection forces — so Freddie Laker duly dispatched to Accra an engineering team with a modification kit, supplied by the Bristol Aeroplane Company, to strengthen the Wayfarer's wing main spar. He also sent two captains and two co-pilots, one of whom was me.

Air Charter had suggested that I would be away from base for about six weeks, but for the whole of January we sat around Accra's Lisbon Hotel and lazed on the local beach (Labadi), waiting for the engineering work to be completed. I was still being paid £850 a year, but the hotel and food in Accra were provided free of charge, and we two co-pilots were paid fifteen shillings a night for expenses. As I didn't then drink alcohol or smoke I was able to save most of these allowances to spend on more important things.

On 2 February, 1956, I flew with Captain Barry Rawlings on a successful Certificate of Airworthiness test flight on Bristol Wayfarer G-AIMA, the first one to be modified with the new wing spar kit; everything went well, and the other Wayfarer, G-AHJD would soon follow her back into the skies.

Most of our subsequent flying (though we didn't actually do very much) was to carry Sir Otway Herbert, General Officer Commanding-in-Chief, West Africa Command, along with his staff, on journeys from Accra to places such as Bathurst (now Banjul) in the Gambia; Lagos, Jos and Kaduna in Nigeria; Freetown in Sierra Leone; and Takoradi, also in Ghana. With no commercial timetable to stick to we could always delay our departures if there was any dodgy weather around; we did have confidence in those upgraded wing spars, but there was no sense in putting them to the ultimate test against a wild West African line squall if we didn't have to.

By the time I returned to the UK in mid-May, travelling on a military charter flight in a Skyways Hermes from Accra to Blackbushe, I had done so little flying in West Africa that I needed to do six take-offs and landings myself to renew my licence so that I could continue flying as a professional pilot; once you're a pilot you have to keep flying regularly, otherwise ratings and licences can easily lapse.

Fortunately, Freddie Laker himself came to my rescue; he leant me his own personal aircraft — a Miles Gemini — in which to do the circuits I needed, so I was soon back in business and keen to do a lot more flying to make up for the rather low number of entries that I'd added to my logbook over the previous few months.

Freddie Laker's Miles Gemini
Photo: MAP

Though I'd not done many flight hours in West Africa I had saved quite a lot of money, and on the strength of this I not only bought a used Jaguar XK120 but also asked Pam if she would do me the honour of becoming my wife; fortunately, she said yes. The wedding would have to wait, however, because by 1 June I was back in Berlin, flying as co-pilot on the Avro York, and I remained there until mid-August before returning to Britain to renew my acquaintance with the Bristol Freighter as I took up flying duties working from Southend on the Channel Air Bridge operation once again.

As well as continuing with the car ferry operations, the Bristol Freighters were now getting some more general cargo work, including carrying cattle and sheep. The sheep would normally be penned using lightweight partitions, with a passageway running along the length of the aircraft on the starboard side, and during flight, a "sheep attendant", normally one of our regular loadmasters, would have to run up and down the aircraft, looking for any sheep that had fallen over and then standing them up again. Sheep were liable to topple over in even the slightest turbulence, and if they were not rescued again they might suffocate in the adjoining sheep's wool, so at the end of a thirty-minute flight, particularly if it was a bit turbulent, the sheep attendant would be utterly exhausted and sweating through his overalls. As those of you of a certain age may recall, in those days there was a very popular television programme called *What's My Line*, chaired by Gilbert Harding, in which a team of celebrities had to guess someone's job based on a brief mime followed by a series of Yes/No questions. I still feel that if one of our loadmasters had gone on the show as an "airborne sheep-stander-upper" he would easily have defeated the team.

In the 1950s, Southend Airport had no instrument landing system, so in low cloud conditions they used a "talk-down" VDF (Voice Direction Finding) approach system, in which the controller would consult a CRDF (Cathode Ray Direction Finder) to determine the location of the approaching aircraft. Pilots would be asked to speak on the radio so that the CRDF could spot them, which normally meant counting slowly from one to five. However, on some Bristol Freighter cattle flights we didn't comply with the usual practice; instead, on receiving the request, "Southend Approach to Golf Victor Romeo, transmit for steer," the response might well be, "Golf Victor Romeo to

Southend Approach: Moo-oo-oo-oo!". Fortunately, our rather pathetic attempt at humour was always taken in good heart by the controllers.

With its bulbous, clam-shell doors at the front of the aircraft, below the flight deck, the Bristol Freighter was not a particularly beautiful aircraft, but it certainly proved its worth as a way of getting cars and other cargo across the Channel. Those huge doors could accommodate large, bulky loads, but on one particular occasion I had cause to silently thank their designer for my continued existence.

We were returning from Calais to Southend on a Channel Air Bridge flight, and as we approached the south Kent coast a red door-warning light suddenly came on. This was followed closely by the arrival through the trapdoor behind my seat of a white-faced loadmaster, who told us that the front doors had opened as far as the backup retaining lock. There was now a visible gap between the doors, through which air was blowing into the aircraft at 160mph, this being our airspeed at the time. We quickly reduced our speed as much as we safely could, and as we were only fifteen minutes from Southend we decided to continue, albeit with fingers tightly crossed. We landed safely, but had those doors opened fully before we were on the ground they would have destroyed both propellers, and we would have found ourselves in an aircraft devoid not only of aerodynamic shape but also of engine power; the only place we would have been going would have been rapidly downwards. The word "relief" is hardly enough to express what we all felt.

Very little in-house training was done in those days, so in November, 1956, I had to return to CAFU (the Civil Aviation Flying Unit) at Stansted to renew my instrument rating in order to remain licensed. After this, I was posted once again to Berlin, because Air Charter were now operating scheduled passenger flights from there on behalf of British European Airways, using a recently-acquired Douglas DC4 aircraft. For the first time in my life I was given, by my employer, a full aircraft technical course and proper flight training, so before I started flying as crew on the DC4 I had passed the Air Registration Board technical exam and had successfully completed the required six take-offs and landings in order to have my licence endorsed with a Group 2 rating on the DC4 that enabled me to fly as a co-pilot. Things were definitely changing for the better as far as pilot training was concerned.

We were based at Berlin's wonderful Tempelhof Airport, a fantastic *art deco* building designed in the 1930s, which even boasted a cantilevered roof over its apron so that aircraft could embark and disembark their passengers under cover. Being the only airport in the post-war American Sector of Berlin it was the only one handling civilian traffic into and out of the western part of the city, and the only airlines permitted to operate flights in and out were Pan American, Air France and BEA. Pan Am and Air France operated their own fleets of DC4s, but BEA, being short of aircraft, had arranged for Transair and Air Charter to operate all its Berlin flights, using DC3 and DC4 aircraft respectively.

I loved the DC4, partly because it was the first aircraft I'd flown that actually had a nose-wheel. I often flew with Captain "Mac" Mackenzie, who was later to become the Operations Director of British Caledonian Airways, and virtually all our flights were along the air corridors to Hanover and Hamburg, requiring very accurate navigation using the fairly rudimentary radio aids available in those days. Straying outside the corridor would have attracted the immediate and unfriendly attention of Soviet fighters, so the incentive to remain on track was strong. Most of the passengers were German-speaking — in fact, many of them were refugees from East Berlin — so Air Charter employed local air stewardesses to look after them, and I'm sure a great many long-held hopes and dreams must have been fulfilled every time we took off from Tempelhof with people heading westwards to freedom.

On 1 December, 1956, Capt MacKenzie and I flew a DC4 from Berlin to Southend for maintenance, and our arrival did not go unnoticed. No aircraft of this size had ever landed at Southend before, so the following day's headline in the local *Southend Standard* was "Giant Skymaster aircraft arrives at Southend". How lucky I was to be flying in the days when a 64-passenger aeroplane could be described as "giant"! Anyway, for the rest of that month (December), I carried on working as a DC4 co-pilot on a new MOD trooping contract, carrying military personnel and their families between Southend, Malta and

An Air Charter DC4
Photo: MAP

Nicosia; this was known as the Cyprair contract, and Air Charter had beaten off strong opposition from other airlines to get it.

After that, in early 1957, I departed with the Chief Pilot of Air Charter, Capt Norman Jennings, on my first trip to Australia, but now I was back in the co-pilot's seat of an Avro Tudor freighter again. Switching from one aircraft type to another completely different one like this was allowed in those days, and although I was fully certificated and rated as a DC4 pilot I had no similar qualifications on the Tudor, nor indeed on the Avro York. Co-pilots on cargo aircraft were still not required to be fully rated on the aircraft they were flying; they only had to do flight tests and written exams if they would be carrying passengers. Presumably no-one had yet thought about the potentially ghastly consequences if the captain of a cargo aircraft had been taken seriously ill in flight.

However, I was actually very happy to go back to the Tudor — tail-wheel and all — because the type of operation in which the aircraft was engaged was far more interesting than what I'd been doing on the DC4. These Tudor trips to Australia would actually start on the night before the aircraft was due to depart, when all the crew — captain, co-pilot, two flight engineers, navigator, radio officer and two loadmasters — would meet at the George Hotel in Bishop's Stortford, enjoy a gently convivial evening of getting to know each other, then stay overnight at the hotel and depart for Stansted after a hearty breakfast.

At the airport a thorough check of the aircraft, equipment, load and paperwork would be made; the aircraft would be in the care of its crew for the next two weeks, and they assumed full responsibility for ensuring that everything was in the best of order before setting off on their journey. The two flight engineers would, understandably, have the most to do at this stage; engines and other components were not terribly reliable in those days, so the more checks carried out before departure the better. Indeed, the main reason for having two flight engineers in the first place was so that one could sort out any serious problems that needed fixing at any of the various stops along the route while the other would be sleeping so that he'd be ready for the next sector. All flight engineers were qualified ground engineers as well, so they all had vast experience of dealing with the many things that could go wrong with a large, piston-engined aircraft flying from one side of the world to the other.

After all the checks had been made, the aircraft would usually depart Stansted mid-morning, and the first stop would normally be at the semi-military airfield at Brindisi in Italy. The flight to Brindisi took six hours in a Tudor, and after arrival most of the crew would go to the very pleasant Mount Joli Hotel. One of the loadmasters, however, would have to stay on the aircraft overnight, as these flights invariably carried sensitive MOD supplies (sometimes including radioactive material) for weapons tests being carried out at Maralinga and Woomera in Australia, which had to be kept under constant guard. After breakfast the next morning the crew would return to the aircraft for the nine-hour flight to RAF Habbaniya, a UK military base in Iraq, and then, after a short night-stop, it would be on to Karachi, then RAF Negombo (in Ceylon, as it then was), followed by Singapore (Kellang Airfield, which is now an amusement park), Djakarta, Darwin and, at last, the final destination, either RAAF Edinburgh Field in Adelaide or RAAF Westbeach at Maralinga.

Short rest-stops were made at most of the airfields en route, but the most memorable ones were definitely at Darwin. In those days Darwin was not well supplied with hotel accommodation, with the result that you could find yourself sharing a room with one of the many itinerant crocodile-hunters who made rich pickings from the local wildlife. These gentlemen kept strange hours and were liable to return rather noisily to the room in the early hours of the morning, having consumed large quantities of beer, so they weren't exactly the perfect room-mates if you needed to be fresh and wide awake in the morning.

If you were lucky, though, you might be invited to stay at the RAAF Officers' Mess; there you would have your own bedroom, built on stilts, but although you didn't need to share your actual sleeping space you would often find yourself accompanied, when using the washing facilities underneath your room, by various examples of the local fauna, though fortunately nothing that would get the aforementioned crocodile-hunters excited.

The aircraft would return to Britain using pretty much the same route, except that as it would be either empty or lightly loaded it could go non-stop from Negombo (Ceylon) to Aden, then next day to Malta and the day after that to Stansted. However, if the aircraft was either on or ahead of schedule by the time it reached Singapore on the return journey the captain would normally authorise a two-day break there, and this was always much appreciated as respite for the crew from an otherwise very tiring schedule.

The whole round trip would comprise 120 hours of flying, mostly during daylight, over twelve or thirteen days, and because this was the maximum flight time allowed each month under CAA regulations the flight deck crew would then have two weeks off. After my first Australia trip on the Tudor I used those two weeks to start studying again at Sir John Cass College in London, this time towards my Senior Commercial Pilot's Licence and my ATPL (Airline Transport Pilot's Licence). I was already looking forward to that magic time in the future when I would move across from the co-pilot's seat on the right-hand side of the aircraft to the captain's one on the left.

I spent the rest of 1957 switching between the DC4 Cyprus trooping contract, the Channel Air Bridge car ferry operation and more time based in Berlin, where I was operating scheduled flights for BEA on the DC4 and cargo trips on the York, the Tudor and the Bristol Freighter. Such variety seems quite amazing now that pilots of large aircraft are usually restricted to operating only one aircraft type, but in those days it was considered quite normal. At least it was impossible to get bored.

During that same year I married Pam, and the local vicar suggested I should wear my airline uniform for the wedding service; it might seem strange today to think of getting married in your work clothes, but I thought it was a good idea, as I felt I'd look much better in my uniform than in a suit (and so did the vicar, I guess). I therefore asked the company if it was OK to do this, just in case they had any objections, little imagining that this simple request would have the effect it did. A message suddenly came through from head office saying yes, I *could* get married in uniform, but that I should also be upgraded from Second to First Officer, which meant an increase in pay and an extra gold bar on my sleeve. I could now get married wearing *two* gold bars instead of a rather puny one, and if I'd had any idea it was that easy to get promoted I might have brought my wedding date forward a bit.

However, on reflection, I decided that this improvement in my pay and rank was really somewhat overdue; at that time, the generally accepted practice in the airline industry was that new co-pilots would be called Second Officers whilst they were under training but as soon as they were cleared to fly as the official co-pilot on the aircraft they should then be upgraded to First Officer rank, with an appropriate increase in pay. Air Charter did things a bit differently, though, and by the time I was promoted to First Officer I had in fact been operating as one for nearly two years. Other young pilots in the company were treated likewise, but at least I had finally got the promotion I deserved, and my salary was now a dizzy £1,250 per annum. My total flying hours had now built up to just under two thousand, and as I had passed both my Senior Commercial and Airline Transport Pilot's Licence technical examinations I was anxious to complete the actual flying hours required for the issue of the Senior Commercial and then eventually of the full ATPL.

Despite the hours I'd accrued, my logbook was still short of night flying hours in command, and I found myself in a kind of chicken-and-egg situation; in order to be able to book any night hours as "pilot-in-command under supervision" in any of the aircraft on which I was currently flying, I would have to be given extra training in order to be allowed to fly the aircraft from the captain's seat, albeit with a training captain beside me. This preliminary training was promised by the company but didn't materialise in time, as I was up against a deadline: like all pilots, I had to complete the flying requirements within one year of passing the relevant licence theory exam, otherwise I'd have to take the exam again.

As the anniversary of my Senior Commercial licence exam was drawing ever nearer I was forced to take drastic — and expensive — action: I hired an Auster aircraft from Southend Flying School so that I could fly round East Anglia in the dark, building up my night hours. By the skin of my teeth I managed to reach the hours I needed for the Senior Commercial licence within the allotted time, but for obvious reasons I was not very pleased that I'd had to spend so much of my own hard-earned cash doing it.

Of course, flying single-engined aircraft at night is not the safest kind of aeronautical activity: after all, if you can't see the ground, what do you do if your engine suddenly stops? Fortunately, the trusty little Auster's engine never missed a beat, though on one memorable flight I did have a generator failure, which plunged all my instruments into darkness and left me with no radio. However, it was a clear, moonlit night, and as I had, as usual, brought along my wife's battery-driven bicycle headlamp, I was able to illuminate the instruments that were still working and thus return safely to Southend.

In November, 1957, I was sent back to Stansted to operate my first transatlantic/transpacific trip on the Tudor. We would be carrying atom bomb components to the test-site at Christmas Island in the Pacific Ocean, and our route took us to Keflavik (Iceland) for our first night-stop, then to Goose Bay (Labrador) for fuel and on to Montreal for our second nightstop. After that we flew into the USAF base at Ellesworth, South Dakota, where we were made particularly welcome, probably because we were "friends" at a time of increasing Cold War tensions. Our next stopover was at Travis Air Force Base near San Francisco, and then we set course on the long over-water flight to Hickam AFB near Honolulu, from where we would be making a short out-and-back flight to our eventual destination, RAF Christmas Island. After landing at Hickam we adjourned to the Reef Hotel on Waikiki beach, and as we would just be doing the short hop to Christmas

Island and back next day the captain suggested we should leave all our luggage in our rooms, as we'd be back by early evening.

Meanwhile, the two flight engineers had decided they would do some light engine servicing while the offload was being done at Christmas Island; they knew the RAF technicians based there would be keen to help, but as an added incentive we took along on the flight a barrel of ice-cream, packed in dry ice, as such luxuries were not normally available in that fairly remote outpost.

We arrived safely at Christmas Island, and during the offload the engineers dropped all four engine oil filters as planned. Numbers one, two and three were fine, but number four filter was definitely not: it was covered with metal shavings, indicating a very imminent engine failure and thus grounding the aircraft. We were therefore stuck on the island until a replacement engine could be air-freighted to us, but of course all our clothes and other bits and pieces were in our suitcases in Honolulu. The captain had to use aircraft funds to buy shorts, sandals and shirts for us from the Christmas Island NAAFI shop, and for the next eleven days we lived under canvas in RAF tents. It was a useful lesson in the ways of aviation: never assume *anything*.

But that wasn't to be the end of it: on the day on which I had originally been scheduled to return to the UK, my wife telephoned the company's office to check whether my flight was on time. Having been assured that all was well, she dutifully cooked a lovely roast lunch and then waited — and waited, and waited — for me to appear. When I failed to do so, she phoned the company again, only to be told that I was still in Christmas Island, literally on the other side of the world. Had I been able to I would have tried to contact her myself, but the only communications systems in Christmas Island were strictly for military use only. I had therefore relied on my employers to let her know where I was, but my trust was obviously misplaced, and my roast lunch therefore ended up in the bin.

Anyway, it would be great to be able to tell you that after having our replacement engine fitted we had a smooth and trouble-free journey home, but unfortunately that is not how it turned out. We duly departed Christmas Island with our newly-installed No. 4 engine, stayed overnight in Honolulu and collected our suitcases, then returned across the Pacific to Travis AFB and onwards across the USA.

When we eventually headed out over the Atlantic we were on a track that would mean night-stops in Bermuda and Santa Maria, in the Azores, where there was a US military base.

On our arrival at Santa Maria, however, we met trouble once again: not mechanical this time but political. Our captain on this trip, a very pleasant chap known as "Pop" Carreras, was originally from Spain, and in his youth he'd been involved in the Spanish Civil War. Although we had landed at a US military base, the runway and other facilities were also used for civilian movements, so there were lots of Portuguese officials around the place. I never quite understood what the problem was, but when these officials inspected our captain's passport we were all suddenly arrested and locked up.

By this time, though, it was late morning, and before long the Portuguese officials decided to go for lunch. In their absence the US Duty Officer came to our rescue: he released us and told us to leave the island as soon as possible, before the Portuguese officials returned. We duly rushed back out to the aircraft and prepared for a very quick departure, but of course we had not had a chance for any food or rest. The prospect of an eight-hour flight to Stansted immediately following a nine-hour one from Bermuda was not attractive, but it was certainly a lot better than the thought of rotting in a Portuguese jail, so we had no choice but to get airborne as quickly as we could, unfed and unrested as we were. We were all very tired and *very* hungry by the time we got back to Stansted, but at least we were all free to carry on our lives as usual. To this day I still don't know exactly why we were locked up, so that little mystery will just have to remain unsolved.

In December, 1957, I became involved in an interesting little exercise to move a "job lot" of Percival Prentice aircraft that Freddie Laker had purchased from the RAF after Training Command had replaced them with de Havilland Chipmunks; he was planning to increase the seating capacity of the Prentices to six or seven seats and then sell them on as ideal aircraft for pleasure or sightseeing flights. Thus on one of my days off I picked up five qualified private pilots from Southend Flying School and ferried them to RAF Swanton Morley, Norfolk, in a Prentice that had already been converted to a six-seater. At Swanton Morley, each of my group of five private pilots was assigned to one of the unconverted Prentices waiting for delivery to Stansted, where the conversion work was to be done, and then the six of us departed in loose formation.

Although I had actually done a check flight in a Prentice I don't think any of the other five pilots had, so it was fortunate that it was a fairly simple aircraft to fly. However, I was flying the only aircraft that was equipped with a radio, so the general idea was that I should get to Stansted first then circle overhead and keep the control tower advised as the others arrived in the circuit; the tower would then give each one a green light to land. Well, it took me just fifty minutes to get to Stansted in the radio-equipped aircraft, and as planned I began circling overhead, ready to shepherd my little flock to a safe landing.

However, I'd rather overlooked the fact that all these private pilots were trying to build enough hours to get their commercial licences, and some of them decided to get as much time in their logbooks that day as they possibly could, particularly as they didn't have to pay for it. The last couple of aircraft to land managed to stretch what would normally have been a fifty minute flight to nearly two hours, by which time I was getting a bit fed up with my shepherding role. Once they were all on the ground I still had to land at Stansted myself, pick up the five ferry pilots and then fly us all back to Southend in the six-seater Prentice, and by the time we got there a fearsome crosswind had sprung up, requiring me to concentrate all of my ability and experience into getting the aircraft safely on the ground whilst being watched by five sets of critical eyes. I was not best pleased.

I continued to operate both the Bristol Freighter and the DC4 from Southend until the end of 1957, a year during which I had not only gained my Senior Commercial Pilot's Licence but had also joined BALPA (the British Airline Pilots' Association), even though at that time the union was only just beginning to take an interest in the working conditions of independent airlines. I have already mentioned how Air Charter had been less than completely fair with its co-pilots by keeping them as Second Officers when they should have been promoted, and unfortunately there were other occasions that showed a certain lack of regard for the company's pilots in general.

One example was a day towards the end of 1957 when I was flying as co-pilot on a Bristol Freighter on the Channel Air Bridge operation from Southend. We would normally do two or three trips in the morning to Calais or Ostend and back and then have lunch in the airport café before doing a couple more return trips in the afternoon. However, on one particularly busy day the captain and I were told we would have to fly an extra trip instead of having our usual lunch break, so we were supplied with sandwiches and coffee to consume in flight. As our flights were so short — just thirty to forty minutes airborne — we had to gobble down the sandwiches and knock back the coffee pretty quickly, and we duly completed a long and very tiring day trundling back and forth across the channel without any proper break. You can therefore imagine how incensed we were when, on our final return to Southend we were presented with a bill for our refreshments, presumably because the company hadn't paid for them. This was definitely *not* the kind of thing that promotes strong feelings of loyalty towards one's employer.

In early 1958 I departed from RAF Lyneham for another Christmas Island flight, this time routing via USAF Offutt, in South Carolina, and Travis AFB in California, returning via Montreal and Monckton in Canada. On reaching Travis we were confronted with a major problem: reports indicated that we would experience a thirty-knot headwind for our onward leg to Hawaii, and this was way beyond the maximum seventeen knots that we could accept for a flight that was at the limit of the Tudor's range. For three days we waited, accommodated as guests in the USAF Officers' Mess, and then our captain decided, despite the misgivings of the rest of the crew, to file a flight plan based on a 25-knot headwind, even though that too was above our limits. Fortunately, this plan was torn up by the US Flight Safety Officer, who told us to return to the Officers' Club and wait for him to tell us when we could depart.

Against a maximum seventeen-knot headwind our flight would take twelve hours and forty-five minutes, and by flying at a constant air speed we could reduce our power setting and hence our fuel consumption every hour as the aircraft used up its fuel load and thus became lighter. For the first couple of hours our "dry-tanks-time" came before our ETA (Estimated Time of Arrival), but as the fuel consumption per hour was reduced the two times would gradually converge until about halfway there the ETA would come before our dry-tanks-time. By the time we actually arrived at our destination we would still have enough fuel to divert to our alternate airfield if necessary. Well, that was the theory, anyway.

After another day's wait we were told that the headwind had dropped to around fifteen knots, so we could finally set off for Hickam AFB near Honolulu with the blessing of all concerned. The flight to Hawaii was uneventful — as expected, our dry-tanks-time was ahead of our ETA for a while but gradually receded until it was beyond it — and our onward trip to Christmas Island and back went smoothly, so just a few days behind schedule we finally set off for home.

The return trip went well until we were approaching Montreal's Dorval Airport, which had just reopened after being closed for some hours due to heavy snow. Snow was still falling and the visibility was very poor, so it was perhaps understandable that our captain became somewhat disoriented, something that could occasionally happen during a difficult approach after a long and tiring flight.

As we broke cloud, looking for the runway lights ahead of us, I suddenly spotted them at about ninety degrees to the aircraft. I immediately told the captain, who reacted by executing a steep, low-level turn, with around sixty degrees of bank — rather more than I'd ever experienced on a large aircraft so near the ground — and managed to get the aircraft lined up with the runway. After we touched down our tail-wheel gave us valuable braking assistance on the thick snow, and we came safely to a halt with no damage to either the aircraft or ourselves, though I'm sure all our hearts were beating rather faster than usual; I know mine certainly was.

Fortunately, the rest of our journey back to the UK went without any further weather problems or hitches, and this time the airline had kept Pam informed of my delayed return, so no more roast lunches ended up being consigned to the bin.

At this time (early 1958) Air Charter was still expanding and was upgrading its fleet to include another new aircraft type, the Bristol Britannia. I was still way down the seniority list, so there was no hope of my being selected for training on the "Whispering Giant", as it was known, and I was naturally envious of those who were. Soon, though, my feelings became rather irrelevant, as the whole airline was left reeling in shock by a terrible accident.

On a flight to Singapore, one of the company's Tudor aircraft crashed into a mountain near Lake Van in Turkey, killing all on board, including not only the crew of the Tudor but also a newly checked-out Britannia crew, who had been travelling to Singapore to pick up one of the airline's first Britannias. The captain of the Tudor was the one with whom I'd done the Christmas Island trip I've just described, and the commander of the Britannia crew was a friend of mine, Captain "Stewie" Stewart-Smith, who had checked me out on the Percival Prentice the previous year. Such tragic events are mercifully rare, particularly now that we have much better airframes, engines and navigational equipment, but when they do occur they are a stark reminder that in aviation the unexpected can always happen, sometimes with traumatic results.

Chapter 4

AT THIS STAGE OF MY CAREER I was becoming steadily more dissatisfied with my employment conditions, and I began to look around for an airline that might be prepared to train me up to a Group 1 Type Rating so that I could build up some P1/S (Pilot-in-Command-under-Supervision) flying hours and thus hasten the granting of my Airline Transport Pilot's Licence. In March, 1958, I met two Australian pilots at Southend, and they told me they were involved in the start-up of a new airline, which was to be called Overseas Aviation and would initially be operating a Vickers Viking passenger aircraft owned by a Dr Erhardt of Basle, Switzerland. As the new company would give me the training I needed I agreed to join them, so I submitted my resignation to Air Charter.

While working my notice I continued to fly the DC4 trooping contract to Nicosia, and as if to confirm the wisdom of my decision I suffered the last unpleasant experience of my Air Charter days when the Ledra Palace Hotel, where our crew were staying, was bombed by Eoka terrorists. None of us was hurt, but it certainly gave us quite a scare.

However, with the benefit of many years of hindsight I now realise it was probably the wrong time to leave Air Charter. It had just acquired its first Bristol Britannia, a modern turboprop airliner in those days, and it was taking over other airlines, such as Airwork, Hunting Clan and Transair of Croydon. Soon the new, larger company would become British United Airways, which later merged with Caledonian Airways to become British Caledonian, which in turn was eventually absorbed into British Airways during the 1980s. Had I stayed with Air Charter I might even have ended up as a British Airways captain, perish the thought!

Anyway, by the beginning of April, 1958, I had gained my Group 2 co-pilot's rating on the Vickers Viking with Overseas Aviation and was operating from Southend on passenger charter flights to Basle, Berlin and various destinations in the Mediterranean. Like most young pilots keen to advance their careers, I was always on the lookout for opportunities to gain extra experience that might be useful in the future, and just such an opportunity came up quite soon after I joined Overseas Aviation, when I discovered that one of their captains, Hugh Dennison, was qualified as a commander on the de Havilland Dove, a twin-engine aircraft that carried eight passengers and was very popular in the executive flying market. In those days any pilot qualified to command an aircraft was also permitted to train other pilots on it, to give them their check flights and to sign up their paperwork so that they could fly in command of that aircraft them-selves, and I decided that this chance of putting the Dove on my licence was too good to miss. Captain Dennison readily agreed to give me the necessary flight training, so after studying the aircraft manual at home and passing the written course I hired a Dove from another company at Southend and only needed a couple of hours of flight training before being cleared to fly in command.

This doesn't sound like much time, but the Dove was a lovely aircraft to handle, unlike the Viking that I was flying in my "day job". The problem with the Viking — apart from the fact that it had a tail-wheel — was that it was terribly unpredictable; you could fly a perfect approach and have everything beautifully under control, and then at the last moment the aircraft would seem to decide that it was going to embarrass you, and you'd find yourself thumping down on

The Vickers Viking: certainly not the best-looking aircraft in the world and also a tricky beast to fly. In fact, it was known by some pilots as "The Flying Pig".
Photo: MAP

the runway so hard it made everyone's teeth rattle. At other times it would be positively docile and would settle onto the runway so smoothly the passengers would be wondering whether they'd actually landed or not. Still, despite all that, I gained my Group 1 rating on the Viking by the end of May, and so from then on I was able to start building that all-important "P1/S" time that would count towards the issue of my full Airline Transport Pilot's Licence. Thus it came about that at the end of July I emerged from the Holborn office of the Ministry of Transport and Civil Aviation with my shiny new ATPL clutched in my hand. Another major career hurdle had been successfully negotiated.

In November, 1958, Overseas Aviation purchased a Canadair CL-4 Argonaut (G-ALHT) from BOAC, and with my previous experience on a fairly similar type — the Douglas DC4 — I was immediately selected to be trained on it. In its BOAC heyday the Argonaut had often carried members of the royal family, most memorably when bringing the new Queen Elizabeth II back from Nairobi after the death of her father in February, 1952. It was now in its dotage but still fit to give a few more years of useful service, even though such large, piston-engined aircraft were rapidly being replaced by new types powered either by turbo-props — jet engines that drive propellers — or turbojets, the ones

Canadair Argonaut G-ALHD was the third aircraft of this type acquired by Overseas Aviation.
Photo: MAP

without propellers that we normally think of when we talk about "jet" engines.

Anyway, now that it had a long-haul aircraft Overseas Aviation started doing passenger charter flights to the Far East, and the crews were very pleased that the company had decided to have most of their Argonaut maintenance done by HAECo in Hong Kong, which meant that a normal crew stopover there was about two days rather than just a night-stop. A second Argonaut appeared in February, 1959, with a third in April and two more in June, and a subsidiary company and base was set up in Copenhagen under the name "Flying Enterprise"; this operation used regular UK-based pilots and mostly local cabin staff, and it flew inclusive tour flights from Copenhagen to Palma and other holiday destinations in the Mediterranean.

I was flying as co-pilot on one of these Flying Enterprise trips to Palma in early 1959 when we had a request from one of the passengers to let everyone know over the PA system as we crossed the south coast of France. The captain duly did so, at which point, as I was later told by the cabin staff, a young lady got up from her seat, went into the toilet and changed into a wedding gown (not the easiest thing to do in an aircraft toilet, but she managed it somehow). She then went and stood beside a rather well-dressed young man and, in front of all the other passengers, including quite a few of their friends, the couple were duly married by a priest whom they'd brought with them. Apparently, the young couple — one of them Swedish, the other Danish — were marrying against their respective parents' wishes, hence their desire to be wed whilst flying over international waters. I always wondered what their families said when they eventually got home, but I don't think the airline ever received a complaint about its complicity in this unusual act of defiance.

On another occasion I was doing a trip with Captain Paul de Vere Stevens, a director of the company, when something rather strange happened before we'd even started the engines. The passengers had just started boarding through the main door, which was located just aft of the port wing, and as usual the cabin staff were positioned near the door to direct the first group of passengers into seats towards the front of the aircraft (seats were not allocated prior to boarding). There was a good reason for this, which will become clear very shortly, but on this particular day it just so happened that the first passengers to board were not only quite large (Danes tend to be tall, strongly-built Nordic types) but also intent on sitting at the back of the aircraft, not the front,

A Flying Enterprise Argonaut

Photo: TAHS

perhaps because they were aware of that famous old adage to the effect that no-one ever hears of aircraft reversing into mountains. The cabin staff did their best, but the passengers ignored them and went straight to the very back of the aircraft to choose their seats.

Captain de Vere Stevens and I suddenly found ourselves rising into the air, which is fine when you're travelling at take-off speed but not so good when you're stationary. Our undisciplined Danish passengers had just demonstrated exactly why the cabin staff had tried to make them move forward after boarding: their combined weight had made the aircraft sit down on its tail, leaving the captain and I looking upwards towards the sky.

Of course, this all sounds rather amusing, but once we were in this precarious position we had to be very careful how we got out of it. The passengers who had gone to the rear were told to stay there for the time being, while lines were put round the fin and tailplane of the aircraft and attached to a very heavy tractor; the tractor then took up the slack, after which the passengers were asked to move forward one by one so that the aircraft could be *gently* lowered onto its nose-wheel. If everyone had rushed forward at once the impact of the nose-wheel hitting the ground could have been enough to cause considerable damage to the aircraft and possible injury to those on board — particularly us two pilots on the flight deck — but everything worked out well, and after carefully boarding all the remaining passengers and distributing them appropriately around the cabin we were finally able to set off on our flight to Palma, feeling mightily relieved. I'm sure all the cabin staff concerned had made a mental note *never* to let *any* passengers defy them again, even if it meant they had to grapple them to the floor.

By early July I had completed my Group 1 training and was now a Senior First Officer on the Argonaut, which entitled me to occupy the captain's seat on a 24-hour crew while he took his rest period. I still operated some Viking flights, but I was mostly flying the Argonaut on long-haul trips to the Far East and southern Africa. These African flights were routed via Benghazi (Libya), Khartoum (Sudan), where passengers and crew would take a night-stop, then Dar-es-Salaam (Tanzania) and finally to our destination of Laurenço Marques (now Maputo) in what was then the Portuguese colony of Mozambique. The majority of passengers were actually bound for South Africa, and they would then make the overland trip to Johannesburg by rail, since no British airline other than BOAC was permitted to land at Johannesburg Airport itself.

The return journey was even longer, as we would route via Livingstone (Rhodesia), Leopoldville (Belgian Congo) and Kano (Nigeria), where passengers and crew would spend the night. The following day we would continue through Niamey (Niger), Agadir (Morocco) and Lisbon, where we would all spend not one but *two* full days. This long stay in Lisbon, during which both passengers and crew would obviously be spending money, was a kind of reward to the Portuguese government for allowing us the use of Laurenço Marques as our destination airport, even though most of our passengers would be travelling to or from Johannesburg.

Meanwhile, Overseas Aviation's Viking aircraft were doing frequent flower flights bringing tulips from Amsterdam, and on these trips, whilst waiting for the aircraft to be loaded, I would often chat to Martin Schroder, the Managing Director of our handling agents, Martin Air Charter, which later became Martinair. In 1959, when I was well established on the Argonaut fleet, I asked Overseas if Martin could come with me on one of our Argonaut trips to Hong Kong. They agreed, so along he came.

Under the Civil Aviation fatigue regulations, a compulsory rest period must be taken after every duty period while operating commercially. However, at that time private flights of empty aircraft were permitted to ignore this rest requirement, and on this particular trip we found ourselves exploiting this regulatory loophole to the full.

On 28 May, 1959, we departed Southend, routing via Brindisi and Ankara, with a load for Kuwait; we didn't usually carry cargo on the Argonaut, but on this occasion it was stuff that could easily be accommodated in the passenger cabin. The cargo was offloaded in under three hours, and we continued as an empty private flight to Bombay, Rangoon and Hong Kong, where we would eventually be picking up a return load of passengers. Our total flying time from Southend to Hong Kong, during which we barely left the aircraft, let alone had any proper rest, came to 37 hours and 45 minutes, during which we watched the sun setting on the first day, then saw sunrise and sunset on the second, then another sunrise on the third, and as we landed in Hong Kong the sun was dipping towards the horizon yet again.

We were, of course, utterly exhausted at the end of all this flying, so I was very glad to collapse onto my bed in our hotel on Cameron Road. It wasn't the smartest of places, but by that time none of us really cared. However, the hotel did have a few special ideas about customer service, and as I pulled the bed-clothes around me I heard something: it was the room boy, perched on a step-ladder outside the door, opening the little glass window above it. "Would you like a young lady for company?" he asked. I can't recall my precise answer, but I'm sure it was not particularly polite. However, I obviously failed to convince him that all I wanted was sleep, for a few moments later he followed up with a supplementary question: "Would you like a boy, then?" I think he got the message that time.

After forty-eight hours of rest and recuperation in Hong Kong we set off on our return trip to Southend, which was quite leisurely in comparison with our outbound one. Our passengers were a ship's crew bound for Athens, and our first day's flying took us from Hong Kong to Karachi, via Bangkok and Calcutta. We then had a full twenty-four hours of rest in Karachi before setting off for Athens via Abadan (Iran) and Ankara, and having safely delivered our seafarers to Athens we had another 24-hour stopover there before taking off for the last (empty) leg of our journey home to Southend. Compared with our schedule on the way out, our homeward trip was like a holiday.

I don't know whether that Argonaut trip was an inspiration to Martin Schroder as he worked to develop his fledgling airline, but it did have certain consequences that could have changed the course of my own career. During my time off at Southend between long-haul flights, I often flew a de Havilland Dove aircraft for a chap called Mike Keegan (the "K" in BKS Aviation and owner of Keegan Aviation at Panshanger Airport in Hertfordshire). Mike had purchased several Doves from BOAC, where they had been used for navigation training, and he had refurbished them to sell on as eight-seat passenger-carriers. I ended up being involved in the sale and delivery of two of these aircraft to Martin Schroder, the first multi-engined aircraft that he bought for his new airline, and later on the company acquired a Douglas DC-3 as well. One day, out of the blue, I had a phone call: it was Martin Schroder, and he had a proposition for me: would I like to leave Overseas Aviation and join Martin Air Charter in Amsterdam as Chief Pilot on the DC3 that they were then in the process of buying?

It was a very tempting offer, but in the end I decided to stay put. I was really enjoying long-haul flying on the Argonaut and was expecting to be promoted to captain before too long, so going back to short-haul flying around Europe did not appeal to me very much. Of course, with the benefit of hindsight, that may have been one of the worst decisions I ever made, as I could have ended up as Chief Pilot of a large international airline (Martinair). However, at the time I seemed to be set fair in a secure job with good prospects. If only I'd had a crystal ball!

In the spring of 1960 things were still going well. My first daughter, Allison, was born in April — I was in Berlin at the time, so I heard the happy news by telex — and now that I was a family man I had commissioned a local builder to construct a four-bedroomed, detached house for us in Leigh-on-Sea, within easy reach of Southend Airport.

However, at that point things began to go wrong. Overseas Aviation decided to move to Gatwick — a long and tiring car journey from Southend in those pre-motorway days — but with our house already under construction it would have been impossible for us to move. However, an answer to our problem suddenly presented itself: a company called Continental Air Services, based at Southend, offered me a job as a senior first officer on DC-4 and Viking aircraft. I was sorry to leave Overseas, but as things had changed so much I decided I had to go.

After joining Continental Air Services I initially flew as co-pilot on Viking and DC4 flights around Europe, but in July I found myself being flown out to Hong Kong as a passenger on a Cathay Pacific DC4 cargo flight from Munich in order to bring home a Continental DC4. This aircraft was G-APID, generally referred to as Rapid Gapid because for some reason it usually flew a bit faster than other DC4s in the fleet, and it had just undergone a major overhaul with Haeco, Hong Kong's famous aircraft and engine maintenance company.

On arrival in Hong Kong we were expecting to take some rest and then do an empty ferry home to Southend, but our company's sales people had done their bit while we were travelling out, and by the time we arrived our empty ferry had turned into a commercial charter. 1960 was, of course, an Olympic year, so after a short test flight in Hong Kong to make sure all was well we flew to Taipei, where we collected the Formosa Olympic team and their national officials for their journey to Rome. (In fact, that team would be at the centre of a controversy at the start of the Games, as they had been ordered by the International Olympic Committee to use the designation "Formosa" instead of their preferred title of "Republic of China", and they gave vent to their indignation during the opening ceremony by parading behind a sign saying "Under Protest".)

Anyway, just to illustrate again the kind of journeys that intercontinental air travellers underwent in those mainly propeller-driven days, our route from Taipei to Rome included refuelling stops at Hong Kong and Bangkok before our first night-stop in Calcutta, then the next day two more refuelling stops, at Bombay and Bahrain, before another night-stop in Damascus, and then on the third day one final leg (for our passengers, that is) from Damascus to Rome, where the Olympic team left us to seek their place in history. Meanwhile, we crew members had the luxury of a night-stop in Rome before continuing our journey back to the UK, though our commercial people had been busy again, so the next morning we flew from Rome to Rimini and picked up a load of returning holiday-makers for the final leg into Southend. The aircraft certainly earned its keep that week, as did we.

It was great to be back on long-haul flying again, but a few weeks later I found myself being trained on yet another new type, though anyone could be forgiven for thinking that this was actually a backward move. In mid-September, my employers were looking likely to acquire a DC3 to back up their Viking operation on European holiday flights, and I was told that if they did get a DC3 there was a very good chance I'd be promoted to captain on it, which was very exciting for me as I felt I was ready to fly in command of a large aircraft. I managed to borrow some DC3 technical manuals, and by dint of much studying at home I soon passed the ARB (Air Registration Board) written exam. Continental then arranged for me to do some flight training on the aircraft they were planning to buy, so I ended up with a DC3 rating on my licence, though as it turned out the DC3 deal never came to fruition, so I never actually flew the aircraft for Continental. Much later on in my life, though, this particular rating turned out to be very useful indeed.

At the end of September, shortly after I'd completed my DC3 training, I was called out from home at 2am one morning because Continental had a delayed DC4 aircraft en route from Palma to Glasgow that had had to divert into Southend for a crew change, as the original crew were running out of hours and would not be legal to continue to their intended destination. The aircraft we were taking over was Rapid Gapid, the one I'd brought back from Hong Kong, and as the captain and I climbed aboard for the fairly short hop to Glasgow we had no reason to think this would be anything other than a routine flight.

We took off as normal and climbed to our cruising altitude of 8,000 feet; most of our passengers were asleep after the long delay they had suffered in Palma — a delay which, incidentally, had not been due to any problem with the aircraft — so the cabin heating system was being used to keep everyone back there nice and warm. That warmth, however, did not penetrate as far as the flight deck, and after about fifty minutes the captain and I decided we needed to turn the cockpit heating on as well, as we were feeling rather chilly. Heat for both the passenger cabin and the cockpit was supplied by those same Janitrol heaters that I've mentioned before, which produced warmth by burning ordinary aviation gasoline from the aircraft's fuel tanks. That does sound a little bit perilous in these safety-obsessed days, but it was how things were done back then, and each heater did have its own little fire extinguisher, operated by pulling a handle on the flight deck, in case anything should go wrong.

Anyway, moments after turning on the heater we heard the dreaded sound of a fire warning bell, while the sudden illumination of a red light in the heater's fire extinguisher handle in front of us confirmed that we had a problem. The captain pulled the fire handle, which should have put the fire out, but it didn't seem to have much effect, and smoke started to fill the flight deck. Things were getting very alarming indeed.

At that point I remembered something from the notes I'd made when I was studying to pass the ARB technical exam for the DC4: as an extra safety measure there was a valve on the cockpit floor, just to the right of the co-pilot's seat, that could be used in an emergency to cut off the fuel supply to the cockpit heater. I reached down to operate it, confident that I'd found the answer to our problem, but try as I might I simply couldn't find it anywhere. As it turned out, G-APID had never been fitted with this particular valve, so my instant solution simply wasn't available to us.

By this time, the smoke on the flight deck was getting denser and could be seen seeping under the flight deck door by the cabin crew in the front galley area. It was clear that if we didn't do something very quickly we would have not only a couple of worried pilots but some very panicky passengers as well.

Having failed to find the non-existent heater cut-off valve, I then remembered that the fuel supply to the heater came from the same source as No. 3 engine; in other words, whichever fuel tank was being used to feed No. 3 engine at any time would also be feeding the cockpit heater. The captain, who was looking after the actual flying of the aircraft while we tried to sort out the situation, had decided to divert to the nearest airfield, so I suggested to him that if we cut the fuel supply to No. 3 engine, thereby shutting that engine down, the fuel to the heater would also be cut off; the captain agreed with me, shut the engine down and feathered the prop. This seemed to work well, as we soon noticed that the smoke in the cockpit was decreasing, so we were feeling rather relieved as we positioned ourselves for an emergency landing at Manchester's Ringway Airport.

But our trials weren't over: we suddenly had a hydraulic pressure warning, which meant we could no longer rely on the assistance of our hydraulic system in our efforts to land the aircraft safely. We were not too worried about lowering the undercarriage — in an emergency, it could simply be released and allowed to "free-fall" into position using good old gravity — but we knew that our brakes would be reliant on emergency bottles of compressed air rather than the usual hydraulics, and that our nosewheel steering would be restricted as well.

Despite all our problems, though, we made a safe landing, and as we rolled along the runway, pursued by a fire truck towing a set of passenger steps, the captain gradually slowed the aircraft down by repeated application of the brakes until the air accumulator bottles were exhausted. At about 20mph, he could no longer maintain directional control of the aircraft without the aid of hydraulics, so we trundled gently off the runway and onto the grass, where we came to a stop. The cabin crew immediately deployed the canvas escape slide from the main passenger door, and passengers began to evacuate down it, but very soon the fire tender arrived with the steps, which they quickly deployed so that the rest of the aircraft's occupants could disembark in a more dignified manner, the fire crew having already extinguished any sign of fire around the nose-wheel.

Though all was well in the end, with no injuries to either passengers or crew, we had clearly come fairly close to disaster, and investigations would obviously have to be carried out to determine what exactly had gone wrong. Subsequent enquiries revealed that it had all started with a small leak of hydraulic fluid (a flammable red mineral oil) from a pipe junction just above the cockpit heater; the fluid had soaked into the asbestos wadding around the heater, and this oil-soaked wadding had started smouldering when the heater was used. The fire extinguisher worked correctly *inside* the heater itself, but the wadding on the outside had continued to smoulder because the extinguishant simply couldn't reach it.

When the captain had shut down No. 3 engine he had not only stopped the supply of fuel to the heater but he had also turned off

No. 3 hydraulic pump, which had been supplying hydraulic fluid to the leak that had kept the outside of the heater smouldering. We had thus inadvertently deprived the fire of its fuel source, even though the fuel we *thought* we were removing was petrol rather than hydraulic fluid.

However, it just so happened that the hydraulic pump fitted to No. 2 engine had already failed for some undetermined reason, so the aircraft had been relying on the pump attached to No. 3 engine. Therefore, when we stopped No. 3 we lost *all* hydraulic pressure, and we had had no warning because pumps were only attached to No. 2 and No. 3 engines, and as we normally started No. 3 engine before No. 2 the hydraulic pressure produced by No. 3 pump would have disguised the fact that No. 2 wasn't working properly. When new problems are suddenly compounded with existing ones in this manner disaster can often ensue, so I think we were all very lucky to come out of this incident completely unscathed.

I didn't have very long to enjoy savouring my good fortune, though, because within a month or so of this incident Continental Air Services went into liquidation, leaving me unemployed. My gamble in switching to an airline based near home hadn't paid off, so I found myself looking for work again.

BALPA, the pilots' union, had an employment section, and they wrote to me as an active but temporarily unemployed member to suggest I apply to Cunard Eagle Airways at Heathrow Airport, who were looking for a few pilots for their DC6 fleet. Eagle gave me a date for an interview, but in the meantime I managed to find some freelance work for Mike Keegan, flying one of the aforementioned de Havilland Dove aircraft that he'd purchased from BOAC. This enabled me to build up my command time, operating flights to Pisa via Lyon, carrying directors of Hepworth's, the famous tailors, on visits to their Italian factory, and doing other flights to Glasgow, Inverness and Antwerp.

When it finally came around, my interview with Cunard Eagle at the company's Heathrow headquarters went very well, as my considerable co-pilot experience on DC4's and Argonauts placed me in an advantageous position for training onto the DC6 fleet. However, the next DC6 technical and flying course was not due to start for some months, but by a remarkable coincidence the Technical Director of Cunard Eagle, a member of the interview board, was married to Mike Keegan's sister, and when he saw that I had flown for Keegan on Doves he told me that one of these aircraft had been sold to Columbia Pictures' British offshoot, Horizon, to operate in support of a film unit that were about to start work on a major production in Jordan. A pilot was needed to deliver the aircraft to Jordan and then to stay on with the film unit for a while, and it was suggested that I should take this rather intriguing job to keep me busy until my training course on the DC6 was about to start. It took me very little time to make up my mind and say yes, and thus I became part of the team making one of the greatest films ever: *Lawrence of Arabia*.

Within days, leaving my family behind in Southend, I was flying the Dove via Nice, Naples, Athens, Beirut and Damascus to Amman. My co-pilot/engineer was H. "Dusty" Miller (in my experience, most British airlines of the twentieth century seem to have had a Dusty Miller, a Chalky White and a Dick Barton on their crew lists), and flying with us, as a passenger, was Wing Commander Jock Dalgleish,

who would be acting as a liaison officer between Columbia Pictures and King Hussein. Jock had once been awarded a Jordanian medal for bravery for managing to evade some enemy jet aircraft whilst flying a Dove with the king on board.

Dusty and I quickly settled into routine flying for the film company; most of our flights were to Aqaba, Damascus and Beirut from their base in Amman, carrying company staff and VIPs such as Sam Spiegel, the film's producer, and David Lean, its director. During the period around Christmas I was left on my own in Beirut, the senior members of the film company having returned to the UK for a few days, but although Beirut

Resplendent in my Horizon Pictures uniform with four gold bars on my sleeve!

was known as "the playground of the Eastern Med" in those days I didn't fancy spending Christmas alone, so I hitched a lift on a Middle East Airlines Viscount to spend a couple of days with some friends in Bahrain; Christmases away always have been and always will be a feature of airline life .

The Horizon Pictures de Havilland Dove
Photo: MAP

Immediately after Christmas I was invited to fly from Bahrain to Kuwait as co-pilot in a de Havilland Heron, which is very much like a Dove but with four engines instead of two, and again I managed to hitch a lift from Kuwait back to Beirut. By 29 December I was back on routine flying for the film company, operating many weekend trips to Beirut for Sam Spiegel. During these weekends I was accommodated in the Penthouse of the St. George Hotel on the superb Beirut beach-front, which gave me a real glimpse of the high life as it was then; it saddens me to think of how things have changed in that part of the world in the intervening years.

I also did a few flights around Jordan carrying other VIPs, including the British Ambassador and his family, and also Colonel Gardiner, the Commanding Officer of the Arab Legion; there was no internal airline in Jordan at the time, so Horizon were always willing to lend me and the aircraft to important people when not needed for anything to do with the film.

In fact, Colonel Gardiner had a daughter, Toni, who worked as a receptionist in Horizon's office in Amman. When I eventually left Amman to return to the UK I said goodbye to all the office staff, including Toni, and she told me, rather mysteriously, that I would probably be reading about her in all the newspapers soon afterwards. And so I did, because a few weeks after my return to Britain Toni married King Hussein and became Queen Muna.

Anyway, while I was in Jordan I did one particular flight that has remained etched in my memory. On 31 January, 1961, we were given special permission by King Hussein to fly around the country at low level searching for film locations, so I had the huge excitement of flying over amazing desert scenery and through the spectacular Wadi Rum, with Oscar-winning cameraman Freddie Young sitting in the right-hand seat of the Dove. We started following the old railway line from Amman towards Saudia Arabia, flying so low that we had to climb to avoid scaring the occasional camel, and we even found the wreck of an old train. At one time this was purported to be the very same train that Lawrence and his followers had destroyed, as depicted in the film, but this was later considered very unlikely to be true. Still, whatever the truth of the train story, that whole flight was one of the most exciting piloting experiences of my life, and I'm sure Freddie Young enjoyed it too.

A few days later, I had yet another interesting experience when, during a routine flight from Aqaba back to Amman with just two of us on board (myself and Dusty, my co-pilot/engineer), I decided to deviate to the west of our normal route in order to stay beneath a lowering cloud-base. Our new route took us over the Dead Sea, whose surface is at some 1,400ft below normal sea level, so when we dropped down to fly at about a thousand feet above the water the altimeter showed that we were at *minus* 500ft, not something you see (or would want to see) very often!

I was certainly very happy working with the film unit, but in February, 1961, I had a message from Cunard Eagle asking me to return to the UK fairly promptly in order to start a course on the DC6 in March and saying that they would be sending out a new pilot for me to check out on the Dove before I departed. This message precipitated one of those big, unexpected decision points that sometimes crop up in life. Sam Spiegel wanted me to stay with the film unit until the end of shooting, and to tempt me to do so he offered to *give* me the Dove aircraft once we were no longer needed. Peter O'Toole and Omar Sharif had already appeared on the scene, and I was very tempted to stay, but the film had been delayed early on by a script problem, and it was clear to me that if I stayed with the film unit my chances of eventually being reabsorbed into Cunard Eagle would be very small indeed. In those days a job with a prestigious company such as Cunard was considered a job for life, so I put good sense before excitement and made preparations to return to the UK.

My final flight for Horizon Pictures was taking David Lean and his wife to Beirut for a spell of "R&R", and I was certainly very sad to be saying goodbye not only to all the film folk but also to G-ARBH, the lovely little Dove aircraft that I had really enjoyed flying. Production of *Lawrence* later moved to Almeria in southern Spain — apparently, the sand dunes there were better for filming than anything that could be found in Jordan — so I presume Bravo Hotel moved there as well. According to information gleaned from the Internet, she was eventually broken up in 1990 (she was built in 1948, so she lasted more than forty years), but she's one particular aircraft that I shall always remember with huge affection.

Chapter 5

DURING MARCH AND EARLY APRIL, 1961, I completed a DC6 technical course with several other new-entry co-pilots at the London Heathrow headquarters of Cunard Eagle Airways, and with no simulator available I was very quickly thrown into circuit training. Along with other trainees and three instructor captains I was sent to Shannon in Ireland, where we would be doing our "circuits and bumps"; this was common practice, as Shannon was always a fairly quiet airport that could easily accommodate these vital training flights without causing major interference to regular commercial traffic.

My first training session on the aircraft was scheduled for the evening, but while waiting in the terminal with my fellow trainees for the previous group to finish their stint I suddenly became aware of bells ringing. We all looked out at the now darkening airfield and saw that the whole length of the runway appeared to be on fire, with a large ball of flames at the far end, and for a moment we thought that it might be an American cargo plane that had crashed on landing, as we knew one was due in at about that time. Of course, we all wondered what on earth had happened and hoped that there were no casualties.

As we soon learnt, though, it was not the American freighter but our own DC6 that had come to grief, but fortunately everyone on board — the training captain, the training flight engineer and their respective trainees — had escaped unscathed. It subsequently turned out that a trainee flight engineer had somehow put the undercarriage lever to UP just after landing, a relatively simple error that led to the complete destruction of the aircraft; in fact, when the wreckage was removed from the runway the following morning the only serviceable part recovered was the anti-collision light from the top of the fin.

Thus before my flight training had even started I was on my way back home from Ireland, and my group was subsequently sent to Filton Airport at Bristol to do the circuits we should have done at Shannon, This time, though, everything went to plan.

During this period, and with Cunard Eagle's permission, I continued to do some Dove flying at Southend, training two Dutch pilots for a new company, Veen's Air Service, of Maastricht. In those days, training regulations were much more relaxed than today, so the fact that I had a captain's rating on the Dove meant that I could both instruct and examine trainee pilots on it. In fact, my role went slightly beyond instructing, because on the night of 5 May, 1961, I operated Veen's first commercial trip, flying from Maastricht to Paris and then picking up a load of newspapers and delivering them to Zurich, Frankfurt and Dusseldorf before heading back to Maastricht. I'd thought I'd done my last Dove flight in Jordan, but this wasn't to be the only time I made a false assumption about saying goodbye forever to a particular aircraft type.

By early June I had done all my circuit flying and was licensed on the DC6, so I was ready to begin my "proper" career with Cunard Eagle, initially as a co-pilot but with hopes of progressing to captain once I'd gained sufficient experience. These were the early days of inclusive tours, and I did lots of holiday flights to European

A Cunard Eagle Douglas DC6
Photo: Aviation Photo News

destinations such as Innsbruck, Rimini, Malta, Pisa and Perpignan, plus some long-haul charters. I did several trips to New York, via refuelling stops at either Gander in Newfoundland or Goose Bay in Labrador, and then from New York the aircraft would sometimes continue to Kingston, Jamaica, to collect passengers bound for a new life in the UK.

On these trips out of Kingston the aircraft would stop at Nassau (Bahamas) and then Gander for fuel before heading out across the pond, so passengers would be on board the aircraft for around seventeen hours in all, though there would be a complete change of crew in Gander. Gander was not the greatest place to stay; in winter it was freezing cold, and in summer it could get very hot, which only encouraged the local mosquitoes to come out and play. Walks around the rather attractive Lake Gander could thus be ruined by the constant and painful attentions of the local insect population, but there *were* certain compensations to be had, including what I reckoned was the best blueberry pie in the world, served at the airport restaurant. Every cloud must have a silver lining, I guess.

I also did one trip down to Mauritius, which proved rather memorable; our crew was "positioned" (i.e. we flew as passengers) to Mombasa, from where, after a rest period, we did a return flight to Mauritius and back before handing the aircraft over to another crew, who would then take it all the way home to London. At that point, in Mombasa, we flight deck crew were given a wonderful choice by our employers: our next flight was to be some six days hence but from Nairobi rather than Mombasa, so the company told us that rather than returning to the UK we could use a certain, fairly generous amount of money to get ourselves to Nairobi by whatever means we wished.

We decided to go the pretty way via a game park or two, so we hired a large, comfortable American car, complete with driver, and drove up from Mombasa to Lake Manyara, where we arrived after nightfall. I'll never forget how wonderful it was waking up next morning to be greeted, on opening the curtains, with a fantastic, panoramic view of the lake and its surroundings, and for the next few days we all enjoyed our free safari holiday as we gradually made our way to Nairobi, where we arrived the day before our flight home and thus with plenty of time for rest. We had stayed well within our budget, and our next payslips actually included a small refund because we hadn't spent as much as expected. What a wonderful company to work for, I thought, and how lucky I was to have found this job!

I also did some trooping flights to Libya, landing at RAF bases such as El Adem and Benina; this was in the time of King Idris, when relations between the West and Libya were very good and the UK still had a strong presence in that country. For trooping flights all the aircraft passenger seats had to face backwards for reasons of safety in the event of an accident — in fact, I'm pretty sure RAF transport aircraft still have rearward-facing seats to this day — so each time a military charter came up our ground crews would have to turn them all round. Occasionally, an aircraft in military charter configuration would then be used for a civilian flight before the seats could be returned to their usual position, so we would apologise to all our passengers that they would have to put up with travelling with their backs to the engine, as it were. I'm sure some of them must have wondered why the general practice was to have passengers facing forward on almost every civilian flight while the military insisted on what is generally considered a much safer arrangement, but I rather suspect that given the choice most people would still prefer to travel facing forwards rather than backwards, whatever the advantages of having a seat behind you to help absorb any impact in the event of something ghastly happening.

By 1962 I was quite often flying in the left-hand (captain's) seat as PIC/S (pilot-in-command under supervision), and in July, with 4,900 hours total time, I was selected for training as a full captain. I completed my final command base check at Stansted with the fleet manager, Captain Jack Peacock, but unfortunately, my fairly quick promotion caused a bit of dissatisfaction amongst some of my colleagues, particularly other co-pilots who were actually ahead of me in the seniority list. However, as the company argued to BALPA when they questioned the situation, Cunard Eagle were in urgent need of more captains, and I'd been favoured because I had accumulated many more hours on similar types of four-engined aircraft —the Argonaut and DC-4, for example — than the company's other DC6 co-pilots at the time. My elevation to command status thus went ahead as planned.

In fact, it was a particularly appropriate time for me to be promoted, because I had recently become a father again with the birth, in April, 1962, of our second daughter, Gaynor. I'd actually been at home this time as I'd booked leave, so I'd been around to help out as needed when Gaynor was born in our house in Leigh-on-Sea. Now that I had a wife and two daughters to support, a regular captain's salary would certainly come in useful.

My first flight on the DC6 as a captain was a "shared command" trip on an MoD cargo flight to Adelaide, Australia, with Captain Frank Nikiel, a Polish ex-RAF pilot. Frank decided that as I was young and enthusiastic I should not only take charge of the technical decision-making but also look after the "ship's funds", the cash float given to all aircraft captains at the start of each trip to cover miscellaneous expenses en route plus meal allowances for the crew. Keeping signed receipts for everything paid out was essential, and captains could accumulate a hefty wodge of paperwork by the end of a longish trip. The need to buy local currency to settle some overseas bills added extra complication, and I'm sure some newly-promoted captains were more concerned about keeping track of ship's funds than about their ability to command the aircraft itself. Anyway, having delegated the book-keeping work to me, Frank, who always took his accordion with him on trips, would be in charge of keeping the crew entertained during stopovers, so with duties appropriately assigned our crew of two captains, a co-pilot, a flight engineer, a navigator and a loadmaster boarded the aircraft and set off.

Our first stop, after a flight of more than seven hours, was at RAF Benina, near Benghazi, Libya, and after refuelling we took off again for the nine-hour trip to Aden (as a British military flight we had to route around Egypt, hence the relatively long flight time for that sector). That's why we had two captains and a co-pilot on board as well as the usual flight engineer and navigator, otherwise we couldn't possibly have done two long sectors like that in one duty period. In Aden we took a 20-hour break while we waited for the next aircraft to come through, then we did another sector of more than nine hours from Aden to RAF Negombo in what was then Ceylon. There we handed over the aircraft to another crew and settled down for four days of rest and recuperation, which we definitely needed after all that flying.

The next aircraft we picked up was bound for Adelaide, but even though we had a "heavy" crew with the extra captain we could not go right through without rest, so we took another brief break of thirteen hours at our first refuelling stop, the Cocos Islands, before flying on to to Adelaide via a further refuelling stop in Perth, Western Australia.

We had three days off in Adelaide before returning to London via a very similar pattern of flights and rest stops, and we finally landed back at Heathrow on 6 August, twenty-eight days after our departure, having flown some ninety hours since we'd left. This was how it was back in the days of piston engines rather than jets, with flight times that were roughly double what they are today, but I count myself very lucky to have experienced it.

Having completed this first command trip I was due to take some leave, so I'd booked Pam, myself and our two little daughters into a very nice hotel in Bournemouth, from which we could just walk across the road to the beach. We were lazing on the sand one day when one of the hotel staff suddenly appeared and asked me to come into Reception to take a phone-call from my employers, Cunard Eagle; I think I'd probably told them where I was going to be, but in any case airline crewing departments have, in my experience, always shown great ingenuity in tracking down off-duty crew members if they needed to contact them, even before the advent of e-mail and mobile phones made such tasks so much easier than they used to be.

Anyway, when I picked up the call I found myself speaking to one of Eagle's operations officers, who asked me if I could help them out with a big problem: they needed someone to operate as an extra captain in a "heavy" crew on a trooping flight to various points in North Africa departing from Gatwick that same evening, and if I would be willing to do it they would send a taxi to collect me and take me straight to the airport. As I didn't have my uniform with me I'd have to operate in "mufti", but that wouldn't matter too much if I could just wear dark trousers, a white shirt and a blazer.

As a newly-promoted captain keen to build up my command hours as quickly as possible I needed very little time to consider my decision; it might be a disruption to my holiday, but I said yes and then went down to the beach to tell Pam the glad news. I don't think she was particularly thrilled at the prospect of my hurtling off to North Africa, but at least it gave her something rather interesting to tell our fellow hotel guests when they enquired why I wasn't around for dinner. I do hope they believed her, especially as I got back to the hotel late the following evening, having completed a long round trip of some twenty-two hours to Malta and then on to Tripoli, Benina and El Adem in Libya before returning to Gatwick and eventually to Bournemouth by taxi again. I certainly slept very well for what was left of that night.

A week later I was back on duty, flying my first trip as sole captain on a DC6: an overnight holiday charter to Rimini and back. It was rather harder work than it should have been because the aircraft's autopilot wasn't working, which meant we had to hand-fly it all the way there and back. Thus by the time I'd completed my first three command trips on the DC6 — the long one to Australia and back, the unexpected one to North Africa in the middle of my holiday and the overnight, hand-flown Rimini trip — I felt I'd had a pretty comprehensive introduction to the business of being captain of a four-engined airliner.

Long-haul trips on the MoD contract, with up to six weeks away from home, were a regular feature of our DC6 programme, but to give us crews a bit of time with our families we would usually be rostered for several European or Mediterranean short-haul holiday flights following our days off after each long trip. Cunard Eagle was one of the pioneers of the new "package holiday" concept, selling inclusive tours through associated companies such as Lunn Poly, and they therefore obtained route permissions into Italy, Spain and other European countries, and even some to the USA, on a charter-flight basis. This meant that they didn't need specific route licences issued by the then Airline Transport Licensing Board (ATLB), which would, without doubt, have been subject to objections from Britain's government-owned national carriers, BEA and BOAC.

In those days the aviation market was far more strictly regulated than now and, when it came to route licences, independent airlines were generally given the scraps that BOAC and BEA didn't want — and if they made a success of a route they might well find that BOAC/BEA wanted it back later on. However, rather unexpectedly, in late 1961, Cunard Eagle gained a full scheduled route licence to operate from Heathrow to New York — the first British independent airline to be granted such a licence in direct competition with the state-owned airline — and they bought two brand new Boeing 707 jet airliners to operate it. Of course, BOAC were very unhappy about this, and they continued to make repeated objections to the competition we posed on that lucrative route. More of that later.

These developments, however, didn't directly affect me — not yet, anyway — and I continued throughout the rest of 1962 as a fairly junior captain on the DC6, flying mainly long-haul trips. 1962 became 1963, and in late January I travelled on a BOAC Comet to Colombo, in Ceylon, as it was still called in those days (it changed to Sri Lanka in 1972), as commander of a DC6 freighter crew; once there, we would have the necessary rest period and then take over an incoming cargo flight from London that was bound for Adelaide via Singapore and Darwin.

Thus it was that on the night of 26 January, 1963, my crew and I were standing in the dark outside the terminal building at Colombo's Katunayake International Airport, awaiting the arrival of DC6 G-APON. We saw the aircraft land and heard reverse pitch on the propellers being selected as normal in order to slow it down, but then everything went terribly wrong. We heard a very loud bang, then we saw the tailfin of the aircraft shoot upwards; flames appeared around the inboard engines as their propellers hit the ground, and it instantly became clear to us that the nosewheel had collapsed. Immediately, John Staite, the flight engineer on my own crew, set off at fast run towards the stricken aircraft, leaping across a fearsomely wide storm drain in his stride. Being of a rather less athletic nature, I hitched a lift on a fire wagon, while the rest of the crew stayed where they were, not wishing to get in the way of any rescue efforts.

On arrival at the aircraft aboard the fire wagon, I was extremely relieved to see that all five crew members (captain, co-pilot, flight engineer, navigator and loadmaster) had already evacuated onto the tarmac; for a moment I could see Captain Phil Taft standing in front of his crew with barely a hair out of place, but then he was suddenly enveloped in a layer of white foam as the fire crew set about dousing the burning engines and everything else in the vicinity. His crew were somewhat protected from the foamy blast by their own commander, who ended up bearing more than a passing resemblance to a snow-man, but at least they were all safe and well, though the aircraft clearly wasn't.

Having scraped off some of the foam, Phil told me what had happened. It had been a perfectly normal landing until the nose-wheel touched the runway, at which point it had started to shimmy — in other words, to move very rapidly from side to side rather than rolling along in a straight line — and the movement was so violent it had caused the whole nosewheel assembly to collapse. The aircraft's sudden deceleration had activated the emergency crash switches, cutting the main electrical circuits to reduce fire risk and leaving just a few lights illuminated by the backup battery system. Had the cockpit been lit solely by its emergency lights it would have been quite dark in there, but it was soon lit up by a bright orange glow coming in from outside: the two inboard engines had caught fire. Both Phil and his co-pilot had immediately reached out to operate the engine fire extinguisher handles — in fact, they almost ended up holding hands — and this quick action helped to prevent a lot more damage in those vital minutes before the fire engines arrived.

As I listened to Phil I remembered something: I had myself flown G-APON six weeks previously, and I had noted in the technical log that the nose-wheel had shimmied a bit on landing, indicating the possibility of wear on the whole assembly. As a result the Eagle maintenance engineers at Heathrow had measured the wear on the nose-wheel's various components but had found everything to be within the manufacturer's prescribed limits, so they had decided to release the aircraft to operate a few more flights before having it back in for a complete nose-wheel change. The aircraft had been due to go back into the hangar at the end of this trip to Australia, but unfortunately the nose-wheel had reached its crisis point a bit earlier than expected.

Anyway, there were no more arrivals expected that night, so G-APON sat on the runway until daybreak. when it became clear that it was not too badly damaged and could probably be repaired. The next step was therefore to get it off the runway so that the airport could reopen and then move it into a hangar so that the damage could be properly evaluated.

The local engineers did a great job of lifting G-APON's nose onto a tractor using large, inflatable bags to raise it from the ground. The main wheels were undamaged, so with the nose supported on the tractor the aircraft was slowly hauled off the runway and towards a maintenance hangar, and everything was going well as the tractor driver carefully positioned his vehicle over the white line that marked the exact centre between the open hangar doors so that the aircraft could be hauled safely inside. However, this particular hangar had apparently never housed an aircraft as big as a DC6, and unfortunately the doors, although opened as wide as they usually would be, were not quite open wide enough to accommodate G-APON's wingspan, with the inevitable result that each wingtip came into sudden contact with the edge of each hangar door. Fortunately, the damage to the wingtips was not too serious, and after the doors had been persuaded to open just a little bit wider G-APON was eventually brought inside. Phew!

But then came the next problem: extricating the tractor from under the aircraft's nose. The first step, of course, was to lift to lift the nose up a bit so that the tractor could drive out, but then someone decided that the nose should be lowered right down onto the hangar floor. However, this had the effect of raising the tailfin much higher than usual, with fairly predictable results: as the nose was lowered, the top of the fin hit the inside of the hangar roof. Again, no serious damaged was sustained, and supports were then put under the nose to keep the tailfin clear of the roof, so eventually this particular exercise in squeezing a quart into a pint pot was accomplished, albeit after several very anxious moments. Once all the freight had been transferred to a replacement aircraft — another Eagle DC6 that had been sent out from Heathrow so that my crew and I could complete our planned trip — repair work could finally begin.

A team of Cunard Eagle engineers came out from London, including one Jock Klacher, who was renowned for his ability to carry out unscheduled "field repairs" virtually anywhere in the world. There was a standing joke amongst Eagle engineers that if any kind of minor repair were needed you should call on Jock to use his "transient shock treatment" — i.e. hitting it with a hammer. I don't know whether or not he used this method on G-APON, but in any case the aircraft was back in flyable condition within a matter of weeks and was then ferried back to London, where further repairs were completed before it returned to full commercial operations.

However, by the time G-APON was back in service a lot of other things had changed. To cut a long story short, a completely unexpected deal had been done by the chairmen of Cunard and BOAC that brought into existence a new airline called BOAC Cunard, which took over the two Cunard Eagle Boeing 707 aircraft and all the Eagle pilots who had been through the Boeing training course. What remained of Eagle had stayed with its original founder, Harold Bamberg, and eventually became British Eagle International Airlines.

Apart from the DC6's, Eagle had acquired some Bristol Britannias for long-haul operations, and the Vikings were being replaced by Viscounts for European work. However, all the transatlantic flying had gone to BOAC Cunard, and as a result pilot redundancies became inevitable. Those made redundant were all junior co-pilots, but of course there were now too many captains, so demotions became necessary as well; I hadn't been a captain for very long so I knew I was vulnerable.

In April, I received a letter from Eagle telling me I would be demoted temporarily to the rank of first officer until the company was able to expand again. Although not unexpected, this was very bad news. Much of my income as a captain was already committed to mortgage and hire-purchase payments, and I wondered how on earth we would manage. However, on the very day that the demotion letter dropped through my letterbox I saw an advertisement in *Flight International* magazine seeking captains to fly Argonaut aircraft on a six-month contract for Aden Airways, a company owned and run by BOAC. I immediately jumped in my car, drove to Eagle's headquarters at Heathrow and went to see John Sauvage, Eagle's Managing Director. I showed him the advert and made him a proposition: if he kept me on my captain's salary with Eagle he could rent me out as a qualified Argonaut pilot to Aden Airways for six months, after which I would return to Eagle with my seniority (and finances) intact. He thought about it for a minute or two, then he picked up the phone and called BOAC.

My idea was welcomed by BOAC/Aden Airways so I was signed up for the six-month contract, on a single-person basis, whilst still being employed by Eagle on my captain's salary and with continuing access to perks such as airline travel concessions. The only big problem was that I knew at the outset that I would be working very hard during those six months, and it was therefore extremely unlikely that I'd be able to get back to the UK to see my family for the duration of the contract. There was only one way to get around this: to take them with me and house us all there at my own expense. To help with the cost of all this we decided to rent out our house in Leigh-on-Sea, so we packed all our possessions into our loft and garage and got ready to leave Britain for a while.

In late April, 1963, the four of us arrived in Aden, staying initially at the Crater Hotel — not the best part of town, but I was planning to find better accommodation as soon as I could. Within a couple of days my aircraft type rating on the Argonaut and my instrument rating had both been renewed, so all I needed then was to do a few route check flights in order to be cleared as a captain. My first one was with Captain Bill Burman, the Chief Pilot, but I was a bit nervous before flying with him because of a minor uniform problem.

On arrival in Aden, I'd been told to buy myself some khaki shirts and trousers, light brown desert boots and matching socks, and although I'd found the shirts and trousers, suitable khaki socks proved elusive. Thus it was that for my first flight with Captain Burman I was wearing my usual black socks, hoping that he wouldn't notice, so when we got to the aircraft steps I stood back and allowed him to go ahead of me. I soon realised, though, that I wasn't the only one who'd had such difficulties, for as he climbed the steps I saw flashes of bright yellow around Captain Burman's ankles, suggesting that any efforts he'd made to find khaki socks had probably proved as fruitless as mine. Anyway, nothing was ever said about my incorrect sock situation, and after further searching around Aden I did manage to find some that were almost khaki and did look much better than my

An Aden Airways Argonaut
Photo: TAHS

black ones. I wondered about buying some for Captain Burman as well but decided that might seem just a little bit undiplomatic.

In fact, Captain Burman became a very good friend to me and my family; he felt we deserved rather better treatment than we were getting as we would be in Aden for so long, so he persuaded Aden Airlines to provide us with a free, furnished flat, just as if I were a permanent employee. We really appreciated that; temperatures in Aden can reach forty degrees centigrade, but as the main bedroom in the flat we were given at Khormaksar was already air-conditioned we just had to purchase an air-conditioner for the girls' room to see us through the summer heat. We had enough money left over to buy a brand new Fiat 600 car, which was relatively cheap in tax-free Aden, and thus we set ourselves up to see out the six months of my contract.

Other temporary captains gradually arrived, but when they met up with me and realised that I had been given family accommodation they quite understandably demanded the same. Aden Airways/BOAC therefore ended up spending rather more on their temporary pilots than expected, so I probably wasn't their favourite employee at the time, and that wasn't the end of it, because when Captain Burman discovered that I had paid for me and my family to fly out to Aden in the first place, albeit on concession fares, he arranged for me to receive full reimbursement, because all the other temporary captains, and subsequently their families, had travelled out free of charge. Bill Burman was certainly one of the best Chief Pilots with whom I've ever had the pleasure of working.

These temporary captains, about six of us in all, were needed because the permanent Aden Airways crews were in the process of being retrained on Vickers Viscounts, which were gradually replacing the ageing Argonauts. During the six months of my contract I flew 600 hours in command on scheduled routes from Aden to destinations such as Mombasa, Jeddah, Cairo, Bahrain, Nairobi, Mogadishu, Riyan (on the south coast of Yemen) and Dire Dawa (in Ethiopia). In the course of this flying I had no fewer than five in-flight failures of the Rolls-Royce Merlin engines that powered the Argonaut, leading to the inevitable three-engined landings, sometimes after dumping fuel to get down to a safe landing-weight. This sounds rather excessive, but it was really only a reflection of the problems involved in operating ageing airframes and liquid-cooled piston engines in severe conditions for which they were never designed. However, it was all good experience for me, though with an engine failure rate of nearly one a month I guess I should consider myself fairly lucky that I came to no harm.

Despite the high temperatures, life was quite civilised and pleasant for Europeans in Aden in the early 1960s. My family and I were members of both the military and civilian beach clubs at Tarshine and Gold Mohr, and we could afford to employ domestic staff to look after our home. First came a tall, good-looking young Somali called Omar, who was very nice but who used to borrow our car every so often. We didn't mind this until one day we discovered what he was doing with it: he was moonlighting as a taxi driver. We decided to dispense with his services and in his place took on a young Yemeni called Ali, who proved to be a wonderful babysitter for our two young daughters, then aged three and one. He was particularly helpful when our younger daughter, Gaynor, contracted monsoon blisters, which caused her great distress. They needed regular bathing with saline solution, and Ali's help proved invaluable. I often wondered later on whether he went into some kind of healthcare career; he would certainly have been perfect for it.

By late October, 1963, my Aden Airways contract had come to an end, so we sold our little Fiat for almost as much as I'd paid for it and prepared to return to England. By this time Aden Airways had received all its new Viscounts, so I delivered the last Argonaut (VP-KOJ) from Aden to its original owners, East African Airways, in Nairobi. My family travelled with me as the only passengers on that final flight, and from Nairobi we flew back to London to see what the future would hold for us.

While I had been away Eagle had acquired more Britannias to replace the DC6's, of which only three were now left. There had been little recruitment, and I was to be reabsorbed on the DC6 fleet, initially as a first officer. However, within a month I was repromoted to a DC6 command, with my previous seniority intact. I was back to where I'd been before Cunard had broken away, so I was hopeful that things would now be rather more settled and predictable.

During January and February, 1964, I continued to operate long-haul trips to Africa and Australia while fleet changes were still being made. In mid-February, John Sauvage, the company's managing director, called me into his office to tell me that two of the remaining three DC6's were to go, but I would be retained as one of four crews to operate the last DC6 as a backup to the expanding Britannia fleet. However, he explained that as the DC6 would occasionally go away on long-haul trips the remaining DC6 pilots would also be required to operate short-haul flights on a completely different aircraft type, built by a different manufacturer. As I've mentioned before in this book, switching back and forth between different aircraft like this would not be allowed today, but it was quite acceptable back then.

I was therefore sent to British European Airways at Heathrow to do a six-week technical course on the Vickers Viscount, and after that I continued flying on the DC6, on the basis that my flight training on the Viscount would be completed at a later date. However, as things turned out I never did a single commercial flight on the Viscount, because by 1964 the company had gained an important MoD military trooping contract to the Far East (Hong Kong and Singapore) and had bought more ex-BOAC Britannias. This, of course, had created a need for more crews, so advertisements for Britannia captains and first officers began to appear in the aviation press.

Now, this annoyed me quite a bit, so I complained to John Sauvage that when the last DC6 was finally disposed of I would probably be left as a short-haul Viscount captain whilst newly-recruited captains would be doing better-paid, long-haul flying on the Britannia. He agreed that this was unfair and immediately sent me to BOAC for a complete Britannia technical course, though he did suggest, and I accepted, that I should afterwards spend some time flying in the right-hand (co-pilot's) seat of the Britannia until considered ready for upgrade to the left. However, in my usual style I *did* make sure that I would continue to draw my pay as a DC6 captain.

After successfully completing the Britannia course I continued to operate in command of the last DC6, G-APON, until early June, 1964, when I delivered it to its new owners, Zantop Airlines of New York. A few weeks before that, however, I had pointed out to the company that the technical course I'd done on the Viscount was about to expire — in other words, if I didn't do the flight training very soon it would no longer be valid — and they decided that even though I was about to become a Britannia pilot it would be useful if I had the Viscount stamped on my licence as well. I was therefore sent to Manston to do the necessary six circuits and landings with Captain Viv Robinson, Eagle's Viscount Fleet Manager, and after that yet another new type was added to my growing list of aircraft ratings, even though, as it turned out, I was never to fly the Viscount again.

A British Eagle Bristol Britannia;
these aircraft were powered by four Bristol Proteus turboprop engines

After returning from the DC6 delivery flight to New York I had another month at home before starting my flight training on the Britannia, but by mid-July I was flying the line as a qualified first officer. In October I was positioned out to Karachi with the Fleet Manager, Captain Peter Busby, to collect a Britannia which had undergone repairs there after being grounded by a technical problem; the required test flight became my final command check, and I flew the aircraft back to London via Istanbul as a full Britannia captain. I was now flying in command of an aircraft equipped with turboprop engines rather than pistons, which marked another significant move forward in my aviation career. I'm sure I felt fairly confident that I would not have to fly on piston engines again, at least not professionally, but that was yet another prediction that ultimately proved to be wide of the mark.

Chapter 6

DURING FEBRUARY OF 1965, I operated an MoD flight into Jesselton (now Kota Kinabalu in the East Malaysian part of Borneo) carrying a squad of Gordon Highlanders. Having dropped them off we came home via Singapore, where we picked up another load of troops and their families returning to the UK, and were then routing home via Bombay and Istanbul. On the flight from Bombay we were battling 60mph headwinds when we received the news that Istanbul was closed due to snow. Our diversion airport was Ankara, which was reporting poor visibility and recent snow, so as we started our descent towards Ankara I briefed my co-pilot, Fred Murray, on the type of approach we were to make, and as normal I asked him to alert me to any perceived deviations. Fred was a real character, and we enjoyed flying together, partly because we came from the same neck of the woods (Southend-on-Sea). He was renowned for two particular things: he always seemed to have an inexhaustible supply of peanuts in his coat pocket, and he always addressed his flying colleagues as "Member"; in fact, he himself became known to us all as "Member Murray".

As we descended, we found ourselves flying through a heavy snowstorm; it might have stopped snowing at the airport, but there was still plenty of white stuff coming down a few miles away. The approach was therefore more difficult than usual, and as there was not a sound from my co-pilot I decided to ask Fred how he thought the approach was looking from his point of view. In reply came a cheery, "You're OK, Member" — not the kind of terminology most pilots used, but on a snowy approach to an airport I'd never actually been to before it made me feel confident that we would make a good landing.

At that moment, however, we had a radio message from Ankara Air Traffic Control telling us to land on the first half of the runway as they had not yet cleared the snow from the other half. Now, suddenly being told that you've only got half the expected runway length available is certainly not ideal, but I was confident we could stop the aircraft within the distance we had left because of the Britannia's excellent braking capability, achieved by putting its very large propellers into reverse pitch — in other words, adjusting their angle to the air-flow so that instead of pushing air backwards they pushed it forwards. As we touched down just beyond the runway threshold I immediately selected reverse on all four engines and, as expected, our speed rapidly reduced; however, as we approached the edge of the snowy half of the runway our propellers, still in reverse pitch, acted like giant snow-blowers, picking up large quantities of the stuff and swirling it around the front of the aircraft, thus blocking all forward vision from the flight deck. I dared not apply any brakes for fear of skidding — not an attractive prospect at any time, let alone when you can't see where you're going — so I decided to hold the reverse power on so that we would stop as quickly as possible.

Then suddenly the white-out conditions cleared, and we could see what was happening: our use of reverse thrust had been so successful we had not only stopped our forward progress but were now actually going *backwards*, with the snow being blown away to the front of us. I immediately cancelled reverse then turned the aircraft round and taxied to the apron as normal, but I'm sure anyone watching this little episode from the control tower or airport terminal must have been amazed to see an aircraft trundling into a mini-blizzard of its own making and then reversing out of it again.

In early 1965, Qantas, the Australian national airline, gave British Eagle an important contract to fly emigrants from the UK to Sydney, Perth, Brisbane, Adelaide and Melbourne. This was in the era of the "Ten Pound Poms", a term referring to British people who took advantage of a scheme that enabled them to emigrate to Australia on payment of that amount; however, it wasn't just British passengers that we carried, as Australia was then welcoming migrants from countries such as Italy, Greece and Turkey as well. As we still had our MoD trooping contract this meant that we had a departure to the Far East or Australia more or less every day.

On one memorable trip to Australia in August, 1965, I had a couple of days off in Darwin, during which I met a young chap called Des Webster, who was keen to make the acquaintance of our female cabin staff (not an uncommon situation when a crew is down-route). On my very next trip to Darwin Des phoned me in my hotel room early one morning and invited me to join him for a game of golf. I told him that although I had on occasion attempted to knock a ball around a golf course I was definitely not a very proficient player, but Des assured me that this didn't matter at all, so I agreed to go along.

We duly arrived at Darwin's one-and-only golf course, and I soon discovered why my ability as a player was not terribly important. Darwin's (very) rainy season was due to start any day, and this was the last day of play before the course would shut down until the expected rainstorms and floods eventually abated. It was also a good opportunity to dispose of any excess stocks of alcoholic liquor from the clubhouse, and a small bar was therefore set up adjacent to every green so that golfers could take a little refreshment after successfully negotiating each hole — in fact, they were absolutely required to do so by the special rules of the day.

For the first nine holes things went fairly well, but it was a whole different ball-game (literally) when it came to the back nine. Those players who had survived the first nine and were still determined to carry on — and Des and I were *not* among them — became ever more erratic as they progressed from hole to hole, and I do remember seeing the few who managed to make it all the way to the eighteenth using their putters like snooker cues to push the ball into the hole from a kneeling position. I don't know who actually won that day or how many strokes he accrued, but I suspect he had a fairly monumental hangover next morning.

Of course, I'd been flying to Darwin since the mid 1950s, and over the years I'd seen many changes. As already mentioned, when I first started going to Darwin we stayed either at the Darwin Hotel, where we'd often have to share a room with crocodile hunters, or we'd stay at the RAAF Officers' Mess, where we would often find ourselves taking a shower under the watchful gaze of the local wildlife. Luxury it was not.

By the mid-1960s, however, that "frontier" Darwin had largely disappeared, and we were now able to stay in comfortable, modern hotels, with our own, unshared rooms and wildlife-free bathroom facilities. There was also an increased understanding of possible threats posed by pests imported accidentally from overseas, so procedures were in place to reduce such risks to a minimum. It was therefore required by the Australian authorities that every arriving aircraft should carry insecticidal sprays to be discharged throughout the cabin before landing in order to kill off any six-legged stowaways that might be potential hazards.

Most of the flights that I operated into Australia would enter the country through Darwin, and although we always carried out the required spraying before arrival, the local Department of Agriculture officials were not quite satisfied with that. To make absolutely sure that we hadn't brought any "nasties" with us from Singapore they would insist on sending out a couple of gas-masked officers, who would board the aircraft as soon as the front door opened and then close it again before bombarding the whole cabin and flight deck with their own preferred insecticide. All windows and doors had to be kept shut, and we were forbidden to use any air-conditioning for at least five minutes while the spray did its work, though I'm sure it was often more like ten minutes before we were allowed to open up again. Those minutes were almost unbearable; with an outside temperature of up to 35°C and the permanently high humidity of Darwin, "stifling" was hardly strong enough to describe the conditions on the aircraft, and the spray made everyone's eyes water, as well as irritating our noses and throats so much that it was almost impossible to breathe, let alone speak. It was horrible.

But even when we opened up the doors and got off the aircraft there was another dreadful trial to endure: as we walked down the steps and across the tarmac, we would invariably be attacked by the biggest mosquitoes any of us had seen in our lives. In fact, we came to the conclusion that the spraying we had to undergo on arrival was designed to ensure that no puny little Singapore mozzies could make it into Australia and dilute the gene pool of the local population of airborne giants. That was *our* theory, anyway.

Another interesting little element of the arrival procedure at Darwin was the regular confiscation of all unused food items that we had brought in with us, *including* tinned fruit. I never quite fathomed what danger there could possibly be in a tin of fruit, but there was clearly some advantage in this confiscation system for the catering people at Darwin Airport, because it meant we had to buy fresh supplies of Australian products from them for our onward journey. Of course, I'm sure the stuff we brought in was *very* safely disposed of!

Although Darwin was our main point of entry into Australia on these emigrant flights we occasionally arrived through Perth, and it was on one of these Perth trips, in August, 1965, that unexpected political developments led to a drastic change in our itinerary. Having arrived in Perth we were expecting, after a 24-hour rest stop, to take the empty aircraft back to Singapore, ready to pick up a full load of troops and their families in accordance with our usual MoD contract. After arriving late morning we had a few drinks as usual and retired to our various rooms to get a good sleep before departing the next day, but during the evening, not long after I'd got to sleep, my bedside phone started ringing; it was our Operations Department in London, and they told me I must get the aircraft back to Singapore as soon as humanly possible, as it was to be officially commandeered, with Eagle's permission, by the RAF. At first I thought someone might be pulling my leg, but I realised it was deadly serious when our Chief Operations Officer, Harry Wyatt, came on the phone, so I jumped out of bed and set about waking and mustering the rest of my crew.

I had soon got hold of everyone other than the first officer and one of our stewardesses, both of whose room phones remained stubbornly unanswered. Bashing on their doors and shouting had no effect either, so I was not totally surprised when the hotel receptionist told me she had seen them getting into a taxi together an hour or two previously. I phoned the taxi company and was told they had asked to be taken to an out-of-town motel for some "privacy", so I then called the motel and told them who I was looking for. I gather my two crew members were very surprised when, shortly thereafter, a barman addressed them by name and told them they must return immediately to the crew hotel.

We understood that as soon as we could get the aircraft back to Singapore another British Eagle crew would be taking it on to RAF Gan in the Maldives; this, of course, was long before the Maldives had become one of the world's top holiday destinations, so it wasn't too surprising that my navigator's first words on hearing this news were, "Where the **** is Gan?". From Gan the aircraft would be going to Dacca — now the capital of Bangladesh but in those days the main city of East Pakistan — to carry out an emergency evacuation of British citizens because war had broken out between India and Pakistan, mainly over their respective claims to Kashmir.

We eventually departed from Perth in the early morning, and after twenty-four hours in Singapore we picked up another incoming Britannia and set off for RAF Gan ourselves, expecting to go on from there to Dacca. On arrival at Gan, the female cabin staff were given secure isolated accommodation, guarded by RAF police, so my co-pilot was definitely unable to pursue his amorous adventures any further. We were also temporarily seconded into the RAF ourselves and given appropriate rankings: mine was Squadron Leader, which I was quite happy with, but my co-pilot suffered even more disappointment when he discovered he was outranked by our No. 1 stewardess; *he* was now a Flying Officer, but *she* was a Flight Lieutenant. He was not very happy at all, but at least the stewardess who outranked him was *not* the one who was the object of his affections.

The aircraft was due to be put into RAF configuration, complete with military registration number and roundels painted on the fuselage, while we waited in Gan for two days, but during that time things calmed down a bit, and in the end we were not required to do a Dacca trip at all. Now that the aircraft was no longer needed by the RAF, Eagle decided to bring it back to London, so we left Gan empty and returned to Heathrow via Bahrain, and by the time we got home I think my co-pilot was just starting to get over what must have been one of the most frustrating trips of his life.

British Eagle had expanded a great deal during 1965, purchasing more Britannias from BOAC and commencing a series of European holiday flights to such destinations as Valencia, Pisa, Barcelona and Rimini. These flights were intermingled with long-haul trips, which gave us crews a rather better lifestyle in that we weren't spending quite such a huge proportion of our time away from home and family. However, I was selected as one of just a few Britannia captains to be checked out as competent to land at Hong Kong's famous — or, perhaps more appropriately, infamous — Kai Tak International Airport, and this meant I continued to do quite a few Far East trips that usually included picking up inbound Eagle flights at Singapore, "shuttling" them to Hong Kong and back and then handing them over

The flight deck of a Bristol Britannia: you can just see the control columns that look more like bicycle handlebars than vital parts of an aircraft, but similar ones were used later on in Concorde.
Photo: MAP

to their original crews so they could set off on their homeward journey to the UK.

Kai Tak's fairly fearsome reputation had come about because it was a coastal airport with a runway built on reclaimed land, with one end pointing out to sea and the other tucked rather worryingly close under a large mountain. Arriving from the seaward end was straightforward, but the prevailing winds meant that aircraft generally came in from the landward end, at which a normal, straight approach was impossible because of the terrain. However, a clever answer to this conundrum had been provided in the form of a large "checkerboard" sign placed on the mountainside above the airport, just beyond the point at which an aircraft would need to turn sharply right in order to line up with the runway. This alone made for one of the most interesting approaches a pilot could ever fly, but added to it was the fact that having made your right-hand turn you continued your descent over the towering apartment blocks of Kowloon, and with flaps and gear down the amount of space between rooftops and rubber was somewhat less than was entirely comfortable. These days, of course, Hong Kong has a huge new airport, and Kai Tak has been closed for many years, but you can still gain a flavour of what it was like in the "good old days" of the Checkerboard Approach if you have access to the internet and simply look for video footage of aircraft arriving at Kai Tak — there's plenty of it to enjoy.

Over the next couple of years I did many trips into Hong Kong, usually arriving via the Checkerboard Approach, and on one occasion, at the end of June, 1967, I had operated a trooping flight into Hong Kong from Singapore, arriving in the early afternoon and scheduled for a quick turn-round. The passenger offload/onload operation went smoothly, and we were soon ready for departure, but we were about to call for start-up clearance when I noticed a large, black, roll-type cloud bearing down on the airport form the north. Roll clouds are associated with extreme conditions, particularly the phenomenon of wind-shear, in which the wind speed and direction can change almost instantly, often with violent updrafts or downdrafts that are almost impossible to cope with when flying at low altitude, such as when approaching or departing from an airport. As we were actually a few minutes early on our scheduled departure time, I asked the army colonel who was in charge of our passengers to come up to the flight deck, where I explained to him that I was concerned about the weather and had therefore decided to delay our departure for a while until it was clearer. In the meantime, I authorised a round of drinks for all the passengers while we waited.

Almost immediately we were swamped by a deluge of rain, the aircraft was buffeted by heavy winds and the visibility dropped to near-zero. How glad I was that we were still on the ground. However, as so often happens in the tropics the storm passed quickly, and as the weather cleared my co-pilot called for start-up clearance, expecting us to be on our way very soon. We were both surprised, therefore, when our request was denied and we were told that the airport was now closed and would probably remain so for twenty-four hours. Clearly, something quite serious had happened during the storm.

Which indeed it had: a Thai International Airways Caravelle — a twin-jet type with a far better rate of climb than our Britannia, even though we had four engines rather than two — had been caught in a vicious downdraft as it was approaching Kai Tak's runway from the seaward end and had been forced down into the water just short of the tarmac. RAF helicopters were quickly scrambled, and although they successfully rescued most of the eighty people on board we learnt much later that twenty-four of the seventy-three passengers had lost their lives.

Anyway, while all this was going on we couldn't actually see the seaward end of the runway from where we were parked, but it became apparent that the fin of the Caravelle was left high and dry when the aircraft came to rest in the shallow water, so no further flights could operate until it was moved out of the way. This must have been accomplished within the 24-hour closure time that was given to us just after the accident, as we were able to depart safely the following day.

This, of course, was the third time I had been on the ground at an airport when an aircraft had suffered a crash; the first two had been the DC-6 accidents at Shannon and Colombo previously mentioned, in which, mercifully, no-one had sustained any serious injury. I was to witness one further major accident in my flying career, one which would prove to be by far the worst of all, but at this time that event still lay far in the future.

Events such as this Caravelle accident bring home to any pilot how fine the line between survival and disaster can sometimes be, but after learning whatever lessons can be taken from them you just have to put any dark thoughts to the back of your mind and carry on with the job. I was therefore able to smile when, a couple of trips later, I found myself rostered for a flight with three other crew members rejoicing in the rather alarming names of Eddie Bendall, Red Breakall and Jim Hazzard. Fortunately, all went well, with no bending, breaking or other hazards to report.

During 1966 and 1967 I continued flying a mixture of long-haul and short-haul trips on the Britannia; one week I'd be off to somewhere exotic such as Borneo, carrying British troops, and the next I might be doing a quick London-Liverpool scheduled service before departing on a transatlantic charter trip the following morning. Eagle had acquired the London-Liverpool domestic route when it had taken over a company called Starways a couple of years previously, and it had also been awarded a scheduled route to Glasgow in its own right, so return trips to both these destinations were on any Britannia pilot's programme; in fact, I remember that on more than one occasion I carried a rather popular Liverpudlian pop group consisting of four young men whose first names were John, Paul, Ringo and George. I wonder whatever happened to them?

By early 1968 I seemed to have it all: a good, secure job that I loved, a growing family and a lovely home. I had been offered a captain's position on the new short-haul BAC 1-11's that were now in service with Eagle, but on the advice of BALPA I'd decided to stay on the Britannia fleet, as they reckoned my seniority would probably get me promoted onto the long-haul Boeing 707's that Eagle had recently acquired from Qantas. These had already begun operating some trans-atlantic charters and a London-Bermuda-New York scheduled service as well.

Of course, not every day, nor every flight, was entirely enjoyable; for instance, on 9 August, 1968, I was telephoned by Eagle's crewing department and told to get to Heathrow as quickly as possible ready to fly. No destination was mentioned, so as I arrived at the airport I didn't know where I would be going, though I soon found out. Earlier that day, a British Eagle Viscount aircraft (G-ATFN) carrying forty-four passengers and four crew on a flight from Liverpool to Innsbruck had crashed near Munich, killing all on board. I was to fly the CAA's accident investigation team and a group of engineers from British Eagle out to Munich so they could start piecing together exactly what had happened on this tragic and terrible day. It was probably the saddest trip I ever did.

On returning, my crew and I had to take another Britannia from London to Liverpool to pick up the flight schedule of the ill-fated Viscount, surely a very real case of filling dead men's shoes. I recall that our arrival there was particularly emotional; the locally-based cabin staff who turned out to greet us were obviously distraught at losing their colleagues in the accident, but they were very glad that the company was going to use Liverpool cabin staff on our Heathrow-based Britannia rather than just sending up a batch of Heathrow crew. They clearly felt that at this awful time it was best to keep working and flying, despite what had happened. My flight crew and I thus spent a week based in Liverpool, staying in the Adelphi Hotel and doing daily flights between Liverpool, Glasgow and London.

The investigation into the crash of the Viscount eventually concluded that a total loss of electrical power had caused the flying instruments to give inaccurate indications to the pilots as they started descending towards their destination, and as a result the aircraft had got into an extreme nose-down attitude of which the crew were unaware because they were flying in thick cloud with no visual reference to the ground. It was found that the outer parts of both wings had broken away before final impact, probably because of the G-forces to which they'd been subjected when the crew had realised, on descending out of the cloud, the dire situation they were in and had pulled back on the control column in an attempt to save the aircraft. Lessons were learned and modifications to the electrical system of all Viscounts were subsequently made mandatory, but like all such accidents it brought home to the rest of us how unforgiving our profession could be if things went seriously wrong.

After my brief sojourn in Liverpool it was back to normal flying for me. British Eagle was now a fairly large company with some 2,500 employees, and with an expanded 1969 programme in mind it arranged financing for a further two Boeing 707's to use for trans-atlantic and other long-haul flights. As I'd hoped, I was soon put on the list for a 707 training course, and I was very glad that my last Britannia trip, departing in early November, was likely to be a memorable one: a round-the-world "air cruise" passenger charter visiting interesting places such as Baghdad, New Delhi, Phnom Penh, Bangkok, Hong Kong, Tokyo, Honolulu, San Francisco, Toronto and New York. We would be picking up our passengers in Frankfurt; in fact, it is very doubtful that we could have run such a trip from London because British people were then subject to a £50 limit on the amount of money they could take out of the country when going on holiday, a sum which wouldn't go very far on a long trip such as this. Germans, however, were not bound by such financial strictures.

Well, things didn't work out as expected, but this time it wasn't the vagaries of aircraft serviceability, or weather, or air traffic control or any similar, practical matters that scuppered our plans: it was politics, particularly aviation politics. To cut a long and complex story short,

BOAC, the state long-haul airline, had complained to the government (as usual) that Eagle was providing far too much competition for them on transatlantic routes, and as a result Eagle's licence to fly to New York and other North American destinations was cancelled without warning and with immediate effect. This was a hammer-blow for the airline: the financing for the 707's was instantly withdrawn, and as the Britannia trooping contracts had, by cruel coincidence, just been transferred to the RAF, who would operate them with their VC10 jets, British Eagle suddenly became an airline whose wings had been severely clipped.

Thus on 6 November, 1968, some five days before I had been due to depart on my final, round-the-world Britannia trip, British Eagle went into liquidation. I remember how I heard the news: I was at home, draining the radiator of my wife's Mini Cooper before refilling it with water and antifreeze so she wouldn't have any problems while I was away. I was just closing the little drain-tap when Pam suddenly called to me from the front door, telling me that the one o'clock news on the radio was saying that British Eagle had gone bust. I hoped she'd misheard, but of course it was all horribly true.

My last act as an Eagle captain was to hand back the ship's funds already issued to me for that round-the-world trip, which I did with a heavy heart. Suddenly, life was looking rather bleak. My wonderful career had come to a shuddering halt, and once again I was looking for a job, but this time in competition with lots of other very well-qualified pilots. I had no idea what the future might hold, but I knew that if I ever again found a job with a company that had such high staff morale as Eagle I would be a very lucky pilot indeed.

I'd been unemployed before of course, but this time I had a mortgage on a four-bedroom, two-bathroom, detached house, two young daughters at private school, a Daimler-Jaguar, my wife's Mini Cooper and a dog to support. As I had mistakenly thought, when I first joined a Cunard company, that I would have a job for life, I had saved little money in the past eight years, and as I discovered to my horror during Eagle's liquidation, much of the company pension scheme had been used, quite legally, to cover some of the airline's operational costs; as a result, younger members of the scheme such as myself would receive virtually nothing from it in terms of future pension provision.

All we got was a refund of our own personal contributions, minus the income tax they'd been relieved of when we made them, so instead of having what in my case should have been eight years of pension saving with contributions from both myself and my employer I was left with an eight-year gap during which, through no fault of my own, I ended up having put nothing aside for my eventual retirement. The law did change in subsequent years, and it became illegal for companies to use their pension funds in this way, though that didn't stop Robert Maxwell from doing a very similar thing with the Mirror Group pension fund in the 1980's. However, that's another story.

Anyway, a week or two after I became redundant I saw an advertisement in *Flight International* magazine seeking a pilot to fly various aircraft for a company called Williamson Diamonds out of its base at Mwadui, Tanzania. Having no immediate prospect of an airline job I immediately sent in an application and was soon called in for interview at the very impressive Rolls Building in London. I was told that there were another forty-one applicants — all from British Eagle — for that one position, so I knew I was up against a lot of competition.

Williamson Diamonds was part of the global Anglo-American Corporation, and its previous chief pilot, a non-family man in his fifties, had been diagnosed with mental health problems. The interviewers were therefore looking for a younger, family-oriented applicant; I was thirty-four, with 10,000 hours in my logbook, and by chance I had both the DC3 and DC4 on my licence, the very aircraft types being used at Mwadui. I fitted the bill, and ahead of all my former colleagues from British Eagle I was offered the job.

I quickly accepted and signed a one-year contract, so we rented out our house to an oil company executive based at the nearby Canvey Island oil refinery, and we sold both our cars. In fact, selling my wife's Mini Cooper proved to be rather easier than expected. I was driving it along Southend High Street one day when I stopped at the traffic lights. Suddenly, someone was tapping on the roof, so I opened the window to find a young chap looking down at me and saying, "Hey, mate, do you want to sell your car?" I told him that by coincidence yes, I did want to sell it, so as the lights started changing he thrust his business card through the window and asked me to call round and see him the next day. When I looked at his card I realised why he might be interested in the car: its number-plate was PK 777, and the gentleman in question was a bookmaker called Peter Ketley with an office in the famous Kursaal building on Southend seafront. I don't know what eventually happened to the Mini, but years later I saw that same registration on Peter Ketley's Rolls Royce.

Thus in mid-January, 1969, my whole family, including our dog, Panda, were en route to Nairobi, flying on BOAC. We arrived in the early morning, and Panda was put in a kennel at the airport while the rest of us recovered from the flight at the Norfolk Hotel downtown. By mid-afternoon we were airborne to Mwadui in the Williamson DC3, with Panda, a rather large collie-cross, sitting on my lap, which I'm sure she preferred after her long trip from Britain in the hold of a Boeing 707. On arrival we were met by the Acting Chief Pilot, Hans Haslett, who handed me the keys of a company Minivan and showed us to our living accommodation, a lovely, three-bedroomed bungalow with a large garden on the edge of the mine's golf course. The mine complex was very impressive with marvellous facilities, including three swimming-pools, two schools, a cinema, restaurants and three reservoirs, one of them with a small fleet of sailing-dinghies, as well as the aforementioned golf course. There was also a farm, with its own milking-herd, beef cattle and pigs, and there was an abbatoir, too, so we had plentiful supplies of excellent fresh meat, along with fresh milk delivered to our doorstep every morning.

The mine employed about ten thousand people, mostly from the local area but with about two hundred European management staff and some Asian technicians. Both my daughters were installed in one of the mine's schools, which had British teachers and mostly European students, though some of the students were the children of African managers who worked at the mine. My wife soon found employment in the administration of the diamond-sorting office, while I started to get involved with the flying.

Initially I was checked out on the DHC Beaver, a seven-seat, single-engined aircraft that was used to fly geologists and technical staff to outlying mines and exploratory sites. Having flown Britannias for the previous five years I found it a complete change to fly a small, tail-wheel aircraft, but after being shown the ropes by Hans Haslett I was sent off to do solo circuits on Mwadui's dirt runway to brush up my tail-wheel skills. I then flew some operational flights, with Hans showing me the routes, and once he was happy that I could fly the aircraft well and knew the lie of the land I started the daily routine of delivering passengers to the gold mine at Bukemba, near the eastern coast of Lake Victoria, in the morning, then spending the day in a very pleasant rest-house there before flying them back to Mwadui in the evening.

I was subsequently checked out on the DC3 and DC4, flying to the international airports at Nairobi and Dar-es-Salaam; on these flights we mainly carried passengers — usually visitors to the mine or Williamson employees — but we sometimes carried mining products such as gold and diamonds, and we would often take back locally purchased supplies, such as fruit and vegetables from Nairobi, or items of equipment that had been sent down from Europe by air or sea. Sometimes I would be able to carry back stuff that I'd bought myself to enhance our lifestyle on the mine; on one occasion it was a complete sailing-dinghy that I'd purchased at Nairobi Sailing Club and with which I subsequently took part in Sunday afternoon races on the biggest of our Mwadui reservoirs, with my younger daughter, Gaynor,

A DHC Beaver, like the one I flew for Williamson Diamonds in Tanzania: it was certainly quite a change from the Britannia.
Photo: MAP

as crew. I'd never sailed before, so we weren't particularly successful, but it was always good fun.

As all the Mwadui aircraft were privately operated for the Anglo-American Corporation, carrying employees and visitors only and with no fares being charged, we were allowed to operate with just one qualified pilot and an engineer/pilot's helper in the co-pilot's seat. Any technical examinations or rating renewals were done with East African Airways at Nairobi, usually during a day-stop. However, it soon became apparent to me, after I'd done several DC3 flights to Dar-es-Salaam with only one passenger — the mine's General Manager, George Hunt — that we needed a smaller, more efficient, light twin-engined aircraft for such duties. The mine's managers agreed, so the local agents for Piper and Cessna flew to Mwadui and allowed our engineers to examine and me to fly their respective products, the Piper Aztec and the Cessna 310.

We'd also contacted Beechcraft, but they didn't seem terribly interested, so on my next visit to Nairobi I, with engineer George Lockhart, visited the Beechcraft agent at Wilson Airport. After a bit of persuasion he arranged for us to have a look at and a flight in the Baron D55, and we immediately decided that despite Beechcraft's reticence it was absolutely in a class of its own. A deal was agreed, and

by late August our brand new Baron had arrived, direct from the USA factory in Wichita and complete with autopilot, coloured radar and lots of other good stuff. No more would we find ourselves bumping along, trying to thread our way round thunderstorms;

The Williamson Diamonds Douglas DC3 (above) and DC4 (right)

Photos:
RA Scholefield (DC3)
and David Welch (DC4)

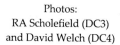

with the Baron's colour radar we could easily find relatively calm air through which to fly, while its state-of-the-art autopilot took much of the workload off the one and only pilot, making life much easier than on the DC3 and DC4.

A Beechcraft Baron: this is not the actual aircraft I flew in Tanzania, but I did fly this one later in my career on air taxi work out of Southend.
Photo: MAP

In March the little DHC Beaver had to go into Nairobi for overhaul, so the company rented in a single-engine Cessna 206 aircraft to replace it while it was out of action. This was a good touring aircraft as well as being capable of handling the kind of rough strips that we kept the Beaver for, so I decided to hire it myself for a day to take my wife and daughters to Lake Manyara to see some wildlife. We landed at Lake Manyara's airport in the early morning, spent the day doing a guided tour of the game park, and then took off for Mwadui in the evening. During climb-out, however, we had a very frightening experience: the engine began to splutter, which made the propeller speed up and slow down alarmingly as the power fluctuated. Turning back towards the airfield was not really an option as we could easily have entered a stall during the turn, so I had no choice but to descend towards the lake itself, the surface of which was considerably below the 4,000ft height of the airport. Fortunately, as we descended, the engine smoothed out and began to run normally, and we were able to continue our flight at low altitude with no further problems.

After landing safely back at Mwadui I asked our engineers what they thought could have happened, and the general opinion was that while the aircraft had been sitting on the ground, the fuel in its wings (petrol, of course) had been heated by the sun, almost to boiling-point. As we'd climbed away from the airfield on our homeward flight, the change in air pressure lowered the boiling-point of the fuel (just as it does for water, which boils at a lower temperature on an airborne aircraft than it does on the ground), causing the fuel to start bubbling and making the engine run rough. As we descended, the boiling-point of the fuel rose as the air pressure increased; this meant that the fuel temperature was no longer so close to boiling, so the bubbling subsided and the engine once again ran smoothly. It had been our great good fortune that we had been able to descend quite low over the lake; if we had been amongst mountains, we may not have come out of that situation quite so well.

In August, 1969, my uncle and aunt visited from the UK, having travelled by ship to Cape Town and then taken a flight to Nairobi. All six of us spent a wonderful two weeks on a game tour of Uganda (this was before the age of Idi Amin), travelling via Mwanza and an overnight ferry across Lake Victoria to Kampala, where we hired a seven-seat Peugeot 404 estate car, in which we ended up doing around a thousand miles of dirt-track driving.

During our little safari we did a boat trip on the upper Nile, and on its banks we could see huge crocodiles basking in the sunshine whilst keeping an eye open for any passing meal. Also on the boat was a group of American tourists, including a couple of young children, and I was amazed when the children, with the apparent approval of their parents, took off their shoes, sat on the side of the boat and let their feet dangle in the water. It was only when their fellow passengers pointed out that this was not a particularly good idea, bearing in mind the very large reptiles with very big teeth that we could see sitting just a short distance away and whose relatives might be lurking in the water beneath us, that the couple realised the danger and quickly instructed their children to get back inside the boat. I presume that family's only previous experience of exotic animals had been within the safety of zoos or wildlife parks, as they were clearly naïve about the risks posed by truly wild animals living in a truly wild environment. I don't know where in the USA they came from, but I suppose it can't have been Florida or any of the other southern states that have their own large, indigenous reptiles to contend with.

The rest of the year passed uneventfully until 4 November, when something happened that set my career on yet another new track. At 9.15am that morning I landed the Williamson DC4 (5H-AAH) at Dar-es-Salaam, and I just happened to park next to a Zambia Airways BAC 1-11 jet airliner that had clearly suffered damage to its nose-cone. Apparently, it had hit an eagle on the approach to land, and it was therefore grounded until a replacement fibreglass nose-cone could be supplied and fitted. The captain of the BAC 1-11 turned out to be a chap called Roy Westgate, who had been British Eagle's Fleet Captain on Britannias, and as I was staying in "Dar" overnight I decided to contact him at the Kilimanjaro Hotel to discuss old times.

At the bar he told me he was now Chief Pilot of Zambia Airways Corporation, an airline that was managed by Alitalia, and that they were shortly to acquire a Douglas DC8 four-engined, long-range jet. As Roy was recruiting pilots he enquired about my future plans; I told him I was subject to renewal of my one-year contract with Williamson Diamonds less than two months hence, and on hearing this he offered me a position as co-pilot on the DC8 with an operational base in London. As the salary was a lot more than I was getting with Williamson, and as the job was based in the UK, I immediately accepted and was told that a contract would be available, ready for me to sign, at the Zambia Airways office in Nairobi next time I was there.

The very next day, on my return to Mwadui, I tendered my resignation with effect from the end of my contract on 31 December, 1969, and then on 21 November, having flown the DC4 into Nairobi for my usual day-stop, I visited the Zambia Airways office in the Hilton Hotel. A young lady at the airline's reception desk confirmed that there was indeed a contract waiting for me in their office and remarked, rather mysteriously, that I'd find something in it that I probably didn't expect. And indeed I did: the contract was as a DC8 captain rather than a co-pilot, with a commensurate increase in the expected salary. Considering the fact that I'd never yet flown a jet airliner (one without propellers, that is) I was both surprised and delighted at this pre-employment promotion; things were definitely looking up.

Nonetheless, as we left the mine to return to the UK at the end of 1969 we were all feeling sad to be saying goodbye to a great place where we'd had a wonderful lifestyle and had met some marvellous people. Had Panda, our dog, known what was awaiting her — six months in quarantine in the UK — she would have been pretty upset as well, particularly as she would no longer be able to enjoy her favourite pastime: chasing a tame "Tommy" gazelle that would often visit our garden at Mwadui but would leap effortlessly out of the way, performing a ninety-degree turn in mid-air, whenever Panda hurled herself across the lawn towards it.

However, we could not deny feeling happy to be going home, and I was very excited that I would soon be going to the Alitalia training centre in Rome to learn how to fly my first big four-engined jet. Another new chapter in my aviation life was about to begin.

Chapter 7

ON RETURNING TO OUR HOME IN LEIGH-ON-SEA on 1 January, 1970, we were delighted to find that our wonderful neighbours had cleaned it from top to bottom before our arrival; they knew the house had been left in a poor state, and they did not want us to come back to a mess at the end of our long, tiring journey. Our dog, Panda, had gone straight from Heathrow to a quarantine kennel in Colchester, but even without her getting under our feet everything was a bit of a rush, as I was about to depart again for Rome to start my training on the Douglas DC8 with Alitalia. We very quickly bought a car for Pam, retrieved our personal possessions from the attic and got ourselves more or less settled back in before I headed off to Heathrow for my flight to Rome, ready to begin my course on 4 January.

The Zambia Airways DC8, acquired from Alitalia
Photo: TAHS

Zambia Airways Corporation had contracted to acquire, by lease-purchase, a DC8 from the Alitalia fleet, which would be flown by non-Alitalia crews and would operate the airline's first route from Lusaka to London via Rome with occasional stops at Nairobi. As the aircraft was to fly a heavy schedule totalling some 4,500 hours a year, Zambia Airways recruited five captains, five senior first officers (who were licensed to take command while the captain was taking a rest period during flight), five junior first officers, five flight engineers and five navigators (astronavigation was required for this route as radio navigation aids were non-existent over large parts of it). A backup aircraft from the Alitalia fleet would be provided during periods when the Zambia Airways DC8 was undergoing maintenance in Rome.

Ninety per cent of the pilots and engineers on the technical course were ex-British Eagle so I knew nearly everyone there, and I also knew all the navigators, who would be joining us later on as they didn't need specific training on the aircraft. The theory part of the course went reasonably well, although at times the Italian instructors had difficulty explaining some of the finer details, and I think the fact that none of us trainees had even set foot on a DC8 flight deck caused a lot of frustration for both them and us. However, by mid-February we were ready to do an oral test in front of a board of Alitalia examiners; fortunately we all passed, and by sheer chance (I'm sure), all the "commandanti" gained higher marks than the co-pilots and flight engineers, the margin of difference being almost the same in every case. What a coincidence!

On 16 February, I had my first lesson on the Alitalia DC8 simulator, and suddenly the answers to all those little practical questions that everyone had agonised over in the classroom became much clearer. I'd done some training in a simulator before — the Bristol Britannia one in London back in Eagle days — but this one was much more advanced; in fact, it was state-of the-art, though back in 1970 the "art" was a long way from what it is today. The Alitalia simulator was completely static — there were no hydraulic legs to reproduce the kind of G-forces experienced in flight — and there were no clever visual displays either, so there was no simulated view of the outside world in the flight deck window. Compared with today's machines, where the instructor can dial up a pilot's-eye view of any major airport with all its surrounding landscape, add in any kind of weather situation, such as turbulence, fog or strong crosswinds, and put trainees through an almost infinite range of interesting situations to see how they respond, the DC8 simulator in Rome was a relatively simple thing: a functioning facsimile of the aircraft flight deck in which trainees would practise various phases of flight and familiarise themselves with all the aircraft's controls, instruments and equipment. It did have sound effects, so if you pushed the throttles forward the simulated engine noise would increase, but the "all-singing, all-dancing" simulators of today were still far in the future.

Our simulator training was complete by 20 February, and we all returned to London for a nice little break of twelve days before the start of our flight training, which was to be done in Tunis. I was certainly glad to have a bit of time to sort things out at home, having left so much for Pam to do following my rushed departure from London just a couple of days after getting back from Tanzania.

I had my first training session on the DC8 on 2 March, the day after my thirty-sixth birthday. My excellent instructor was a Corsican, Captain Giovanni Salle, and on that very first flight I found myself doing stalls, steep turns and even an emergency descent, which on a DC8 is one of the more exciting things one can ever do in life.

Most jet airliners that have ever been built have spoilers (or air brakes) that can be used during flight, but the DC8's spoilers were designed purely for use on the ground to help slow it down after landing. Of course, all pressurised aircraft have to be able to descend rapidly to a survivable altitude of around ten thousand feet in the event of a sudden loss of cabin pressure, and the DC8 had been developed with its own rather novel way of doing this: using reverse thrust on *all four engines*.

Thus on my first ever flight on a DC8 (I'd never even been on one as a passenger), I found myself, under Captain Salle's direction, climbing the aircraft up to forty thousand feet over the desert and then, on his command, launching into the designated emergency descent procedure. First, I had to don the captain's emergency oxygen mask, then I had to select "idle reverse" on all four engines before putting the two inboards into full reverse thrust and pointing the nose of the aircraft downwards at an angle of twenty degrees below the horizon. I'd never seen a vertical speed indicator winding down at a rate of sixteen thousand feet a minute before, so this was certainly one of the more exhilarating experiences I'd had in my career so far.

The legal requirement for any aircraft was to reach ten thousand feet within two minutes, but at around thirteen thousand feet I had to start raising the nose of the DC8 to slow our rate of descent so that we could level off at ten thousand and put the power setting back to normal. It all went exactly to plan, and I began to realise that here was yet another Douglas aircraft that I was going to love flying.

Having read books on handling large jet aircraft I knew about the need to anticipate the longer "spool-up" times of jet engines compared to the much quicker responses of the piston engines and turboprops I'd been flying before, but the Rolls Royce Conway engines fitted to Alitalia's DC8's (and thus our Zambia Airways one) were far more responsive than I'd imagined they would be — almost like a piston engine, in fact. The Conway was a really good piece of kit, and in its day it powered VC10's and Boeing 707's as well as DC8's and some military aircraft types. Over time, as newer engines with better fuel consumption came along, the Conway became too expensive to operate and gradually became obsolete, but I have always considered myself very lucky to have done my initial jet training on Conways, as their responsiveness was so good they made a potentially tricky transition very much easier.

At this stage we trainees were living in the Tunis Hilton, being paid subsistence allowances at the standard, quite generous, Alitalia rate, and these were apportioned out to us, in cash, by the hotel's front desk manager every few days. The pile of lira notes given to our instructor, Captain Salle, always looked considerably thicker than ours — and quite rightly so — but one day I plucked up the courage to ask him how much he actually received. "Enough", came the instant reply. There was clearly no point in asking for more details.

I completed my final check flight prior to line training on 19 March after some twelve hours of actually handling the aircraft myself and around fourteen hours of watching the efforts of fellow students (there were always two or more trainees on each flight, and after each had done his share of take-offs and landings there would be a general swapping of seats so that the next trainee could start his own session). By the end of March I'd started my line training, doing an Alitalia trip out of Rome to Athens, Bombay and Bangkok, and between Athens and Bombay I was rather surprised when the training captain invited me to join him for dinner in the first-class section of the aircraft, leaving the co-pilot and flight engineer in charge.

The training captain ordered food for us both along with a small glass of wine each, but when I remarked upon this rather unusual arrangement — such consumption of any alcoholic beverage being strictly forbidden under British regulations — the training captain assured me that a little drop of wine would help to make my landing in Bombay even better than the one I'd done in Athens! I did drink the wine — when in Rome, as they say — but whether it improved my landing technique I really don't recall.

On another of my line-training trips I operated from Rome to Khartoum, Addis Ababa and Mogadishu, where the whole crew stayed overnight in a beach-house owned by Alitalia. The house was comfortable and in a lovely location, the staff produced freshly caught fish straight out of the ocean to barbecue on the beach, and all in all it was probably one of the best night-stops I ever had. How sad it is to think about what has happened to Mogadishu and indeed the whole of Somalia since those long-gone days.

On 7 May, 1970, having successfully completed my route training, I operated my first trip as a fully-qualified DC-8 captain for Zambia Airways on the standard route from London to Lusaka via Rome, and barely a week later I found myself flying southbound from London on a regular scheduled service that had been completely booked out by Zambia's president, Kenneth Kaunda, and his entourage. I'd never carried a head of state before, and as I was still fairly new on the aircraft the company decided to put one of the Alitalia training captains on the flight as well, though he actually spent most of the flight asleep in one of the passenger seats down the back.

In the middle of the night, as we were over the Libyan desert, the president's private secretary came up to the flight deck and told me to arrange an unscheduled stop at Dar-es-Salaam, then capital of

Tanzania, as Dr. Kaunda had decided to take breakfast with President Nyerere. It was clearly up to me to communicate this change of plan to the Tanzanian authorities, so I called the controllers at Benghazi's Benina Airport and let them know that I had an urgent diplomatic message to be passed to the Tanzanian president.

We had a reply back within an hour to say that President Nyerere was out of the country, but would the vice-president do as a substitute? Dr Kaunda agreed, so I rerouted the aircraft to Dar-es-Salaam, but as we started our descent the training captain awoke from his slumbers and came up to the flight deck, where he quickly realised that we were *not* on the approach to Lusaka. I'm sure that for a few moments he was convinced I'd made some ghastly error while he'd been asleep, so he looked extremely relieved when I quickly reassured him that all was well and we had diverted to Dar for a breakfast stop on the president's instructions. We eventually got back to Lusaka three hours later than planned, and the president was given his usual ceremonial welcome by a host of army personnel and dignitaries, none of whom, I'm sure, made any comment about the delay.

My work for the next few months was fairly routine, flying the London-Lusaka route via Rome and, on some trips, Nairobi, but also flying occasional Alitalia trips landing at Athens and Entebbe en route to Lusaka and back from Rome. However, one flight did throw up a rather unexpected situation: on 6 September, I arrived in Nairobi en route from London and Rome to Lusaka to be told that amongst my first-class passengers for the remainder of the journey would be no fewer than three heads of state: King Hussein of Jordan, Lon Nol of Cambodia (the chap who had deposed Prince Sihanouk earlier that year) and Fidel Castro of Cuba, all of whom were travelling to Lusaka to attend a summit meeting of non-aligned nations. One might have thought that there would be all sorts of extra security measures in place, but it was all very low-key, and the three VIPs came on board with very little fuss or fanfare. The rest of the trip was absolutely routine, but since then I have often wondered how many airline captains have ever done a normal, scheduled flight with not just one or two but *three* heads of various states on board. I didn't actually meet any of them, but I was assured they were back there in First Class.

During this period of my career I was getting plenty of days off both at home in the UK and in Lusaka, so I started looking for things to do in between my DC8 trips. At Southend Airport I came across a small air taxi company called Baron Air Charter — as you might expect, they operated a Beech Baron aircraft — and they were looking for another experienced pilot who could operate occasional flights in order to give their full-time pilot a day off now and then. As I already had experience on the Baron from my days with Williamson Diamonds I was an ideal candidate, so after doing all the necessary tests and exams to put the Baron on my British licence (I'd previously flown it on an East African one), I started doing a few trips for Baron Air Charter to destinations in Britain, Scandinavia and even the shores of the Mediterranean. Of course, I made sure I never jeopardised my allowable monthly flying-hours limit, but flying the Baron made a very enjoyable change from my usual long trips on the DC8, and Pam just had to get used to the fact that even on my days off I might be away somewhere on the Baron. At least she couldn't get fed up with having me under her feet, and of course the additional income was always very welcome.

Meanwhile, in order to save on hotel expenses for their air crew, Zambia Airways had built a crew rest-house in Lusaka, complete with restaurant, bar and swimming-pool. I was spending roughly similar amounts of time at each end of the London-Lusaka route, and as I would qualify for a substantially higher salary if I agreed to be based in Zambia I volunteered for, and was granted, a change of base from London to Lusaka.

Some of my fellow crew members did likewise, and we were all offered comfortable, detached villas, complete with gardens, in a very good part of the Lusaka suburbs. All the others accepted, as they were planning to bring their families down to Zambia, but I wasn't going to uproot Pam and the girls again, so I swapped the villa for a permanent room in the new crew rest-house. It was an excellent arrangement: when I was in Zambia I had very comfortable accommodation, and while I was in the UK I was living at home with my family in Southend whilst receiving allowances from Zambia Airways because I was away from base. In the UK I was doing my occasional flights on the Baron, while in Zambia I teamed up with one of our navigators, Steve

Osborne, to build a four-berth wooden sailing-boat, which we constructed in a disused hangar at Lusaka's City Airport.

The boat was a Peter Blandford design (a Lysander), and we planned to bring all the required materials and equipment, including a Seagull outboard engine, down from the UK. We had already started building the boat when we realised that the import duty on some marine equipment, particularly engines, was very high, but a possible answer to our problem suddenly presented itself when we found an old Seagull outboard lying discarded in the mud at the edge of the Kafue River, where we would eventually be sailing our new boat once it was finished. We retrieved the engine and cleaned it up a bit, and then next time Steve and I did a flight to London we took it with us through the airport and drew the Customs Officer's attention to the fact that we were taking it up to the UK for repair.

Now, I would love to be able to say that once back in Britain the old Seagull engine was lovingly restored to full working order, but I'm afraid that's not what happened. No, as soon as we got back to London we dumped it at the nearest scrapyard and then went out and bought a new one, straight off the local yacht-chandler's shelf. Then, some weeks and several trips later, we took the new engine down to Lusaka with us and passed it through Customs with no problems at all!

Steve and I spent many happy hours during 1971 and '72 working on the boat, and it gave us something constructive to do during our days off in Lusaka. By the time it was finished, though, towards the

This is Coriolis, the boat I helped to build in Zambia; unfortunately, I ended up leaving Zambia Airways before she was launched, so I never had the pleasure of sailing her myself.

end of 1972, my contract was coming to an end, and as a result I never actually got to sail it on the Kafue at all. At Steve's suggestion, we'd named it Coriolis (as in the Coriolis Effect, because the boat had a slight curvature in its keel), and after I eventually left Zambia it was used by some of my friends down there. Some years later, though, I heard that all the private boats on the Kafue had been blown up by the Zambian army for fear they might be used by invaders from Rhodesia, but at least I'd enjoyed the effort of putting Coriolis together, even if I never managed to sail her before her sad demise.

During the three years that I flew the DC8 for Zambia Airways I fell completely in love with the aircraft and was delighted by its performance, its flying qualities and its high level of operational serviceability. That said, I did have a couple of unexpected situations to contend with. On one occasion I had to do a precautionary shutdown of one engine soon after take-off northbound from Nairobi, but as we still had three good ones I decided we should continue to Rome, where I knew that the excellent Alitalia engineers would be ready to do an engine-change as soon as we arrived. Now, in my experience before and since that time, engine-changes could normally be expected to take anything from ten hours upwards, so the airline would have to give the passengers and crew a night- or day-stop in a hotel while the work was done.

However, on this occasion things happened rather more quickly than that; as the problem had occurred soon after we departed Nairobi, Alitalia had about five hours' notice that we were coming, so they pulled out all the stops to get everything ready before our wheels even touched the tarmac. Then, as soon as we stopped, all passengers and crew were disembarked from the aircraft and sent not to a hotel but to the transit lounge, where we would await further developments. I don't recall now exactly how long the engine-change took, but I'm sure it was no more than three hours or thereabouts, as we still had plenty of time left in our crew duty period to fly on to London. We didn't even need to do a test flight with the new engine because we still had three others that were in perfect working order anyway, which was one great advantage of having four engines rather than two. The brilliant Alitalia engineers had done an amazing job that enabled the aircraft to get back on its normal schedule very quickly, and I'm sure our passengers were pleased to reach London after a much shorter delay than they might have experienced with other carriers.

The other, more serious problem happened on a southbound flight from London in the summer of 1971. We arrived at our first stop, Rome, around nine-thirty in the evening, and within an hour we had refuelled, picked up some passengers and were taxying out to the runway. Senior First Officer Jim Strong, my very competent co-pilot, was to do the take-off, and in due course we got our clearance and set off along the runway. As our speed increased to around 100 knots we suddenly heard a loud bang, so Jim abandoned the take-off and applied the brakes. As we slowed down, a bright light suddenly appeared on the left-hand (port) side of the aircraft, which we later discovered was caused by a tyre in the left main undercarriage that had burst and caught fire. Flames had started licking the underside of the port wing, which at that point was filled with around thirty tons of aviation fuel, so quick action was needed to get everyone out of the aircraft and away from danger.

Fortunately, the fire service were there very quickly, and our own cabin staff did an excellent job of evacuating the cabin through the starboard exits only, even though quite a number of our passengers, presumably feeling rather less sense of urgency than was appropriate in the circumstances, tried to take their coats and hand baggage with them. A few people decided that they'd rather run down the escape-slides than sit on them, and it was one of these who sustained the only injury experienced by any of our passengers or crew: he tripped over near the bottom of the slide and badly bruised his nose.

As captain, I was the last person to leave the aircraft, but by the time I reached the tarmac the firefighters had done their job with great efficiency, and the undercarriage fire was already out. The passengers had been taken to the terminal by coach, and my crew and I joined them in the transit lounge shortly afterwards, leaving the aircraft in the hands of the engineers who would arrange for it to be removed from the runway and taken to a hangar. As I entered the lounge one of our first-class passengers, a chap who travelled with us regularly, put a glass of whisky in my hand and thanked me and the crew for getting everyone out of a sticky situation, and knowing that it would be quite some time before our aircraft would be cleared to fly again I gladly accepted this little gift. It was strictly against regulations to drink alcohol whilst in uniform, as Zambia Airways followed British rules rather than Italian ones, but when you've just escaped from a potentially very dangerous situation, and there's no immediate prospect of further flying, I thought a little bit of rule-bending was reasonable.

However, the burst tyre wasn't to be the only surprise that evening. As I took a few sips of my whisky, the Zambia Airways duty manager, an Alitalia employee who looked after our operations in and out of Rome, suddenly appeared. He told me that Alitalia happened to have a spare DC8 immediately available, so we could continue our journey straight away! Now, as I'd been sipping whisky in front of all our passengers I really didn't think this was a very good idea, and in any case I had serious doubts that having just been evacuated from one aircraft our passengers would be happy to get straight back onto another one. I therefore suggested to the manager that everyone should be put in a hotel for the night to get over their experience, and fortunately he agreed.

The next morning, every single passenger rejoined the flight, and we completed our journey to Lusaka on the replacement DC8 with no further mishaps. Within days our Zambia Airways aircraft had been fixed — in fact, I ended up flying it from Lusaka to London on my next trip — and a brief investigation into what had happened concluded that the tyre-burst was due to a malfunction in the aircraft's brake system, so there was no fault whatsoever on the part of the crew. In fact, all of our crew received company commendations for the actions we had taken during the incident, and mention was even made of my brilliant suggestion that the passengers should be given an overnight stop in a hotel to recover their equilibrium afterwards. As all of them had continued their journey with us this was considered a great piece of public relations, and I suffered no repercussions from my little transgression in the bar.

During 1972 I did some freelance flying, again between my DC8 commitments, on Beech Baron and Piper Aztec aircraft around Zambia and to neighbouring countries such as Malawi and Rhodesia (as it then was), and in May of that year I was offered the chance to ferry a privately owned Piper Twin Comanche from Zambia to the UK. I had a seven-day break between scheduled DC8 flights, and as I'd already done a check flight on the Twin Comanche I decided to do the trip. As co-pilot I took John Louch, a member of the local aero club, and I have to admit we set off with relatively little advance planning.

Our first stop was at Dodoma, in Tanzania, where we picked up fuel, and then we flew on to Nairobi, where we took an overnight stop. We left early next morning for another refuelling stop at Lodwa, in northwestern Kenya, not far from the border with Sudan, but to our dismay we discovered that the only fuel there was strictly reserved for the Flying Doctor service. We were a bit concerned for a few moments when a group of local men, wearing very little in the way of clothes, suddenly appeared from the bush and surrounded the aircraft, but they were very friendly and helpful, and they advised us to go on to Juba, in southern Sudan, if we had enough fuel to do so. Fortunately we did, so we took off and headed across the border.

Having arrived safely in Juba, we thought we could just pick up fuel and then continue on our merry way northwards to Khartoum. However, things turned out to be a bit more complicated than that, and we had to wait more than three hours while the very helpful airport manager negotiated with the authorities at Khartoum to allow us to land there; in our haste to set off from Zambia, we had omitted to apply for permission to either fly over or land in Sudan, but eventually we were given the nod, so by that evening we were on the ground in Khartoum. Even though the sun was going down it was still pretty warm, so we were glad that our taxi-driver knew exactly where to take us, and we were soon checking in at the Acropole Hotel, the only air-conditioned one in the city, where we spent a very restful night.

Which was just as well, because the next morning another interesting problem confronted us: the aviation authorities at Khartoum told us that the only flight plan they would accept was non-stop from Khartoum to Cairo, which at our speed would take us six hours. Unfortunately, the maximum endurance of the Twin Comanche was exactly that — six hours — so had we been foolhardy enough to attempt the trip non-stop the best result we could have expected would have been to land with nothing but vapour in our tanks; the other and perhaps more likely possibility was to run out of fuel just short of our destination. Neither scenario was very tempting.

We checked around to see if any local engineers could possibly fit an extra fuel tank to the Comanche, but there was no hope of having that done within a reasonable timescale, so we decided there was nothing for it but to submit the flight plan as instructed, thus enabling us to continue our journey. Of course, we didn't mention that we intended to divert to a suitable airfield en route for fuel, and nobody asked us, so off we went. We knew we

A Piper Twin Comanche, similar to the one I ferried from Zambia to the UK.
Photo: Wikipedia

might have trouble negotiating our onward journey from wherever we might eventually decide to land, but we'd just have to cross that bridge when we came to it.

The weather was clear, and at our cruising height of 12,000 feet we were cool, comfortable and quite relaxed. After about two-and-a-half hours we were approaching Lake Nasser in Egypt, and below us was the airfield at Abu Simbel, close to where the famous temple had been reconstructed to save it from inundation following the building of the Aswan Dam. We could see aircraft on the apron and decided this might be a very good place to stop, so we called them up and were given permission to land.

Once on the ground we explained that although we'd expected to make Cairo non-stop from Khartoum (a little white lie, of course) we had run into unexpected headwinds and had decided to land for fuel before going any farther. Luck was not with us, though: first, we were told that where was no fuel available anyway, and then we were placed under arrest and taken to the local jail.

However, once again, a friendly airport manager came to the rescue: we'd hardly settled into our cell when he suddenly appeared and got us released. He then put us in his car and gave us a wonderful tour around the whole Abu Simbel complex before taking us back to the airport. Once there he got on the phone and negotiated a clearance for us to the military base at Luxor, roughly half-way between us and Cairo, and well within range with the fuel we still had on board. We would be able to refuel at Luxor, and we eventually arrived there in the early evening of what had been a very interesting day. As we landed we got a bit worried as the whole place seemed to be on some kind of alert — we could see pilots sitting in the cockpits of their military jets looking like they were about to go off on a mission — but we knew better than to ask any questions, and although we weren't exactly greeted like old friends we were quickly refuelled and were on our way again within ninety minutes.

We arrived at Cairo after nightfall, and once there we refuelled again and spent the night in the airport hotel. We took off early the next morning, heading initially for a refuelling stop in Heraklion (Crete), then another in Naples before our final planned landing of the day in Lyon. However, the Mistral was blowing hard down the Rhone Valley, so we had to divert to Marseille, where it was so windy we had to get the aircraft hangared overnight. Once that was sorted out we set off for a nearby hotel, where, as you might expect, we enjoyed the best food, drink and accommodation that we'd had for the entire trip.

Next day, on the final leg of our journey, we departed Marseille at 7.30am and had to fly quite low, around 1,500 feet, to avoid the strong headwinds above us and the risk of possible airframe icing if we had gone into cloud; having spent its recent life in Africa, the Comanche didn't have much in the way of anti-icing equipment. All went well, and we landed at Southend Airport before noon. Pam was there to meet us, and she took us home and gave us a very good lunch before John set off to wherever he was going in the UK to enjoy a bit of leave before returning to Zambia. I, meanwhile, had to get back to Lusaka ready for my next DC8 duty, so later that afternoon Pam drove me to Heathrow so I could jump on the next southbound Zambia Airways service. I duly arrived back in Lusaka the following morning, having slept for much of the journey, and that same evening I was travelling north again, in command of the next flight to London. That was certainly one of the busiest weeks of my life!

My three-year contract with Zambia Airways finally came to an end in December, 1972; I had half expected it to be renewed, but due to promotions of people lower down the pecking order, some of whose contracts still had a while to run, I was no longer needed and was given a "golden handshake" of a full year's salary. I therefore returned

Chapter 8

AFTER SPENDING CHRISTMAS AT HOME I was offered a temporary contract by a company called BIAS (Belgian International Aviation Services) to fly Muslim pilgrims from Rabat, Morocco, to Jeddah, Saudi Arabia, for the annual Hadj. BIAS had two DC8's, so this was an excellent opportunity to keep my hand in and earn a bit of money while I figured out where my career would take me next.

The Belgian authorities had agreed that during this Hadj period pilots could fly a maximum of 200 hours throughout the whole operation, which was expected to last for a month in each direction, with about a week's break between the completion of the inbound flights to Jeddah and the start of the homeward ones. I joined BIAS on 4 January, replacing a captain who had had to pull out through illness, but by that time the flights to Jeddah had been going for three weeks already. However, even as a "late joiner" I was still allowed to fly the full quota of 200 hours, which I accomplished in just five weeks, in the process earning more salary than I would expect to amass in six months of normal flying.

One of the two DC8 aircraft that I flew for BIAS

Photo: TAHS

On one of my last flights for BIAS, carrying a full load of 186 pilgrims out of Jeddah, I suffered one of those problems that all pilots train for but which they hope won't ever happen: an explosive engine failure shortly after take-off. Fortunately, it was an outboard engine (No. 1) that disintegrated, so none of the debris did any damage to other parts of the aircraft, and with three good engines still going strong we made a plan to fly down the Red Sea, dumping fuel as we went, so that we could land back at Jeddah at a weight that was well within our maximum for landing. To avoid the danger of igniting the fuel as it was being jettisoned, the aircraft would have to fly in a straight line, and the crew would have to shut down as much of its electrical equipment as possible to reduce the risk that a stray spark could change a difficult situation into a disastrous one. I told the controllers at Jeddah exactly what I was doing and warned them that I would be out of radio contact for the next half-hour or so in order to comply with standard procedures, so I was therefore rather surprised when, having successfully completed our fuel-dump and called Jeddah again to say we were now inbound to the airport, I was told that they'd been calling me over and over again and were wondering whether we were still in the air. I assured them we were, and that we would be back with them shortly, so they called out the fire trucks so they'd be handy when we touched down, just in case we needed them.

As it turned out we were able to do a virtually normal landing, and as there was no immediate threat of fire we were allowed to taxi to the terminal and disembark our passengers as if nothing had happened. The aircraft was obviously not going anywhere for a while, so my crew and I flew back to Rabat as passengers, and the very next day I operated the last BIAS flight of the whole Hadj operation from Rabat to Jeddah and back again on the company's other aircraft.

The contract had clearly been very profitable, as the company's owner, Charlie van Antwerpen, took over a whole floor of the Hilton Hotel in Rabat and laid on a big "thank you" party for everyone who'd been involved. Sadly, though, there was to be no permanent job for me with BIAS, so for the rest of February and March I did some freelance flying for Pomair, another Belgian airline, based at Ostend and operating a single DC8.

One trip with them — a passenger charter to Los Angeles with refuelling stops in Keflavik (Iceland) and Chicago — was rather interesting, not because of anything that happened in the air but because of a couple of things that happened on the ground. First, after landing at Chicago's famously busy O'Hare Airport we were told to go to the "penalty box", a far-flung area of the apron normally reserved for aircraft whose crews have done something wrong during approach, landing or taxying and are therefore ordered by Air Traffic

Control to take an enforced "time-out" before being allowed to carry on with their day. I had no idea what we'd done, and I wasn't looking forward to having to explain things to our passengers, but I was soon reassured by ground control that we weren't at fault ourselves. The problem was some kind of bomb scare in the terminal, so they had decided to send us over to the other side of the airport for refuelling to keep us away from any trouble. After picking up our fuel we carried on to LA as planned, and as I heard nothing further about the bomb incident I assume it was a hoax.

The Pomair DC8

Photo: TAHS

We were then scheduled for a night-stop in LA, and after the usual meal and a few beers with the rest of the crew I retired to my room at the Hacienda Hotel, looking forward to a good night's sleep after what had been a very long and tiring three-sector day. I was woken early the next morning — around 6.45am, in fact — but not by my little alarm clock, which I'd set to wake me up in time for breakfast, but by the sound of the bedside lamp crashing onto the carpet. I was immediately aware of a strange, shaking sensation, as if my bed had suddenly started trying to dump me onto the floor, and drowsy as I was I quickly realised what was happening: it was an earthquake, not a very serious one, but enough to make me don my dressing-gown and head outside.

There I met up with the rest of my bleary-eyed crew and most of the other hotel guests, and for a while we all kept a wary eye on the hotel building in case the whole place should suddenly start cracking and crumbling. Eventually, however, it was somehow decided that it was safe to go back inside, and we all returned to our rooms, some of us for another hour or two of shut-eye while others got dressed and headed to breakfast. Of course, there was no way of knowing whether or not the little shaking we'd had was just a small, isolated movement of the ground or the precursor to something massive and catastrophic, but then you could spend your whole life worrying about things like that, and I was keen to have a bit more kip before tucking into the most wonderful ham and eggs in the world at a nearby coffee shop.

During this time I was constantly looking out for permanent job opportunities both in the UK and overseas, but only one reasonable possibility presented itself. Dan Air Services, the well-known airline based at Gatwick, needed co-pilots for its fleet of Comet 4 aircraft (the Comet 4 had superseded the Comet 1 after the original design had proved vulnerable to metal fatigue, with disastrous results). At this stage, I had logged a total of some 13,000 hours of pilot time, including over 2,000 hours in command of four-engined jet aircraft (i.e. the DC8), but in early 1973 employment prospects for experienced pilots in the UK were not great. I knew I couldn't be too choosy, and as Dan Air was renowned as a good, solid company with strong finances I was ready to compromise if necessary.

At the Dan Air interview I was duly offered a position as a Comet 4 co-pilot based at Manchester, as there were no positions open at Gatwick, where the company had its headquarters. I was disappointed that I was to be based so far from home, but I was assured that I'd probably get a command fairly quickly, and in any case I really needed a job, so I said said yes.

My technical course and simulator training were done at Horley, Surrey, right near Gatwick, and for the six weeks they lasted I was accommodated in the nearby Copthorne Hotel. Each weekend I was given cash to cover a return rail fare to my future base at Manchester, which comfortably covered my petrol costs to go home to Essex, and I decided to delay finding any accommodation in Manchester until I'd completed all my flight training and had some idea of how much time I would be spending there. By mid-May I'd finished my circuits-and-bumps and was starting my route training, so my move to Manchester was now very imminent.

However, while I was doing my route training I discovered that Dan Air had recruited another co-pilot for the Comet fleet but had offered him a base at Gatwick; presumably someone had left the company since I'd been recruited, thereby creating a space that hadn't been there when I was interviewed. I was obviously rather vexed about this, so I suggested to the fleet manager that as I was senior to this new employee I should, in all fairness, have been offered the option of taking the vacancy at Gatwick before it was offered to the new chap.

A Dan Air Comet 4
Photo: MAP

Some companies might have ignored me or even marked me down as a potential troublemaker, but Dan Air saw things from my point of view, and I was duly transferred to Gatwick while the other guy was posted to Manchester. In fact, he didn't mind at all, as he was a single man with no family, fresh out of the RAF, and he wasn't too bothered where he was based so long as he had a job on which to found his new airline career. For my part, I felt very pleased to be working for a good, well-run company, based fairly near to home, with prospects of a reasonably quick command and even a long-term job that would perhaps take me through to my retirement. However, once again things did not turn out as I'd expected.

At the initial interview it had been explained to me that although there were, at that time, no vacancies for captains, the Comet fleet was expected to expand during the summer, thus creating several more command vacancies. With my experience, and as holder of an Airline Transport Pilot's Licence, I would be about number five in line for a command, as only four other co-pilots on the Comet fleet had the ATPL needed for promotion to captain. The rest had Commercial Licences and were working towards gaining their ATPLs as soon as they had flown enough hours and passed all their exams, but if everything continued as planned I would be safely ensconced in a captain's seat before any of the others had qualified.

In fact, I was given plenty of chances to get used to flying the Comet from the left-hand seat by the captains I flew with, many of whom had far fewer hours than I did. As mentioned previously, the Comet 4 had been designed and built to overcome the disastrous design problems that had afflicted the original Comet 1, and it was a very safe and powerful machine that was a delight to fly. Indeed, its four Rolls Royce Avon jet engines generated more power than the aircraft really needed; the Comet had originally been designed to operate at altitudes above forty thousand feet, but because of the problems with the Comet 1 the CAA had decreed that the Comet 4 should not go that high, even though its engines would have been more efficient up there. As a result, the aircraft used rather more fuel than it might have done, and this simple fact ended up having a rather serious effect on my career.

The relative thirstiness of the Comet 4 became a really major problem for Dan Air when, in October 1973, the world oil crisis came along. The company's plans to expand the Comet fleet were put on hold while they tried to find ways to make the aircraft a bit more economical, and someone came up with what I thought was a great idea: because the aircraft was clearly over-powered, why not shut down one engine on reaching cruise altitude and then fly on three engines until starting up the fourth again for the descent and landing? With the CAA's approval (of course), it was decided that we could try out this idea on some of our regular flights, and I flew as co-pilot on several of these test trips. Everything went perfectly: there were no problems with in-flight engine shutdown or start-up, we were easily able to maintain the required speed on three and we were saving lots of fuel.

Unfortunately, though, the CAA had a sudden attack of cold feet and put a stop to the whole idea, mainly because it would have made record-keeping much more complicated. Accurate records of aircraft engine-hours have to be kept so that servicing is done as and when necessary, but keeping track of which engine out of four has been shut down and for how long during a particular flight would not be straightforward, and I can understand why the CAA decided that to permit such fuel-saving techniques, whilst they were attractive in the short term, could lead to eventual problems in terms of administrative accuracy. Such is often the fate of great ideas when they come up against the obstacle of regulatory requirements.

As regards my own situation, while all this was happening other Comet co-pilots who had been with the company longer than I had were able to complete their ATPLs and thus jump ahead of me in the promotion stakes, and by late autumn my position in the list had slipped back from number five to number twelve or thereabouts. In terms of career development I was actually going backwards, and it soon became clear that my salary as a co-pilot was simply not enough to support me and my family, particularly as I was now commuting by car almost daily from Essex to Gatwick. I was having to eat into my savings, which was something I really hated to do, and clearly this was a situation that needed to be remedied as soon as I could.

Naturally, I was looking in the situations vacant columns of *Flight International* magazine every week, and I sent off replies to any adverts that seemed reasonably attractive. One letter I'd sent had been to a new airline — Air Malta — and in December, 1973, I got a telegram from them offering me a job as a captain. I accepted immediately and, having negotiated a friendly release from Dan Air, which apparently saved another co-pilot from redundancy, I operated my last Comet flight at the end of January, 1974. In many ways it was a shame to be leaving, but no pilot in his right mind would stay in a job where he's going *down* the seniority list rather than up it. I really had no choice, so on 1 February, 1974, I arrived in Malta, without my family, to join a course of about ten complete crews.

As a new airline, Air Malta needed captains, first officers and flight engineers, and I soon discovered that most of my colleagues were from Scandinavia. The company was to acquire two Boeing 707-720B's from Pakistan International Airways (PIA), and flight operations were to be run initially by PIA managers on secondment, while day-to-day engineering support in Malta was provided by PIA as well. Some PIA pilots and flight engineers were also brought over from Karachi to help get the airline into the air.

The aircraft itself was a high-performance version of the ubiquitous Boeing 707; it had a much shorter fuselage than the big intercontinental 707-320 series, and it carried only 140 passengers as opposed to the 180 or more that could be accommodated on the larger aircraft. However, it had the same engines as the full-size 707, so with its much lighter take-off weight it could climb rapidly to flight levels above forty thousand feet where air traffic was relatively light. When I eventually came to fly the 720B I was delighted to have so much power available, which meant I could accept ATC clearances that other aircraft on

An Air Malta Boeing 707-720B
Photo: MAP

similar trips had to reject because they couldn't get up there until they'd burnt off some of their fuel load. Flying-wise, it was great.

Anyway, soon after arriving in Malta we started our technical training, with instructors being brought in from Karachi week-by-week to cover the various topics — hydraulics, pneumatics, electrics etc. — that we needed to master in order to pass our technical exams. By late February, having completed all our written tests, we were sent to Karachi for our simulator and flight training. As always, I was eager to get on with it, but it soon became clear that nothing much had been organised for us in terms of simulator time, so it was very frustrating.

After about two weeks I was champing at the bit to get on the simulator, especially as I'd made friends with one of the Danish captains, a chap called Soren Kanne, who had already flown the Boeing 707 in a previous job and had been telling me all about it. One day we could bear the enforced inactivity no longer, so the two of us wandered down to the simulator building and talked our way onto the 720B simulator for a bit of "self-tuition".

I, of course, had never flown a 707 of any sort, but the DC8 I'd flown in Zambia was a similar kind of aircraft and, like the Air Malta 720B's, it had been equipped with instruments made by a company called Sperry. Soren had flown the 707, but it had had Collins instruments, which differed from Sperry ones in various important ways. Between us, therefore, we managed to spend the whole day teaching each other, which came in useful the very next day when we finally started our simulator training proper. Although it was a completely new aircraft for me I needed just three sessions on the simulator before being cleared for flight training, and within another five days I had completed all my circuits and my final command check. Then it was back to Malta to start my line-training, and on 6 April I did my first commercial flight on the 720B, from Malta to Paris and back, under the supervision of a PIA training captain. By early May I'd been cleared to fly as pilot-in-command and was looking at the possibility of buying a home in Malta for me and my family. Things were looking pretty good.

It was not long, however, before they started to go wrong. The frequency of Air Malta services, particularly the one to London, made it possible for European-based crew members to arrange their schedules so they could accumulate four or five days off and then travel home to spend time with their families, but this soon created tensions between us and our PIA managers. Certain cultural differences also began to surface, and probably the best example of this was something that happened to me.

I had been sent to Manchester for a couple of days to sort out a noise abatement problem with the airport authorities on behalf of the company, and I returned to Malta as supernumerary crew on a flight out of London. As we were flying over the Paris area, with the sun going down off our starboard wing, I suddenly heard the senior PIA captain ask the copilot to turn down the cockpit radio speakers and to remain silent while he, the captain, said his prayers. I immediately made it obvious that I strongly disapproved of this situation; it is a legal requirement in commercial aviation that, in normal circumstances, all aircraft maintain a constant radio watch, a principle that is of particular importance in the crowded skies over Europe. The captain's instructions on this occasion meant that, for a short time, the crew on that Air Malta flight would be unilaterally isolating themselves from the air traffic controllers who were responsible not only for their own and their passengers' safety but also the safety of all other aircraft in the area, and to me it was simply unacceptable for any airline crew to do this deliberately unless there was very good reason (such as, for example, when dumping fuel, as I mentioned in the previous chapter), and it should certainly never be done without telling the controllers first. I made my views abundantly clear, and on my insistence the first officer did maintain a radio watch via his headset, and if necessary he would have responded to any calls.

The next day, I was summoned before the Chief Pilot to explain my attitude, and we had what would now be called a "full and frank" exchange of views. Then, a week or so later, when I returned to Malta from a few days off in the UK, I was met by some of my Scandinavian colleagues, who were in a state of considerable agitation. Management had issued an instruction to the effect that all crews were to be confined to Malta on their days off and could only leave the island on official annual leave.

I was quickly chosen as crew spokesman to discuss the situation with the Chief Pilot, and he confirmed that the new rule would henceforth apply to all of us. At that time I was planning to buy a sailing boat, so I asked if I would be allowed to sail it off the coast of Malta on my days off. The Chief Pilot thought I was being flippant and said that he needed to have crew members available at short notice to fill in for others who might go sick, so in reply I pointed out, in my own inimitable way, that it would actually be much easier to contact me on a day off by phone at my home in the UK than it would be if I were sailing my boat, and I could then jump on either of our daily flights from London to get back quickly. (This was, of course, in the days before nearly everyone had a mobile phone.)

Unfortunately, though not surprisingly, the Chief Pilot failed to see my point of view, and I must admit I probably didn't endear myself to him when I ventured the opinion that he was turning a very pleasant island into a kind of prison for crew members.

This perhaps rather hasty statement was misreported to the airline's Maltese owners, who were given the impression that I regarded the whole island of Malta as something akin to a penal colony, and I soon realised that my career prospects there were very limited as long as PIA remained in control. It was also now confirmed that Air Malta crew members were definitely *not* allowed to leave the island except during their annual leave, a restriction that I felt was very unfair and shortsighted.

However, I could see a small chink of light at the end of that particular tunnel. I had already heard on the aviation grapevine that a Gatwick-based cargo airline, International Aviation Services (IAS), was about to upgrade from Britannia aircraft to DC8's and was looking for pilots. With all my DC8 experience I was hopeful of finding a job with them, so in mid-July, abandoning the non-returnable deposit I had put down on a nice little house in Malta, I packed all my belongings into my Peugeot 504, took the ferry to Sicily and then, over the next couple of days, drove up through Italy, onwards to Calais and thence by ferry to England. On arrival at Southend I submitted my resignation to Air Malta by phone. It was immediately accepted.

I spent August and September unemployed in the UK, but by October I had been recruited by IAS at Gatwick and was off to Denver, Colorado, to do a DC8 requalification course with United Airlines. The future was looking good again.

Chapter 9

BY LATE 1974 IAS had been operating out of Gatwick with Bristol Britannias for some years but had decided to take the plunge and upgrade to bigger, faster, four-engined jet aircraft capable of carrying 40-ton loads over long-haul distances.

The natural choice for such a move would perhaps have been the Boeing 707-320C, as this type was already on the UK CAA register, being flown by airlines such as British Airways and British Caledonian. However, Boeing 707's were difficult to obtain and expensive to hire or purchase, but a number of used DC8-50 series cargo aircraft were beginning to become available on the international aircraft market, and as these had very similar capabilities to the 707 in terms of load capacity and fuel burn IAS decided to go down the Douglas route rather than the Boeing one.

A deal was duly agreed between IAS, American Airlines and the finance company Guinness Peat, and IAS thus acquired its first DC-8, registration N-8782R. As this aircraft was still on the American register and would continue to operate on it for as long as the CAA would accept the idea of a British company operating a foreign-registered aircraft in and out of Gatwick (which turned out to be until the following summer), all the pilots who flew it had to have full American pilots' licences; in other words, we couldn't just validate our British (CAA) licences but had to do proper American (FAA) courses from scratch.

This prospect proved to be a bit worrying for some of IAS's existing Britannia crews, who were told that if they volunteered for DC-8 training but didn't make the grade their Britannia positions would probably have been taken up by newly hired people in the meantime, so if things went wrong they could end up jobless. For me, though, there was no such dilemma, as I was recruited specifically to fly the DC-8. Sometimes life is much easier when you have no choice.

Anyway, by late October the initial course of five crews — four other captains, five co-pilots, five engineers and myself — had settled into the United Airlines Training Centre in Denver, Colorado (for some reason, United was chosen over American as the supplier of our training, but as both were top-notch airlines it didn't matter two hoots which one we went to). The technical course, which I used as a refresher but which nearly all the others were tackling with no prior knowledge or experience of flying large jets, was followed by four sessions in the DC-8 simulator followed by a simulator check ride with an FAA examiner. Once we'd finished all that — and I'd had an easier time of it anyway, because I'd not been required to sit the DC-8 technical exam again — we pilots broke off from our training course at United to attend a special "crammer" ground school in order to pass the technical exam for the FAA ATR (Air Transport Rating) licence, the equivalent of the British ATPL.

This kind of technical exam is a general one, not related to any particular aircraft type, and for three relentless days, from eight in the morning until six in the evening, with only short breaks for coffees and lunch, our tutor lectured us solidly about all the things that would come up in our written test. We were told *not* to write anything down, just to listen, which seemed rather odd to us, but the instructor was confident he could get virtually anyone through the exam so long so they followed his instructions. In fact, he said that we as a group were already qualified to a much higher standard than necessary anyway, but there are always differences between the way various govern-ments run their aviation administrations, so we had to learn what the FAA wanted us to do in the exam so that we could appreciate any contrasts with what the CAA would expect. It was non-stop, high-pressure stuff, but it certainly did the trick, because we all passed the exam at our first attempt.

As I already had lots of experience in command of DC-8's I needed only three flights between Sacramento and San Francisco before being cleared as a fully FAA-qualified DC-8 captain, and everyone else — including all the former Britannia pilots who had taken a bit of a gamble to do the course — came through the training successfully as well, so by Christmas we were all back home enjoying some paid leave before the "new" IAS aircraft could be brought over to the UK.

In January, 1975, I was a member of the DC-8 crew who were flown out to San Francisco, along with a group of IAS engineers and manage-ment staff, to do the delivery flight to the UK. The owner of the airline,

Alan Stocks, was also with us as we departed San Francisco on that flight, which for various reasons was bound for Prestwick via Winnipeg. I'm pretty sure the aircraft could have made it all the way without stopping, especially as it was empty except for a few people plus a stock of spare parts, but also on board was a finance team from American Airlines, who would be officially signing the aircraft over to IAS during the flight.

The reason for doing an en-route handover like this was simple: lots of money could be saved if the actual sale took place over a state that imposed little or no sales tax. I can't remember now exactly which state it was that we had to overfly on this particular trip — it may have been Nevada, Idaho or perhaps Montana — but as the moment of signing approached I had to get confirmation of our exact position from air traffic control and then had to ask them to log the fact that the transaction had taken place. With everything signed and sealed the American Airlines finance team left us as soon as we arrived in Winnipeg, where we were taking a night-stop before continuing our journey to the UK.

During the night the temperature at Winnipeg fell to minus forty (it doesn't matter whether you prefer C or F: minus forty is the temperature at which the two scales cross over), and it thus required some effort the next day to get the aircraft started and warmed up for the long flight to Prestwick. Jet engines love cold air, though, so the aircraft almost leapt off the runway, and we were soon heading out across Canada and then over the Atlantic.

During the Atlantic crossing, however, we received bad news of a meteorological kind: the runway at Prestwick was experiencing forty-knot crosswinds, well beyond the safety limit not only of the DC-8 but of any other normal aircraft as well. I broke the news to Alan Stocks, who was rather upset; he'd arranged a big reception for the aircraft at Prestwick, with representatives of both the local press and various aviation publications in attendance to see the aircraft arrive, but there was no imminent prospect of a lull in the weather, so he agreed that we should continue to Gatwick instead. This was no problem as we had plenty of fuel, and we duly landed there around 6am, but as we'd arrived more or less unexpectedly there was no-one to meet us, and it took more than an hour just to get steps up to the aircraft so we could disembark. It was not the most promising start for the new DC8 operation, but in aviation, as in other things, the weather can sometimes mess up the best of plans.

Thus, with little fanfare, the first IAS DC-8 arrived in Britain to start its new career, and within days it was flying on cargo charter operations to various destinations, mostly in Africa. There was still some training to sort out, as the ex-IAS Britannia captains had to do their DC-8 line-training, flying on commercial operations with training captains to make sure they were thoroughly competent. American Airlines had sent over a few of their own training captains to help us get started, but at this point the company gave my career a bit of a boost by appointing me as a line-training captain as well. Our new captains still had to fly with American Airlines guys, but once they'd been cleared I was able to do route training and final line checks on our co-pilots, and in due course I would be doing renewal checks on both captains and co-pilots when needed.

By mid-July IAS had arranged to buy a second DC8 freighter from the USA, and I was one of the crew that flew out to Dallas, Texas, to collect this addition to our fleet. By this time the CAA had decreed that IAS must transfer its DC8's onto the British register, so this second aircraft had already undergone some required modifications and had actually been given a British registration: G-BDDE. However, it was still not licensed for commercial operations as it would need to undergo some fairly stringent flight testing in the UK before being released for normal service, so we ferried it back to Gatwick as a private, non-commercial flight.

A couple of days later I was to fly with Gordon Corps, Chief Pilot of the UK Air Registration Board, and Keith Perrin, their Chief Test Observer, on that all-important test flight, and I knew that as the DC8 had never been on the UK register it had to be treated as if it were a newly designed type, straight out of the factory. G-BDDE would therefore be flown right up to its limits, even though it had already clocked up many years of service, so I wondered what was in store for me as we did our departure checks and taxied out for take-off.

As an ordinary airline pilot I had always flown well within the limits set out in the aircraft flight manual, but test pilots are a special breed, of course, and they do things rather differently. It was fascinating, if not a little alarming, to be sitting there on the flight deck as Gordon Corps pushed G-BDDE not only up to but often beyond some of the limiting speeds laid down by the FAA and carried out manoeuvres that just wouldn't be done in any other circumstances. I soon realised, though, that Gordon was an exceptional pilot — as all test pilots have to be — and I marvelled at his skill in getting the utmost out of an aircraft that he was flying for the very first time. Happily, I was to have many more experiences of flying with Gordon, and every one of them proved yet again what a brilliant flier he was.

Within a couple of days G-BDDE was cleared to start commercial operations on the British register, and just over a month later I happened to do a trip on it to Lagos, Nigeria. My crew and I had a brief rest stop in Lagos while our cargo of luxury goods was offloaded, and we then took off in the early hours of the following morning with no freight on board but with our fuel tanks full; because of a favourable exchange rate it was cheaper overall to fill up in Lagos, as there would still be more than half the fuel left as we landed back in the UK and the amount of extra fuel burnt to carry it home would be relatively small. Our weather radar on the outbound leg had been working rather intermittently, but we were not too concerned about it as the forecast we were given before departure was reasonably good.

Soon after take-off we noticed that our weather radar seemed to have packed up completely, but with no particular warnings about bad weather, and with no guarantee that we'd be able to get the radar fixed even if we went back, we decided it was safe to continue. However, just over an hour north of Lagos, in the area of Niamey, we were cruising at around 35,000ft in thin cloud when suddenly all hell let loose: with no radar to warn us, we had flown straight into an "embedded" thunderstorm, the kind that is impossible to spot visually because it is hidden by other clouds that are relatively benign. Hailstones the size of large marbles began hitting the aircraft with such force that the outer protective layers of our windscreens cracked under the onslaught, and the noise was such that it was well-nigh impossible for us to hear what we were saying to each other.

There was almost deafening static on the radio, caused by the huge electrical charges generated within the storm, but the worst thing of all was the turbulence, which was so bad it made the flight instruments virtually impossible to read. The autopilot couldn't cope and very quickly "dropped out", so I had to wrestle with the controls in an attempt to keep the aircraft flying more or less straight and level. At one moment we'd be carried upwards through 40,000ft which, being unable to read the altimeter, we only knew about because it caused the cabin pressurisation warning horn to go off, adding to the general cacophony, and then seconds later we'd be dropping at 2,000ft or more per minute. As I couldn't keep to our cleared altitude I decided to concentrate on trying to keep us in a level attitude whilst limiting the speed to within 0.7 and 0.9 on the Machmeter, the only instrument I could read properly, so I kept shouting at the engineer to put on full climb power and then pull it back almost to idle to keep us within this range and prevent the aircraft from either stalling at low speed or exceeding its maximum permitted airframe speed, which might cause serious structural damage from which it would be impossible to recover.

After a few rather terrifying minutes we emerged from the storm, but unfortunately we quickly ran into another one, and then two or three more after that, but after a quarter of an hour or so that had seemed like an eternity we came out into calmer air as we flew north, out over the Sahara. The aircraft was now flying perfectly, and apart from the windscreens, through which we could see only a rather dim and incoherent picture of the sky ahead, we seemed to have sustained no major damage, so we decided to carry on to Gatwick rather than divert to anywhere else en route. Our radios were fine, and apart from our weather radar everything was working as it should, so the only little adjustment I had to make to our normal flight procedures was, on final approach at Gatwick, to open the little sliding window on my side of the cockpit so I could get just enough clear forward vision to make sure we were lined up with the runway (in fact, such openable flight deck windows are called "direct vision" or "DV" windows, but not all aircraft have them). Anyway, we landed safely and taxied to the parking area, with me looking out of the side window to make sure we didn't hit anything.

My co-pilot, Leon Swanepoel, a man with some ten thousand hours of flying experience, later told me that at one point he was convinced the aircraft was in grave danger of falling apart, and our flight engineer has always maintained that his hair was several shades greyer after that flight than it had been before it. However, I probably had something of an advantage over them because of that test flight I'd done with Gordon Corps some weeks previously. I had seen first-hand just how much the DC8 could cope with, and this had given me considerable reassurance as we'd fought our way through the storms.

Afterwards, it occurred to me that also on our side was the fact that the aircraft was flying in its optimum configuration for dealing with turbulence: the wings were full of fuel while, with no cargo, the fuselage was empty, so there was no huge downward force in the middle of the aircraft competing with the lift generated by the wings. It's impossible to say what would have happened had we been carrying a full load of forty tons of cargo, but as we came through with no major damage I believe we would still have survived — just about. As it was, the only major repairs needed to the aircraft were replacement of all the windscreens and a new radome on its nose, the outer covering of the previous one having been ripped away during our encounter with the storm. In fact, after the repairs and a thorough engineering check had been completed the aircraft was airborne again the following day with the very same crew; well, they always say that if you fall off a horse you should get back on straight away, so this, I guess, was the aviation equivalent.

This next flight was, in fact, the first IAS service that went beyond Africa, and it thus represented a significant extension to the company's operations. The first leg of the trip was a normal freight run to Lagos, but from there we flew across Africa to Ndola in Zambia and thence to Perth, Australia, via a refuelling stop in Mauritius. This was the start of a fairly regular contract based on flying freshly killed and chilled lamb from Australia to destinations in the Far and Middle East, and on this trip we flew the meat from Perth to Singapore. From that point on, though, we were "tramping", picking up loads that the company had successfully bid for on the Baltic Exchange (which handles air freight contracts as well as shipping) and taking them to wherever they were needed. By the time we got there, the company would have found us another load to go somewhere else, and so it would go on. On this particular trip we ended up flying from Singapore to Colombo then to Hong Kong and back to Colombo before handing over to another crew to bring the aircraft, with us on board, back to Gatwick. On such occasions we would travel in a set of rather battered passenger seats located at the back of the cargo compartment; not for us were the pleasures of travelling on a passenger flight unless it was absolutely necessary.

In January, 1976, I was told by the Managing Director of IAS that the company had purchased the passenger DC8-43 which I had flown from 1970 to 1972 for Zambia Airways. The operating contract for that airline had been taken over by Aer Lingus, Ireland's national airline, who had replaced the DC8 with a Boeing 707, so the DC8 (9J-ABR, otherwise known as Bravo Romeo) had been grounded and had sat at Lusaka Airport for a couple of years. This was a great shame, I thought, as Bravo Romeo was a really lovely aircraft, and even though IAS had bought it it was definitely *not* going to be joining the IAS fleet. Unfortunately, as an airframe built purely for passenger work, its floor and undercarriage were not strong enough for cargo operations, and its Rolls Royce Conway engines were also incompatible with the existing fleet's Pratt and Whitneys. In an age when both DC8's and Boeing 707's were rapidly being replaced by newer types of passenger aircraft, Bravo Romeo's greatest value was as a source of spare parts.

Because of licensing requirements it was necessary for one of IAS's three former Zambia Airways pilots to do the delivery flight back from Lusaka to the UK, and I was glad that the job fell to me. Thus on 24 January, 1976, I flew out to Lusaka as a passenger — along with the company's Chief Flight Engineer, a co-pilot and a large cheque — to complete the purchase of the aircraft and bring it back to the UK.

Fortunately, Zambia Airways had kept the aircraft up to date in terms of maintenance in the hope that they'd find a buyer, but in any case we decided to do an air-test before setting off on the long ferry flight home. However, before we did that test flight I was approached by two ex-DC8 Zambia Airways captains who were now flying the Boeing 707. As I was a company-approved line training captain on the DC8 they asked if they could come on the air-test and handle the aircraft for a little while themselves; a bit of recent experience is always useful if one has to look for a new job at short notice, so this was a way of boosting their appeal to any future employer if the need should arise. Thus the quick test flight we'd planned eventually included no fewer than eight circuits and landings, with me in the right-hand (co-pilot's) seat while the two Zambia Airways captains took turns to do the landings from the left. That gave me and the flight engineer a chance to check all the radios and systems really thoroughly, and afterwards the two 707 captains thanked us profusely and said how much they'd enjoyed flying the DC8 again. Both said they still much preferred it to the 707.

On the evening of 26 January, we filled all our tanks and took off from Lusaka bound non-stop for Bournemouth (Hurn) Airport, where we landed after an uneventful flight some ten hours later. Parking at Hurn was fairly cheap — it had a shortish runway and limited facilities, so it was a relatively quiet place in those days — and IAS had decided to leave the aircraft there while various possibilities for its future use were explored. Had any airline expressed a wish to buy it for passenger use its existence as a viable whole could have continued, but as expected there were no takers, and it was ultimately decided that in early June the aircraft would make its final flight from Bournemouth to Luton, where it would be broken up for spares.

By this time, though, Bravo Romeo was no longer Bravo Romeo; its Zambian registration had lapsed, so it was now de-registered and therefore stateless. In order to move it, IAS had to arrange for the CAA to issue a "Permit to Fly", a special kind of certificate that usually covers small, experimental or home-built aircraft allowed to operate under very specific conditions and restrictions. The permit we were given for the ferry flight from Bournemouth to Luton specified that I, and only I, was authorised to fly as captain and that IAS's Chief Flight Engineer was the only person allowed to fly as engineer. We also had to avoid flying over any heavily populated areas, so it all sounded rather dramatic.

Anyway, the aircraft was still in good flying condition because its engines had been started up and run for a short while every month, so on 4 June my crew and I travelled down to Bournemouth by taxi, ready to take the ex-Zambia Airways DC8 to Luton. We thought it would be a fairly routine flight, albeit a rather short one, so we were a bit surprised to see that the local press had congregated outside the perimeter fence near the end of the runway to watch the take-off. We wondered about this for a moment, but then we came to the conclusion that they had gathered there to watch our take-off in the expectation that we would only get airborne just before the end of the runway (or even fail to get airborne at all). We'd been told that the DC8 was the biggest aircraft that had ever landed at Bournemouth, as Hurn's short runway was unsuitable for anything larger than a short-haul passenger jet at that time, so we were sure that the press had decided to take advantage of our departure as a potentially exciting photo opportunity.

However, they probably ended up somewhat disappointed. We had a very light fuel load, of course, and with no cargo or passengers on board, the aircraft virtually leapt off the ground. By the time we were overhead the photographers we were already several hundred feet in the air, so I rather doubt they got the exciting photos they were hoping for.

Having set course for Luton we called London Radar, expecting them to give us headings that would keep us as clear as possible of any large settlements on the ground beneath us, so we were surprised, to say the least, when they routed us right over the centre of London. It was a bright, sunny day, so we had a wonderful view of our capital city before bringing the aircraft safely to its final landing at Luton.

I'm not the sort to get overly sentimental over things like aircraft — which are, after all, just so many pieces of metal bolted together — but I did feel a twinge of sadness as we taxied this particular DC8 to its parking-spot outside the hangar and shut down its engines. I'd always felt it was a particularly good example of its type, and during my Zambia Airways career I'd spent many happy hours flying it. I therefore decided I should take a few little souvenirs home with me, and thus some of the life-jackets plus the curtains that had once separated the First-Class cabin from Economy ended up on yet another small sailing-boat that I had put together from a kit and was now keeping on the River Crouch in Essex. No-one ever complained, so I think I can safely admit this now.

By this time the original IAS DC8 had also been transferred to the British register; in fact, I'd flown it out to Dallas at the end of January to have all the modifications done. Three weeks later I flew it on a test flight over Texas, with Gordon Corps again; there were a few things that didn't quite come up to scratch — three-engined climb performance, for example — but the aircraft was given a temporary

Certificate of Airworthiness so that it could be flown back to the UK and operated commercially for a limited period, though more test flights would eventually have to be completed within a certain time.

Thus it happened that during May, 1976, I found myself on another flight with the CAA flight test team, and this time things went much better than they had in Texas. In fact, it was on this flight that I reckon I travelled faster than on any other flight before or since; at one point we were doing a maximum speed test, flying eastwards in a shallow, powered dive over the North Sea, when I noticed that the Machmeter was showing us at just below the speed of sound (Mach 0.96). Of course, that's less than half the cruising speed of Concorde, but as I never had the pleasure of flying on that amazing aircraft this "nearly" moment was the closest I ever got to supersonic travel. In any case, I'm sure it was rather more exciting being on the flight deck of a DC8 in a powered dive like this than it would have been just sitting in a passenger seat on Concorde sipping champagne, especially when ATC called us to say that we were getting rather close to Dutch airspace, so would we please execute an immediate course reversal and head back towards the English coast.

Of course, making sharp turns in aircraft travelling at or near their maximum design speed is not a good idea — you can give yourself all sorts of very serious problems doing that kind of thing — but Gordon had a great way of getting around the problem: he simply activated the thrust reversers on all four engines to slow it down and then put the aircraft into a beautifully balanced descending turn with sixty degrees of bank so that we were very soon heading back towards Norfolk and away from any possible conflict with traffic bound for Schiphol. Again I marvelled at his flying skills and was grateful for the chance to observe them so closely.

During the rest of 1976 I did lots of flights to Africa and the Middle and Far East on the two IAS DC8's, both now on the UK register, and in early 1977 the company acquired a third one, which enabled them to take on extra charter work to the USA and farther afield, including a series of horse flights carrying bloodstock to New Zealand via Canada, Hawaii and Fiji. For obvious reasons there was always a vet on board the aircraft for these trips, as well as half-a-dozen grooms to take care of the very valuable cargo, and the flights normally went without any major problems, which was perhaps quite surprising considering the fact that we were carrying up to twenty highly-strung thoroughbreds each time. However, on one trip, as were heading out over the Pacific, we suddenly heard a lot of banging and crashing from the back end of the aircraft, which was rather worrying, to say the least. The vet for that trip, a delightful Irish chap who spent most of the flight sitting in the spare crew seat behind me telling me lots of wonderful Irish jokes, immediately jumped up and said, "Don't worry, Captain, I'll sort that out", and left the flight deck.

Very soon afterwards the din suddenly stopped, and shortly after that the vet came back on the flight deck again. Peace reigned for another hour or so, but then the banging started again, so the vet once more departed the flight deck, only to return a few minutes later, with quiet once again restored. Another hour or two passed before the racket started up once more, and the vet went back yet again to do whatever it was he was doing to calm whichever horse was causing the trouble. Things went quiet again, and when the vet returned to the flight deck I asked him what the problem was and what he was doing to solve it.

"Well," he said in his soft Irish voice, "in this load we have a mare in season, that we've put right up the front, and a stallion, that we've put right down the back, but the trouble is he keeps getting a little whiff of the mare every so often, which gets him a bit excited."

"So how do you calm him down?" I asked.

"Well," said the vet, "a bit of this stuff inside the nostrils seems to do the trick with most stallions most of the time."

And at that point he produced from his pocket a large jar of Vicks Vapor Rub. I'm sure that the good people at Vicks had never imagined this particular veterinary use for their product when they invented it, but I now understand that it's a fairly common remedy for masculine over-excitement in the equine world.

At this time I was still doing line training for the company — in other words, supervising new captains and co-pilots who needed to get a bit of experience of flying the line before being cleared as fully-trained DC8 pilots — but in September, 1977, IAS had me checked out by the CAA and approved as an official Type Rating Examiner on the DC8. This meant I could now do both *ab initio* training on the aircraft for new pilots and regular six-monthly base checks for existing ones, and with no simulator available all of this training was done on the aircraft itself, usually at Shannon Airport in Ireland. The famous Durty Nelly's bar in Bunratty, near Limerick, thus became a favourite place for IAS pilots to either drown their sorrows after a particularly tricky training session or celebrate successful completion of the various exercises, such as two-engine approaches and flapless landings, that were thrown at them in their six-monthly checks. Lots of other companies used Shannon as well in those days because of its long

G-BDHA, one of the IAS DC8 fleet
Photo: MAP

runway, good facilities and relative lack of normal traffic compared to other airports of its size, and I'm sure Durty Nelly's must have done very well over the years out of its visiting aviators. Nowadays, of course, such training is almost always done on high-tech simulators that can replicate real flight conditions with amazing accuracy, so I guess that famous bar no longer resonates quite so much with chat about flap settings, engine temperatures and missed approaches.

By February, 1978, the company's third DC8 had been accepted on the UK register as G-BIAS, and in April it was joined by a fourth one, G-BSKY. Then, in September of that year, IAS bought another "new" aircraft, this time from Air Ceylon, which had been Sri Lanka's national airline but had shut down earlier in 1978 due to bankruptcy. Again I was the captain who was chosen to go, with a crew, to Colombo to do the necessary checks and test flights, complete the purchase formalities (i.e. hand over the cheque) and then bring the aircraft back to the UK, but I wasn't going to have the luxury of travelling out on a passenger airline, being pampered by smiling cabin staff. Oh no, the very clever IAS crewing people decided I could work my passage as far as Sharjah in the United Arab Emirates on a regular IAS flight and then continue as a passenger on the same aircraft until it stopped for fuel in Colombo. There I got off, along with one of IAS's most senior flight engineers; we were short of a co-pilot, but we'd been promised that one would be despatched to us forthwith.

The aircraft we were to collect was a passenger version of the DC8, and again it was not one that could be readily modified for cargo use. However, it did have four very good, low-houred engines on it, and it was these that IAS really wanted. The airframe itself was of no use to us, but it did represent the most convenient way of transporting four Pratt & Whitney power units back to the UK.

During the several days it took for the engineer and I to make sure the aircraft was in good enough condition for us to do the required flight tests, another IAS captain was positioned out to Colombo by air, but when he appeared he told me he was in need of a routine, six-monthly base check, which would have to be done before we set off on the ferry flight back to the UK. We therefore decided to kill two birds with one stone by making the test flight into a training flight as well; all we'd have to do would be to add in a three-engined approach and overshoot and then a three-engined landing, with him doing all the handling. Assuming everything went OK I could endorse his licence accordingly, and then we'd be thoroughly legal for the homeward flight.

One minor concern was that the Sri Lankan Minister of Aviation was going to be on board for the test flight, but he would be sitting in the front of the passenger cabin, not on the flight deck, and I was therefore quite happy that we could do the training without making it obvious; there were lots of possible reasons why we might want to do a go-around during the test flight, so I was pretty confident that no awkward questions would be asked.

Thus during the evening of 23 September, 1978, we duly got airborne in the Air Ceylon DC8 (registration 4R-ACQ) and flew it around for an hour or so to make sure everything necessary actually worked; it did, so we headed back to the airport to put our little plan into action. I pulled back the power on one engine, and we flew the approach with the other captain doing the handling whilst I looked after the things such as radio calls, flap settings, landing-gear etc. that the non-handling pilot would normally do. As we reached 200ft above the ground I issued the command "Runway obstructed, go around" (it wasn't really obstructed, of course, but it's normal to give a reason in such situations, even when it's just a check flight). The other captain then put full power on the three engines we were using, which made things quite noisy as the aircraft climbed away, so anyone sitting towards the rear of the cabin would have found it uncomfortably loud. We were therefore very glad that the Minister of Aviation was sitting up at the front rather than farther back.

Having completed the overshoot and a circuit of the airport to bring us back onto the approach, still on three engines, we completed our landing safely and then taxied back to the parking area. The steps soon arrived at the aircraft door, ready for the Minister of Aviation to disembark, but someone else rather unexpectedly beat him to it.

As the Minister and his small entourage started rising from their seats and gathering their possessions together, a frightened-looking figure rushed up from the rear of the cabin, hurtled down the aircraft steps and ran off into the night. As it turned out, one of the airport cleaners had decided that the back row of the unused DC8 was a great place to get some shut-eye after a busy shift, and as the aircraft had had boarding-steps in place for some days before we did our test flight he would have found it easy to get on board. I guess he was fast asleep when we went out to the aircraft for the test flight, and he probably didn't wake up until we started the engines for what was almost certainly his first ever flight. I can imagine how he felt when we took off, having no idea where he was going to end up, and the fact we did a noisy overshoot before landing must have made it all the more terrifying for the poor man. I suspect he vowed there and then *never* to fall asleep on a parked aircraft again.

Although things had gone well on the test flight, the Air Ceylon DC8 didn't actually get airborne again for another couple of weeks. The problem was that before it could set off on its ferry flight to London it was to be transferred onto the US register and, as usually happens, this re-flagging operation required various modifications to be done and lots of paperwork to be completed. While we waited for everything to be sorted out I received a confidential message saying we would not be returning to Gatwick after all but instead would be landing in Luxembourg — and I wasn't to tell anyone about the change of plan, not even my crew. In fact, I was to file a flight plan to Gatwick as originally intended, but over Bahrain we would be contacted by Air Traffic Control and told to divert to Luxembourg. As my crew members had been planning to buy a bit of furniture in Colombo — beautiful "peacock chairs" are a speciality there — I did tell them that our final destination could possibly change to somewhere in mainland Europe, so I managed to prevent them pitching up at Luxembourg with a couple of chairs each and no obvious means of getting them home.

I wasn't sure of the reasoning behind all the cloak-and-dagger stuff, but I knew that the general process of buying and selling second-hand aircraft could be quite complicated, so I just got on with the job of organising the flight home. Once we got airborne everything went according to plan; as we flew towards Bahrain we got the message about diverting to Luxembourg, and some hours later, after a very long flight of 11 hours 45 minutes (probably the longest one I ever did on a DC8), we landed at Luxembourg and taxied to a hangar where the engine swap and other modifications to the Air Ceylon aircraft were due to be carried out. My crew and I flew back to Gatwick on a passenger flight, and I understood I'd be going back to Luxembourg some days later to ferry the same aircraft to its new owners in Miami. In the meantime, another IAS DC8 had flown to Luxembourg with four higher-time engines attached so that it and the Air Ceylon aircraft could undergo something I think is quite rare in the aviation world: a quadruple engine-change.

I ended up having a week at home before heading back to Luxembourg, along with another co-pilot and flight engineer, to do the flight to Miami. We got a taxi to the hangar but were rather surprised when we got there to see no sign of the Air Ceylon DC8; no matter, I thought, perhaps they've parked it on some faraway stand now that all the work on it had been done. But when I asked the hangar staff where the aircraft was and how we could get to it they looked at me in amazement. Apparently, an American crew had arrived at the hangar sometime beforehand, and after producing some paperwork to show that their company now owned the aircraft they'd climbed aboard, started up, taxied out and taken off. Our trip to Miami was thus instantly cancelled.

However, it just so happened that the IAS DC8 with the former Air Ceylon engines on it was still sitting in Luxembourg, waiting for a crew to come out and collect it later that day, so I phoned IAS headquarters and told them not to bother sending an extra crew as we'd bring it home ourselves. I thus had the very unusual experience of doing consecutive flights on the same four engines but on two different airframes. I don't know whether I can claim to be unique in that regard, but I rather hope so.

By this time (late 1978), IAS had started using a DC8 simulator in Amsterdam that belonged to KLM, who were still operating a DC8 fleet of their own. However, like the Alitalia one on which I'd been trained for Zambia Airways, this was not the kind of all-singing, all-dancing simulator we see today; it didn't move at all, and the only "visuals" it had were a set of runway lights that could be switched on when required to represent the view from the cockpit in the final stages of a simulated approach. The whole thing was powered through a huge system of glowing valves, and it bore about as much resemblance to the simulators of today as the wartime Colossus computer does to the latest iPad, but it would save us many hours of very expensive training on the aircraft itself, and IAS were therefore willing to pay a considerable amount of money to the UK CAA for them to approve it for the company's use.

In fact, this simulator, primitive as it was by today's standards, helped me make another "great leap forward" in terms of my career; by the autumn of 1978, IAS was operating a busy programme of worldwide cargo flights with its four DC8's, and with a normal staffing complement of four crews per aircraft, plus a few extra captains to handle training duties, we had around forty pilots who needed regular checks. I was already a Type Rating Examiner on the DC8, but IAS wanted me to become an Instrument Rating Examiner (IRE) as well; this would mean that I could renew pilots' instrument ratings, the essential qualification that all professional pilots need. As I've mentioned before, the instrument rating certifies that pilots are able to fly almost entirely by reference to the aircraft's instruments rather than looking out of the window, and it demands a thorough knowledge of navigational equipment, radio procedures and general flying skills that makes it a serious test of any pilot's capabilities.

In November I was scheduled to go to Amsterdam to do a normal six-monthly simulator base check on a couple of pilots, so the company arranged for an inspector from the CAA to come along and observe how I conducted these checks, with particular emphasis on how I briefed and debriefed the pilots before and after the simulator session and how well I picked up and explained to them any errors they made. The inspector would then report back to IAS as to whether he felt I could complete the IRE course successfully; should the answer be no, IAS would save themselves several thousand pounds in course fees and other expenses, and they might even reconsider whether to keep me on as a Type Rating Examiner. It was therefore something of a relief to hear that the inspector was sufficiently impressed to recommend me for inclusion on the next available IRE course, due to start in February, 1979.

There were piles of snow on the ground when I arrived at the Civil Aviation Flying Unit at Stansted to start my course, but that didn't worry me too much, as the only "flying" I'd be doing would be on a simulator. There was one other pilot on the course with me — a chap called Jim Snee, from British Midland Airways — and both of us had done as much preparation as we could, which mainly involved learning about the HS125 executive jet, as this was the kind of simulator we'd be using. Fortunately, the CAA had been kind enough to send us a copy of the aircraft manual a couple of weeks beforehand, so both of us had spent many hours studying a type we'd previously known nothing about.

However, no amount of studying could have prepared us for what happened when we first set foot on the 125 simulator. The arrangement was that while one trainee flew the simulator from the left-hand (captain's) seat the instructor would be in the right-hand one, and the other trainee would be sitting behind them, observing what went on. For our first session Jim was chosen to go first, so I settled in to watch and learn, hoping to pick up some tips that would help me out when it was my turn. I felt confident that I would do well; after all, this was our first training session, so surely the instructor would let us get accustomed to the unfamiliar flight deck layout and give us a reasonably easy time. The tougher stuff would surely come later, when we felt secure enough to handle it.

However, my hopes of that gentle start to the course were soon dashed. Jim was a good pilot, but soon after take-off the instructor started giving him a whole series of instrument and system malfunctions to deal with, as well as weather problems such as icing. The harder Jim worked to cope with all these things the more problems the instructor threw at him, until the poor chap was completely overwhelmed. When I eventually climbed into the captain's seat myself I was feeling a lot less confident than before.

As expected, I got exactly the same treatment as Jim, and at the end of that first session we had both, inevitably, failed. Our licences were taken from us, and we were told quite bluntly that if we didn't pass the IRE course we might not be relicensed at all, which would, if it happened, mean the end of our flying careers. We were already feeling rather exhausted and demoralised but now we were really alarmed as well.

To what extent this was just an amusing little psychological trick to test our resolve I'm not sure, but it certainly didn't seem like a joke at the time. I had never ever met anyone who'd actually lost their licence in this way, but then only a very small minority of pilots are selected for IRE training anyway, so it's not likely that I would have come across a failed one. I understand that this system of inevitable failure at the outset of the IRE course has now been changed, so trainees no longer go through what Jim and I did, but fortunately we were tough enough to survive it, and we both completed the rest of the course successfully. At the end of it I was not only a Type Rating Examiner on the DC8 itself but also an Instrument Rating Examiner on *any* aircraft, a qualification that was to prove very useful to me for many years to come.

I spent the rest of 1979 doing normal line flying punctuated by regular visits to the Amsterdam simulator to carry out checks on other pilots; things were looking good, but it wasn't long before the storm clouds began to gather again. During the autumn of 1979, IAS bought out a company called Trans-Meridian Air Cargo (T-MAC), which had previously been owned by Cunard (yes, *them* again). T-MAC had been our main long-haul cargo competitor, but in response to market conditions in the late 1970s they had reduced their cargo rates and profit margins so much that IAS simply could not compete. If IAS was to survive they had to do something drastic, and the answer was to take the other airline over, even though it was a much bigger company with a fleet of two DC8's and nineteen Canadair CL44's (a swing-tail turboprop aircraft rather similar in appearance to a Bristol Britannia). The larger airline thus created took on a new name: British Cargo Airlines.

Everything was fine for a while, but as 1979 turned into 1980 a lot of outstanding bills started to land on British Cargo's doormat. Rumour had it that a number of T-MAC's creditors had held off presenting their accounts until the takeover was safely completed, but whatever the truth of the situation might have been it was clear that by the end of February, British Cargo was struggling to stay afloat. On Thursday, 13 March, 1980, I was operating the empty return leg of a trip from Gatwick to Kano (Nigeria) when my crew and I got a radio message that confirmed our worst fears: we were told to take the aircraft to Stansted rather than Gatwick. We knew this was an ominous development as Stansted was T-MAC's original base, and many of their aircraft, particularly the rather underused CL44's, were already parked there.

After landing we were told to taxi to a parking spot in the main-tenance area (*not* the cargo-handling apron), and we got a further instruction to remove the Omega navigation set, which didn't actually belong to British Cargo, and bring it with us in the taxi that was being arranged to ferry us back to Gatwick. The end was clearly very much nigh, and as it turned out I had operated British Cargo's very last flight.

I'd enjoyed working with IAS/British Cargo, and I was very sad to see it go. And once again, of course, I had no idea where my future career would take me.

Chapter 10

I WAS UNEMPLOYED YET AGAIN, and I knew there was little, if any, chance of my getting another flying job in the UK. I was therefore very interested to hear that a recruiting team from Overseas National Airways of New York would be in London during April, 1980, just a month or so after IAS had gone bust, seeking to recruit experienced DC8 captains. The only problem was that these captains were to be based in Jeddah, Saudi Arabia — not a place I particularly wanted to work in — but with no likely alternative on the horizon I felt I had no real choice. Thus towards the end of May I flew to Denver, Colorado, to do a four-hour simulator evaluation at the United Airlines training centre, after which I was, as expected, offered a DC8 command in Jeddah, on the basis of doing sixty days' duty followed by twenty days off at home, with free accommodation in Jeddah and free flights in each direction. I had little choice but to take it, so that's what I did.

The basic salary was good, as it would need to be for such an operation, but if we flew more than sixty hours per month we could earn overtime, which was quite a boost to our incomes. We were operating passenger flights which Saudia, the national airline, could not quite cope with using their own aircraft and crews, particularly during the Hadj season, so we wore full Saudia uniform. Most of the flying was within Saudi Arabia, although we did some international flights to other parts of the Middle East and North Africa, especially when carrying pilgrims.

The crews were mainly American and British nationals, and of course we were all subject to the general limits imposed on life by the strict Islamic regime that governs all things in Saudi Arabia; Jeddah was certainly not the most interesting or exciting place to be living, so we were all happy to do as much flying as we possibly could during our two-month stints in the Kingdom. We were housed in an apartment block called Luna 1, and towards the end of every month it was quite common to see pilots forming a line each evening at the company's crewing office, located on the ground floor of the building, in the hope of being scheduled for a flight the following day and thus grabbing any overtime that might be available once most of the pilots had done their sixty hours. I have a feeling that some of the American pilots paid a little bit of "commission" to the crewing staff to ensure they got a good slice of the available overtime each month, but after my first couple of months there I found I was getting as much flying as I wanted anyway, so I never had to resort to such methods.

Although most of the DC8's we were flying were of the standard types (30 and 50 series aircraft), ONA also had three "stretched" DC8's (DC8-61's), which had a longer fuselage than the standard model and could carry 251 passengers as against just 170 in the 50 series. Extra pilot training was needed in order to fly these DC8-61's, as they required slightly different take-off and landing techniques in order to

One of the ONA "stretched" DC8-61 aircraft that were operating for Saudia
Photo: Wikimedia

avoid scraping the tail-skid on the runway either during rotation or when rounding-out for landing, but by July I'd gone through this training and was therefore cleared to fly the 61's as well. I had always loved flying the DC8, so getting my hands on the stretched version was the fulfilment of a dream I'd had for some time, and at least it was some compensation for having to put up with the lifestyle restrictions of being in Jeddah.

In that same month, July 1980, I was scheduled to come home to the UK for my usual twenty days' leave, but by now it was not the Southend area that I was calling home but Haywards Heath, in West Sussex. My marriage to Pam, which had lasted some twenty-five years, had broken down, partly due to the ever-increasing unpredictability of my own career, and I was now living with Larraine, a stewardess with British Caledonian Airways. My two daughters were by now grown up and living their own lives, so Pam and I had agreed to begin the process of ending our marriage.

By mid-1980 Larraine, with encouragement from me, had got herself a British Private Pilot's Licence; she had learnt to fly at Shoreham Airport in West Sussex, an achievement which I felt was all the more admirable as her own mother had been killed in a light aircraft accident when Larraine was just four years old. We'd decided that we would do a trip to the USA for her to gain some more pilot experience — flying has always been much cheaper there than in the UK — so when my leave period started I arranged to travel to New York rather than London, and once there I went up to Danbury, Connecticut, and arranged a ten-day rental of a single-engined, four-seater light aircraft, a Beech 19 Sport. Larraine flew into New York from London the following day, using her BCAL crew concessions, so I met her there and then we headed back up to Danbury to start our little jaunt around quite a large chunk of the USA.

From Danbury we headed south, with Larraine doing almost all the flying, heading for our first overnight stop. One of the things we wanted to do during our trip was to visit the Smithsonian Air and Space Museum in Washington DC, and as the USA was — at least in those days — quite relaxed about the idea of mixing small aeroplanes with big ones, we had decided to land at what was then Washington National Airport (now called Ronald Reagan Washington National Airport). Larraine had done some previous flying in the USA at a general aviation airfield near Atlanta, Georgia, called Peachtree de Kalb (BCAL had a regular service to Atlanta, so she was able to do a bit of flying during stopovers), but while Peachtree was a lot bigger and more impressive than Shoreham, Washington National was a busy commercial airport with lots of aircraft movements. I had never landed there before either, so it was all rather exciting as we flew down the approach; not only were we much closer to "big" aeroplanes than Larraine had ever been before whilst flying as a pilot, but we also had fantastic views of the whole downtown area of the city, with all its impressive monuments and government buildings. What a wonderful way to arrive for our first ever visit to Washington DC! And the Smithsonian was pretty good, too.

We were off again the next day, still heading south towards our next overnight stop, which was to be on more familiar ground: Peachtree de Kalb Airport in Atlanta, where we spent a couple of nights before turning westwards on the next leg of our roughly rectangular itinerary. Our plan was to spend a couple of days at the big Oshkosh Air Show in Wisconsin, but we were going there "the pretty way", across the southern states as far as Texas before turning northwards. We made overnight stops at Greenville (Mississippi), Fort Worth (Texas) and Tulsa (Oklahoma) before landing in Wisconsin, at a place called West Bend, around sixty miles from Oshkosh itself.

We had briefly considered the idea of flying into Oshkosh Airport for the show, as it is primarily a get-together for people who own — and in many cases have built — their own light aircraft, but when we discovered that during the show the Oshkosh control tower becomes, temporarily, the busiest one in the world we decided to take the easier and more relaxing option of landing at West Bend, hiring a car and finding a nice little motel nearby for a couple nights, leaving ourselves just a comfortable one-hour drive to get to Oshkosh next day.

Our plan worked a treat. Having landed at West Bend we were advised by the car rental people to go to a little place called Jackson, just south of West Bend, as there was a small and very comfortable motel there. We followed their advice, and after checking into the motel we looked round for somewhere to have dinner. Just along the road we found a lovely little "supper club", where we ended up dining on both nights of our stay. Apparently, these establishments are a bit of a speciality in Wisconsin — they are generally small, family-owned businesses serving good, home-cooked, traditional food — and when we walked in and asked, in our English accents, whether we had to be members in order to dine there, we suddenly became the centre of attention.

It appeared that British people of any description had only rarely, if ever, pitched up in Jackson, Wisconsin, and our hosts and the other diners were fascinated when we told them that we had flown into West Bend earlier that day in a light aircraft. One of them did ask us if we had flown all the way from England in it, so we quickly explained that we'd used big airliners to get to New York and then picked up a much smaller aeroplane in Connecticut. However, when we told them that we had, by that time, flown three sides of a rectangle in our trip around the USA they were still amazed; one lady said, "You mean you've come all that way in that little plane and ended up in Jackson, Wisconsin?". I think her incredulity was a reflection not so much of how far we'd flown but the fact we'd found the little town of Jackson at all.

The Oshkosh show was great, but when we saw how busy the circuit (or "traffic pattern", as it's called in the USA) was at the end of the day we were very glad we hadn't flown in, and after our second dinner at the supper club and another night in the lovely little motel we headed back to West Bend Airport the next morning and took off on the last long leg of our journey: the west-to-east journey back towards Danbury. We'd scheduled ourselves a spare day at the end of the trip in case of any delays on the way round, so if all went well we were expecting to land back at Danbury during the afternoon of the day before we were due to return the aircraft. However, things didn't quite work out that way; as we flew eastwards the cloud-base was steadily getting lower, and it was soon quite obvious that we could not expect to get to Danbury under VFR (Visual Flight Rules) that day.

A Beech 19 aircraft similar
to the one we flew around the USA
Photo: Wikimedia

Fortunately, as we had routed to the south of Lake Erie, we found a suitable diversion airport just ahead of us: Youngstown, Ohio, very near the border with Pennsylvania. Youngstown is not exactly a tourist destination; in fact, it is located in what became known as the "Rust Belt" after the decline of the American steel industry in the late 1970s, but as a sanctuary from unhelpful weather conditions it was fine. We had been somewhat spoilt in Jackson by the wonderful people we'd met at the supper club, but in this rather down-at-heel industrial city we didn't necessarily expect to find such a warm and friendly welcome as we'd had there.

However, even Youngstown exceeded our expectations; we found a lively and quite crowded restaurant, and as we waited for a table we went to the bar to order drinks. There was a tall, well-dressed chap standing next to us, and as we put in our order he suddenly turned to us and asked where we were from. We went through the usual story about our trip round the USA, and as our drinks arrived on the bar he said to us, "Hey, let me get those for you," and insisted on paying. We accepted his generosity, thinking that we could reciprocate when it was time for a top-up, but just as we were thanking him our new friend spotted some people he was waiting for, so he apologised to us and off he went. We then sat down for our own dinner, but as we were finishing, our friend appeared again; we thought we'd be able to buy him a drink now, but he'd only popped back to apologise yet again for the fact he was leaving with his friends and so couldn't spend more time with us. We were sorry too, but this gentleman's courtesy and generosity had given us a very warm feeling about a city that relatively few Britons will probably ever have cause to visit.

The next day we managed to complete our flight back to Danbury, though the weather was still far from perfect, and by the end of the trip we had clocked up over thirty-six hours in the air. We'd been to places we would probably never have visited under any other circumstances, and we'd been warmly welcomed almost everywhere we'd stopped, whether just to pick up fuel or to stay overnight. To this day it remains in both our memories as one of the best holidays we've ever had, though not exactly the most relaxing.

By mid-August I was back in Jeddah; the workload had increased, and I was told I was now on the company's permanent staff, which was good news, as despite the problems of being based in Saudi Arabia it was far better than sitting at home earning no money. I would also be flying the DC8-61 on most of my trips, so I was as happy as I could be in the circumstances.

On 19 August, not long after my return from the UK, I was doing a long day of flying; we had done a Jeddah-Amman-Jeddah round trip in the morning before setting off from Jeddah again to Beirut and then Riyadh, after which we were due to return empty to Jeddah again. It was late evening by the time we started our engines at Riyadh for our last sector, and we were looking forward to getting back to Jeddah for a well-earned rest. We asked for permission to taxi, but were told to hold our position because an incoming aircraft had declared an emergency; it's normal practice, of course, to stop all aircraft movements until any aircraft with a problem has landed safely, so we sat and waited.

Shortly thereafter we saw the lights of the aircraft in question — a Saudia L-1011 Tristar — on the approach, and we watched it as it made what looked like a good landing. By this time the fire trucks had run up the runway and were positioned at the far end, ready to meet the Tristar as it came in, and as the aircraft passed us on its landing roll my co-pilot told me he'd noticed smoke coming from its aft end. We presumed that the fire trucks would be able to deal with the situation once the Tristar had reached them after turning off the runway onto the taxiway, so we continued sitting there on the apron, awaiting further instructions.

As we listened on the Tower frequency we heard the Tristar captain ask the tower controller to enquire whether the fire section leader had spotted any visual sign of fire on the aircraft, and shortly afterwards the controller replied that there was no apparent fire and the aircraft was therefore cleared to taxi to the apron. However, the captain responded that he did not wish to taxi but was shutting down engines and initiating an emergency evacuation of the aircraft.

In the DC8 we were still sitting on stand waiting for taxi clearance, and although we were obviously a bit concerned to hear that the Tristar was being evacuated we knew that if there's any doubt about an aircraft's situation immediately after an emergency landing then it's better to go ahead and start an evacuation rather than wait for things to develop further and potentially become a lot more serious. After a few minutes we were given clearance to taxi, but as we were heading towards the runway we were told to taxi across the runway and wait on the far side, as there was another aircraft behind us that had priority (it belonged to the Saudi Crown Prince). In fact, we heard the captain of the royal aircraft on the radio, telling the tower that the Crown Prince was prepared to remain at Riyadh if his presence could be helpful in light of the problem with the Saudia aircraft, but the controllers told him to depart as planned, which he did.

We then called for our own take-off clearance, but were again asked to wait; an executive jet had declared a fuel emergency because it had been held overhead whilst the Tristar was given priority for landing, so it now needed to land as a matter of some urgency. We watched it land, and as it rolled along the runway we called again for take-off clearance, expecting to be cleared immediately. This time, however, we were told that the airfield was closed until further notice and we were to taxi back to the apron. It seemed we were not to get back to Jeddah after all that day.

It was not until we were leaving the aircraft and standing on the top of the steps that we could see across the whole airfield, including the Tristar with all the fire trucks around it, but things were looking rather more serious now, as there were flames coming out of the top of its fuselage. We were obviously concerned, but as it was now some considerable time since the captain had started the evacuation we felt there was a good chance that most, if not all, of those on board would have got out of the aircraft before the worst of the fire had taken hold.

We went to a hotel near Riyadh Airport, but as we settled into our rooms and turned on the TV we became aware that what we had witnessed at the airport was a great deal worse than we'd thought. It turned out that *no-one* on the Tristar had escaped; everyone on board — all 301 passengers and crew — had perished in the fire. Naturally, we were all rather stunned.

The next day we got up and returned to the airport, ready to fly back to Jeddah, but as we entered the crew check-in area we were taken aside by local representatives of the NTSB, America's National Transportation Safety Board; the Lockheed Tristar, of course, was an American-built aircraft, so the NTSB would inevitably be involved with the crash investigation. All three of us flight deck crew were interviewed about what we had seen and heard, so we didn't get away from Riyadh until the evening, by which time we had been rescheduled to do a flight to Amman, then on to Dharan and eventually to Jeddah. Our long day had turned into *two* long days, and as we returned to our apartments we were in a pretty reflective mood.

How, we wondered, could an aircraft have landed in one piece at a well-equipped airport, with emergency vehicles in close attendance, yet no-one on board had survived? In fact, I came to the eventual conclusion, when I heard more details of what had happened, that it might have been better if the aircraft had made a crash landing and broken up; at least *some* of those on board could then possibly have escaped through breaks in the fuselage instead of perishing inside it. So what, in the ultimate analysis, had gone wrong?

The cause of the fire itself was never established with certainty, but it was suspected to have been a hydraulic leak below the centre engine. However, this kind of thing does happen from time to time, which is why aircraft are equipped with extinguishers to deal with such problems, though in this particular incident it seemed they did not put the fire out completely. Smoke got into the cabin, causing panic amongst the passengers, so things were already in a bad way as the aircraft came in to land, and some experts feel that had the aircraft done an emergency stop on the runway and started the evacuation immediately, rather than rolling along to a taxiway and turning off onto it, then at least some people could have been saved. However, my own view, having watched the incident unfolding, was that the captain did his best to get the aircraft to where the fire trucks were waiting for it, so I don't agree with this particular criticism.

There was also the question of why, even after the captain had shut down the engines and initiated an evacuation, it was more than twenty minutes before the first door was opened — by rescue teams from the outside, not by crew members from the inside — by which time everyone on board had died from smoke inhalation rather than burn injuries. It was subsequently discovered that the aircraft had been pressurised when it landed and that the pressurisation control had been set to manual rather than automatic, which prevented the pressure inside and outside the cabin from equalising automatically immediately after touchdown. This could have made it very difficult to open the doors, assuming anyone in the cabin had been able to attempt such action, but for whatever reason none of the doors were opened until the fire service managed to open the second door on the starboard side some twenty-three minutes after engine shutdown. Around three minutes after that the aircraft burst into flames and was destroyed.

It was ultimately concluded by the accident investigators that the flight deck crew's responses to the emergency situation in which they found themselves was inadequate in various ways, and this case ultimately became an important example in the relatively new field of Crew Resource Management (CRM) training for airline crews. Learning from the mistakes of others is an invaluable tool in aviation, as it is in many other activities, so the disaster at Riyadh, tragic and terrible as it was, did provide useful lessons that I'm sure have played a major part in reducing the likelihood of anything similar happening again.

I continued to fly our regular programme, mostly on the DC8-61, taking my regular twenty-day break in the UK in October and then returning to Jeddah to work through November and December. By then our flights in the DC8-61 were becoming rather less regular, and in mid-December I operated a flight to Khartoum, Sudan, on a smaller DC8-55, after which my crew and I stayed on in Khartoum to do a series of flights for Sudan Airways. It was now getting close to Christmas, and I was hoping to see Larraine, as she was due to be in Dubai for a day or two as part of a BCAL DC10 trip to Hong Kong that she had requested to do during the festive season.

Fortunately, I was able to arrange a free ticket to Abu Dhabi on Sudan Airways, and when I got off the aircraft the duty manager there very kindly arranged a free taxi to take me to Dubai, where Larraine and her colleagues on the BCAL crew were staying for a couple of nights before the next stage of their trip. Dubai is a very tolerant part of the Arab world, so people are free to celebrate Christmas, and on a trip to the souk Larraine and I were even able to buy a small, inflatable Santa Claus to help decorate the party room that the hotel had set aside for the use of BCAL crews during their stay. In fact, that strange little memento eventually became an essential part of our seasonal decorations at home until, several years later, he developed a fatal leak.

In early January, 1981, I returned to the UK straight from Khartoum as a passenger on a Sudan Airways Boeing 707 for my usual 20-day break. I was expecting to be called back to Jeddah later that month, but the days came and went, and I heard nothing. As the end of January was looming I decided to phone ONA's head office in New York to find out when they were likely to need me, and it was only then that I learnt what had happened while I had been enjoying my time off.

Apparently, one of the DC8-61's, N913R — a very good aircraft that had done service with Japan Air Lines and that I'd particularly enjoyed flying — had been flown up to Luxembourg for major maintenance, but while it was in the hangar a fire had broken out, and both the hangar and the aircraft itself had been completely destroyed. That was the rather bad news, but even worse was to come. With an aircraft gone, and as the airline had no immediate intention of replacing it, ONA suddenly had four crews more than it actually required, and they had therefore decided to employ a simple but brutal method of dealing with that sudden glut of pilots and flight engineers: those who were in Jeddah would keep their jobs, but those who were relaxing at home were suddenly redundant. At the age of forty-seven, with some 17,000 hours of flight time, I was jobless yet again.

There was no realistic chance of getting anything in Britain, but within a few weeks I spotted an advertisement in Flight magazine that I felt I had to reply to, and it was in a location with which I was already familiar: Jeddah. This time, though, it was Saudia itself that was

A Saudia L-1011 Tristar
Photo: MAP

looking for pilots, as it was in need of more crew for its L1011 Tristar fleet, so I sent them my CV. Quite soon afterwards I was called for interview at Saudia's London office and was subsequently offered a Tristar command based in Jeddah and starting in April, so at least I was back in employment again.

However, I have to say that the prospect of being based in Jeddah permanently did not appeal to me. At least when I'd been working with ONA I'd been getting three weeks off in the UK every couple of months; with Saudia I would have to move to Jeddah, and Larraine would not be able to join me immediately because we were not yet married. Quite frankly, I also had my doubts as to whether Larraine would ever settle in a country like Saudi Arabia, bearing in mind she would have to put up with all the restrictions with which women of any nationality had to comply whilst there. For an independent young woman like her I knew that not being allowed to drive or go out anywhere on her own, particularly when I was away flying, would be very difficult indeed, and I found myself wondering whether living in Saudi Arabia would put our intended marriage under serious pressure right from the start.

Anyway, I tried to put these concerns to one side as I embarked on my Tristar technical course in Jeddah, and after I'd finished that I did thirty hours of training on the Tristar simulator, followed by twelve hours of flight training at a little-used airfield at a place called Wedjh, located on the Red Sea coast about four hundred miles north of Jeddah. I was then given a type-rating for the Tristar on my American licence, and with most of my training successfully completed I was allocated a two-bedroomed flat in the Saudia City housing complex where most of Saudia's ex-patriate crew members and their families were accommodated. I bought a new car and was all set for the line-training I would have to complete before being confirmed as a Saudia Tristar captain.

For some reason, though, and for the first time in my life, I had a few difficulties with the line training. Though the Tristar itself was a very good aircraft to fly, it did have a rather complicated Flight Management System (FMS) and was a far more "technical" aircraft than any I had flown before; in other words, I felt I was learning to fly the computer system rather than the aircraft itself. Perhaps, too, my attitude and diligence weren't all they might have been — I was still having misgivings about how Larraine and I would adapt to the ex-pat lifestyle once we had married and moved to our new home in Saudi — and I know that at times I said things I probably shouldn't have done.

On one early trip, for example, I got rather cross with the Saudi Arabian captain of a flight on which I was rostered as third pilot, mainly to observe the use of the FMS (we all had to do several of these observation flights so that we could learn how the FMS was used before being let loose on it ourselves).

Anyway, this particular trip took place in July, which also just happened to coincide with the Muslim holy month of Ramadan in that particular year. We were to fly the Jeddah-Geneva-London route, returning non-stop from London to Riyadh the following day. As we flew north towards London, one of the senior cabin staff, a young Jordanian lady, came up to the flight deck and asked whether, as it was now dark in Jeddah, she and her Muslim colleagues could break their fast and at least have a drink of water. The captain's answer was a stern "no"; they would have to comply with strict Islamic rules and wait until after sunset in London before they could eat or drink anything whatsoever.

I was absolutely incensed by this, but quite frankly I was already feeling pretty angry before this incident even happened. During the long hours of our flight from Jeddah via Geneva, the captain had made it clear that neither he nor the co-pilot would be able to tell me very much about the FMS because they were both observing their fast and would be neither drinking nor eating until the sun had gone down. This situation was obviously not very helpful to me, seeing as I was supposed to be observing what they did and asking them any relevant questions, but in any case I am utterly convinced that pilots have an absolute duty to keep themselves properly fed and hydrated whilst flying as a matter of safety. The air you breathe on an aircraft at altitude is much drier than what you find at ground level, which is why people often feel the need to drink more fluids whilst airborne, and when you're in charge of the aircraft and the safety of all its occupants it is simply irresponsible, in my opinion, to deprive yourself of liquids and thus risk suffering from such possible effects as fatigue, muscle weakness, poor concentration, headaches, dizziness or light-headedness.

Anyway, having heard the captain's ruling the flight attendant returned to the cabin, and as she left the flight deck I could see tears in her eyes. This was the moment when, if I'd *really* wanted to make a success of my career with Saudia I should probably have clamped my hand firmly over my mouth and pretended I was stifling a cough, but I didn't. Instead, I just opened my mouth and said something along the following lines:

"Captain, may I just point out that at the moment we still have enough flight duty hours and fuel left to continue as far as Iceland if we want to, haven't we?"

"Yes, I suppose we do," came the rather puzzled reply.

Again, I should have stopped right there, but now my blood was up I blundered on regardless.

"Well," I continued, "in Iceland at this time of year the sun doesn't go down at all, so I just wonder how you'd deal with that."

The captain was clearly not impressed with my little observation, and the rest of the flight was conducted in stony silence except when the checklists and other necessary talking had to be done. I knew that my apparent lack of respect for the laws of Islam would not count in my favour; it may not have had any effect on what ultimately happened to me in Saudia, but I'm sure it can't have helped, and in any case it must have shown that my attitude to this particular job was not quite as positive as it should have been.

I also think that when you've become a very experienced instructor on one kind of aircraft it may be that little bit harder to switch to another type and assume the role of the "new boy" again. Anyway, my line training continued, but I was doing mainly internal flights within Saudi Arabia and was seeing very little of Europe. Larraine and I did start making plans for our wedding, which would have to wait until I could get some leave and come home, but as I had had to spend so much time on line training, particularly all those observation flights, I was beginning to get very frustrated that I wasn't yet checked out, and in the end I probably started getting a bit over-confident and thus took my eye off the ball.

The result was that on one bad day I just didn't perform as well as I could and should have done; my Saudi training captain told me I simply hadn't made the grade and he was therefore recommending that my employment with Saudia be terminated forthwith. This could have been a terrible blow to my confidence and self-esteem, but on the very same day another new pilot, who had already flown with a well-respected airline for several years as a captain on another type of wide-bodied, three-engined aircraft (the McDonnell Douglas DC10) was also terminated, so I could at least reassure myself that I was not alone.

In any case, I was not terribly upset to be leaving Jeddah; I didn't want to be out of work, but I had this odd feeling that somehow this would all turn out for the best. Of course, I was now very keen indeed to get home as soon as possible, and although I'd heard that it would normally take ten days or more for a departing foreign pilot to extricate himself from the various bureaucratic entanglements of working for Saudia I managed to do it all — and to sell my car — within three. As I arrived back at Heathrow in early October I was unemployed but not discouraged. Something, I thought, was bound to turn up.

Chapter 11

VERY SHORTLY AFTER MY RETURN TO THE UK that "something" did turn up. One day, I went to meet some friends I'd worked with in IAS/British Cargo; they had been in the commercial and marketing side of things, not flying, and we were just going to have a general chat about this and that and who was doing what where. They told me they were thinking of getting involved in a new airline project overseas, but they didn't really expect me to be interested, thinking that the operation they were planning was rather too small for a "big jet" pilot like me to bother with. However, when I heard the details of what they were considering, I instantly pointed out to them the folly of this assumption, and in return was almost immediately offered the job of Chief Pilot of the new airline, assuming it got off the ground.

After the lifestyle restrictions and oppressive social atmosphere of Saudi Arabia, this new proper job was to be somewhere that could hardly be more different — the British Virgin Islands — and the aircraft I would be flying was a world away from the highly technical Tristar I'd been trained on in Saudia. After an interval of some twelve years, I would once again be flying one of the most iconic aircraft of all time: the Douglas DC3 Dakota.

With a new job in the offing I felt very cheerful, but as the startup of the new airline was not planned until sometime in early 1982, and as, having recently returned from abroad, I was not entitled to claim any benefits despite being unemployed, I took a temporary job as a delivery van driver, working for another former IAS colleague who was now managing a branch of a courier firm down in the Brighton area. By now we were in the run-up to Christmas, 1981, so there was plenty of work coming through, but once the festive season had passed it started to drop off, and by the end of February I was living on my savings and getting rather worried about how long it was taking to get the new Caribbean operation up and running.

I therefore decided that I might as well try to push things along a bit, so I pulled a few strings and managed to hitch a lift on an Overseas National DC8 flight from Gatwick to New York, whence I caught a

Greyhound bus to Miami, where my new employers — now named British Caribbean Airways — had rented a small office, from which they were co-ordinating preparations for the launch of the airline. They were rather surprised to see me, but they put me to work straight away, helping a chap called Jim Waterman, a former IAS flight engineer with whom I'd flown many times, in finding us a good aircraft to purchase. At that time Jim was already working in Miami for one of the main cargo airlines based there, but he was thinking of moving, so he'd agreed to help British Caribbean with a view to possibly joining them if they did eventually manage to get airborne.

It wasn't very long before Jim and I located an aircraft that sounded just right: an ex-US Navy RD4 version of the DC3 (or C-47 to use its military designation). In those days, Miami Airport had an area known as "Corrosion Corner", so named because of the many old aircraft of various types and conditions, mostly owned by small cargo airlines, that were always parked there. The aircraft we'd found had flown relatively few hours for its type and age, so we approached its owners, Conner Air Lines, whose CEO, Gus Conner, was definitely one of aviation's more notable characters. He was in the habit of holding regular "happy hours" in his office on many evenings, during which a large bottle of Ballantine's whisky would normally be consumed, and I remember that our negotiations over the price of the aircraft were fairly well lubricated by this particular Scottish product. After three or four evenings we agreed on a price of $90,000 for the aircraft and a whole stack of spares, and thus the deal was done.

There were various things to do before taking the aircraft down to the British Virgin Islands — getting it painted, getting me checked out on the DC3 again and finding another pilot to work with me for the new company — but by late April all these things had been sorted out. N8666 had a fresh coat of paint, I'd done some refresher training and a flight check to add the DC3 to my American licence, and we'd found an experienced co-pilot in the shape of Tony Trent, who had flown DC3's with Air BVI, the passenger airline of the British Virgin Islands, and was also an occasional skipper for one of the many yacht charter companies based there. On 23 April, 1982, after a delivery flight from Miami that had included picking up a commercial load in San Juan, Puerto Rico, and dropping it off in St Maarten, in the Dutch Antilles,

Above: the British Caribbean Airways DC3 (N8666)
Below: the DC3 flight deck, with me in the left-hand seat

we landed at Beef Island, the BVI's main airport. For me, another new adventure was about to begin.

British Caribbean Airways was already established in a downtown office in Road Town, the BVI's capital, and had started operating flights on behalf of the company's major shareholder, a local supermarket. These flights had been done in a Beech 18 aircraft, flown by another pilot who already worked for the company, so with the newly-arrived DC3, British Caribbean now had two freight aircraft to offer to customers. Its main activity would be to collect cargo that had been brought from the USA or Europe to San Juan, Puerto Rico, on various international airlines and then to distribute it around various Caribbean destinations: places like St Maarten, Antigua, Barbados, Dominica, St Kitts, Montserrat, St Thomas and St Croix. The company also offered a purchasing service, so that if a customer in one of the islands we served needed to buy three cases of widgets, the BCA manager in San Juan — a wonderful lady of Cuban heritage called Lourdes — would contact a widget-supplier somewhere in the USA, place an order and then arrange for the goods to be flown to San Juan. On arrival they'd go into the BCA cargo-shed, where they would stay until the next available DC3 or Beech 18 flight to the relevant destination.

It was a great system, and working for BCA had one particular advantage over every other flying job I'd ever had: almost all the work was done on weekdays, as most airports around the Caribbean just didn't want to handle cargo at weekends. In those days, very few island airports had cargo sheds or anywhere safe and dry to store goods for any length of time, so the normal practice was that the recipients of any freight we carried had to come to the airport with their vans or trucks as soon as we landed so they could pick up whatever they were waiting for. Van and truck drivers tended not to work at weekends, so our general flying schedule was defined by this happy combination of island culture and lack of storage space. I guess things may well be rather different now.

Soon after I arrived in the BVI I rented a small house in an area called Brandywine Bay on the south coast of Tortola and acquired a car in the shape of an old VW Beetle. Larraine had meanwhile resigned from British Caledonian, had packed up and rented out our home in Haywards Heath, and had spent a while in Atlanta, Georgia, doing her US Commercial Pilot's Licence, just in case she had any opportunities to use it in the BVI. She then joined me in Tortola, and in July, once the decree ending my first marriage had been made absolute, we organised our wedding, to be held at a restaurant with a very large garden, just above where we were living.

July can be rather wet in that part of the world, and on the morning of our nuptials we woke to a fairly heavy rainstorm. However, it relented during the morning, and at the appointed hour Larraine was driven up the hill in our rather battered Beetle by my old friend, Jim Waterman, who by now was the Chief Engineer of Air BVI, the passenger airline; as expected, he'd moved down from Miami but had decided to join Air BVI instead of British Caribbean.

At the top of the hill were waiting around fifteen guests plus myself and the BVI's Chief Registrar, and within a very short time Larraine and I were duly wed. For the reception, held outside under clear blue skies, we had engaged a local band called "Trouble". No-one really wants trouble at their wedding, of course, but we took the chance, and throughout the afternoon everyone ate great stacks of fried chicken and salad whilst getting gently inebriated to the band's lilting West Indian rhythms. It was gloroius.

*Our wedding in Tortola; and this time I **didn't** wear uniform!*

In fact, Larraine has a rather unusual memory of that day: at one point, a small lizard with a frill round its neck popped out of a crack in the wall next to her. It seemed to be interested in what was going on, so she broke off a sliver of chicken and held it out for the little creature, which quickly grabbed it and gobbled it up. She offered it another piece, and then another, each of which was gently taken from her fingertips and quickly swallowed, until at last the little reptile's appetite was satisfied and it disappeared into the wall once again, probably to sleep off the feast it had just enjoyed. Ever since that day, Larraine has told people that although we had a fairly low-key and low-budget wedding, the location — a beautiful headland looking out over a calm, blue sea and neighbouring islands — could hardly be bettered, and she doesn't imagine there are many other women in the world who can say that during their wedding reception they had the pleasure of feeding tiny bits of chicken to a friendly little lizard with a frill round its neck. I think she's probably right.

We didn't need to go away for our honeymoon; when you live somewhere as beautiful as the BVI there's not much point in going anywhere else, and at that time I didn't want to take much leave as we were planning to make a trip back to the UK in the autumn. I was now doing some flying on the Beech 18 aircraft with the company's other two pilots, Michael Sabine and Tony Trent, who were both very experienced on it and could therefore ride shotgun while I gained the necessary hours on type. In August I went over to St Thomas in the US Virgin Islands and was cleared by the US FAA to fly the aircraft commercially as its single pilot, and I began to feel well settled into my new job.

Larraine started looking for work as well, and as word got around that a well-qualified and experienced secretary/PA was on the loose (Larraine had been doing that kind of work before she joined BCAL) one or two interesting offers came in. Larraine had done an intensive secretarial course, with shorthand, after leaving school, and her skills were still in good shape even after six years as an air stewardess (in fact, she still uses her shorthand to this day). She eventually got a job as PA to a chartered accountant in Road Town, and soon after that we moved from our rather hot and "buggy" little house at Brandywine Bay to a gorgeous hillside residence at a place called Maya Cove, with wonderful views towards the airport at Beef Island and, below it, to a mangrove-fringed anchorage that was home to a small yacht charter company and a number of private boats, many of them "live-aboards".

My income as a pilot was obviously not as good as it had been with other companies, particularly when I was working in Saudi Arabia, but Larraine's salary was rather better than she might have expected

The 26ft sailing-boat and the Cessna 150 aircraft
that we owned while we were in the BVI

to get in the UK, so all in all we were pretty comfortable. Thus, during 1983, we decided to add a few little embellishments to our lifestyle: we bought a lovely little 26ft yacht and a two-seat Cessna 150 light aircraft. Both were second-hand, of course, but with a little bit of work they were soon looking great, and we were thus ready to spend our weekends either sailing between the various islands in the BVI group or perhaps flying over to St Thomas (in the US Virgin Islands) or San Juan (Puerto Rico) if we wanted to do some serious shopping or perhaps see a film in a proper cinema. Life was very good indeed.

Of course, flying old aeroplanes such as the DC3 and the Beech 18 was not without its little problems and surprises. In November, 1982, I'd suffered a starboard engine failure on the DC3 on take-off, fully loaded, from San Juan; losing half your power with a full load of either passengers or cargo can lead to serious or even catastrophic results, but the one remaining engine kept us going round the circuit until we could do an emergency landing back where we started. On another occasion, again on the DC3, I suffered a serious braking problem after landing at Beef Island with a very heavy load. Our particular DC3 had things called "bag brakes", which relied on being pumped full of hydraulic fluid, and although they might work well when first applied they did have a tendency to fade, thus resulting in a serious loss of braking action as the aircraft progressed along the runway.

Beef Island Airport Tortola, with sea at both ends of the runway!
Photo: BVI Airports Authority

That's exactly what happened after this particular landing, and I quickly realised that the far end of the runway — and the sea beyond it — were coming towards us rather too rapidly for comfort. There was only one thing I could do: as we were running out of tarmac I knew I somehow had to find some more, so I yelled at the co-pilot to take his feet off the rudder pedals (which doubled as brake pedals, and in a normal landing would be used to help to keep the aircraft straight), then stamped on the right rudder/brake pedal myself so that the aircraft swung round in a ground-loop and came to a halt, facing the opposite way. Of course, you wouldn't want to do that sort of thing too often, but it was a much better solution to our problem than taking an unscheduled dip in the sea.

However, that was not to be my only ground-loop experience whilst working for BCA: I had one on the Beech 18 as well. I had arrived at San Juan early one morning with an empty aircraft to pick up a load of cargo for St Maarten. There were several boxes of various sizes, most of which were fairly light, but there were also some small but very heavy oil pumps packed on small wooden pallets, so I asked the loaders to drag them up to the front of the cabin, then place the boxes behind them and then put a cargo net over the whole load. I was sure they understood exactly what I wanted, so I left them to it and went off to have some breakfast.

The BCA Beech 18

On returning to the aircraft I looked at the load through the rear door, and everything seemed fine, so I got into the pilot's seat — which, by the way, entailed climbing up the trailing edge of the wing, inboard of the port engine, and lowering oneself through the side window — and started taxying out. The aircraft felt a bit odd, but the Beech 18 had what was called a "walking undercarriage", which could sometimes feel a bit strange if the aircraft was loaded to anywhere near its maximum weight. Having reached the runway and been cleared for take-off, I started bringing up the power fairly slowly, as usual, and then as the speed increased I gently eased forward on the control column to lift the tail.

Almost immediately the world around me starting spinning as the aircraft swung violently to the left, so I immediately closed the throttles and pulled the control column back towards me to keep the tail down; by the time it came to rest the aircraft had gone through about three hundred degrees, but at least I'd managed to keep it on the runway. I called up the control tower and told them I'd had an undercarriage problem and was returning to the ramp — the undulations of the ground between the tower and runway meant that they hadn't actually seen what had happened — and then I taxied rather gingerly back to the apron, where I demanded that all the cargo be offloaded.

As soon as the cargo-net and a couple of large boxes had been removed it became clear what the problem was: the loaders had decided it was rather hard work to drag the pumps up the slope of the cabin to the front so they'd simply hidden them under the boxes at the rear, thereby causing the aircraft to be extremely tail-heavy. Had I actually managed to get airborne that take-off could have been the last I ever did, but as it turned out there was no lasting harm done, and after the aircraft had been reloaded — under my strict supervision this time — I was able to complete the flight successfully.

Our wonderful lifestyle continued throughout 1983 and into 1984, with both of us working during the week and sailing our boat on most Sundays. We usually sailed over to Peter Island, which meant an exhilarating beat to windward on the outward leg and a lazier, down-wind run on the way back, and we'd often have friends along with us and take a picnic to enjoy onboard whilst riding gently at anchor just off a beautiful, sandy beach. There was a small coral reef between the anchorage and the beach, where we would snorkel and see lots of gorgeously coloured little fish and, quite often, a barracuda that seemed to be a permanent resident there. Though barracuda are quite fearsome to look at they are not generally considered very dangerous to humans, though as a precaution we always removed any jewellery before getting in the water. Barracuda can sometimes mistake the glint of a metallic object as the flash of a small fish and might therefore launch an attack, so the "no shiny stuff" rule was one that we all followed when swimming.

Larraine would also do some occasional charter flights, either on our own little two-seat Cessna 150 or on a four-seat Cessna 172 owned by one of Air BVI's pilots. In the bigger aircraft she did a couple of trips down to Montserrat, landing at the airport that was, some years later, destroyed by a volcanic eruption, while in our little Cessna she did one rather interesting trip with the starboard door removed so that a local photographer could take some aerial shots of yacht anchorages for a sailing guide he was publishing. After we'd removed the door, and before the day of the flight itself, we each did a test flight in the Cessna just to see how its aerodynamic properties were affected, and we were amazed to discover that the doorless side of the aircraft created less drag — in other words, it flew more efficiently — than the normal one. This seemed quite ridiculous, but we did wonder for a while whether we'd save fuel if we flew around with *both* doors off all the time!

On another occasion, a very distinguished-looking Englishman appeared at the airport one day when Larraine was tying down the Cessna after a flight and asked if he could charter the aircraft for a trip around Tortola and its outlying islands; he was an ornithologist studying frigate birds, and he wanted to find out, from the air, exactly where they were nesting so that he could rent a boat to go and see them at closer quarters next day. After a short flight he duly found what he was looking for, but while he was taking photos through the aircraft window of the birds that were on the ground Larraine was busy dodging any that were airborne, as meetings between large birds and small aeroplanes can be rather messy.

On some weekends we would fly over to Puerto Rico for a night or two, often to go to the cinema. We did have a cinema in Tortola, but it simply couldn't match the big screen and air-conditioned comfort of the one in San Juan, so if there was a film on that we really wanted to see we would jump in the Cessna and head off to San Juan. We did sometimes go to the picture-house in Tortola, though, and one day we noticed in the local paper that the week's big film was *The Texas Chainsaw Massacre*, though this was something neither of us wanted to see. We were, however, were rather amused when we drove past the cinema a couple of days later and saw that the sign outside, made up of those slide-in plastic letters as used by American motels and fast-food joints, was proudly advertising *The Texas Chainsaw Massage!*

Our social life in the BVI was always very good, but the best fun was to be had during occasional visits by Royal Navy frigates that were on their way back from duty in the South Atlantic; the Falklands War was over, of course, but the Royal Navy had to maintain a continuing presence in those cold and rather bleak islands, so it was an established practice for their ships to call in at the BVI on their way home to get some warmth back into their crews' bones for a couple of days before setting off across the North Atlantic. We often socialised with the petty officers, taking some of them sailing with us on our boat or even flying in our little Cessna. Most of them had never been on a sailing-boat of any description before, despite having spent many years at sea, but they soon got the hang of winding winches, furling sails and other tasks that never cropped up in their day jobs.

One of the chief petty officers who came up with me for a flight in our Cessna was a senior radio technician, and he was particularly fascinated by the airborne radio navigation aids we could use when flying to other islands. I explained to him that although there were various official air navigation beacons around the area, the most useful aid to finding a particular island was a much-photocopied list of the frequencies of all the commercial radio stations around the Eastern Caribbean, as the music and news programmes from these stations could often be heard hundreds of miles away simply by tuning in the radio-compass equipment (otherwise known as ADF, which stands for Automatic Direction Finder) fitted to virtually every aircraft, large or small. The glory of this now rather old-fashioned ADF technology is that the radio set has a little dial with a needle on it that points straight to the source of the broadcast: simple, but very effective. In fact, this Chief Petty Officer was quite envious, as he reckoned the ADF on our little Cessna was more efficient than the similar but much larger equipment he had on his frigate!

The summer of 1984 came and went, and we were still enjoying our life in the BVI even though we'd had to move out of our lovely rented house at Maya Cove because the owner had wanted to move back in, at least for a while. The apartment we moved to, which was in Road Town, the capital of the BVI, was not a patch on the house on the hillside, but it was acceptable, and by that time we were thinking of buying a plot of land higher up the hill at Maya Cove and putting an American log-cabin style home on it, which we could import quite easily from Puerto Rico. It was therefore, perhaps, rather fortunate that before we actually started putting money down or signing on any dotted lines everything suddenly changed when, in early November, 1984, Klaus arrived.

Klaus was a tropical storm that turned into a hurricane, and although it wasn't outstandingly powerful it did something rather unusual: it came out of the west rather than from the Atlantic, the first recorded storm to hit the Leeward Islands from that direction. The morning after the main part of the storm hit, Larraine and I set off to drive rather gingerly in our car towards the airport on the main road that would also pass Maya Cove, where our yacht was anchored. As we neared Maya Cove we met the Managing Direction of Air BVI driving the other way, and he flagged us down to give us some bad news: our little Cessna had been picked up by the storm and flipped over, causing lots of damage.

It was not the news we wanted to hear, but we'd rather expected it; a week or so beforehand we'd been asked to move the aircraft from its normal parking-place on the grass near the perimeter fence so that work could start on a new taxiway, so we had put it onto the tarmac apron in front of the terminal. In its original position on the grass we had had three tie-down points to which we could attach the aircraft when returning from a flight: two heavy lumps of concrete under each wing and a strong ground-screw at the back to which we could tie its tail. With help from the company's forklift we'd been able to move the concrete blocks onto our temporary parking-spot on the airport apron, but you can't put a ground-screw into tarmac, so we had to forgo the extra security of having the tail tied down as well. As we were near the end of hurricane season we weren't too worried — but then came Klaus.

After hearing the bad news we continued our journey to the airport, but as we rounded the bend at Maya Cove we saw that it was not just our Cessna that had suffered: our yacht had been swept off its mooring and was lying at a steep angle against a jetty on the far side of the cove. We immediately thought that it too must have suffered major damage, but when we eventually got round to it along a waterlogged path we discovered that the boat was actually quite secure where it was, despite its crazy angle, and there was very little damage that we could see. There was nothing much we could do, so we left the boat as it was and headed to the airport.

We already knew, of course, that the aircraft would be a mess, and so it was. The only slightly pleasing thing was that the knots Larraine had tied after flying the Cessna a few days previously had held firm, so the aircraft had simply been turned upside-down; if the knots or ropes had failed it could have been picked up and carried along the line of aircraft parked there, causing loads of damage, but as it was it had simply spun vertically on its ropes and landed on its back with its wheels in the air. It looked like a write-off.

However, it was not just our Cessna that was damaged. As I looked around the airport I noticed that there was something very wrong with the British Caribbean Airways DC3: its entire rudder was gone. I knew this would probably mean a lengthy repair, but at that point I didn't appreciate how serious the implications might be for the future of the whole company.

I'd known that BCA had so far been running at a small loss, but this unexpected turn of events quickly precipitated a sudden rethinking of the whole situation by the airline's backers, and within days they reached a decision to put the company into receivership. The staff were kept on by the receiver for a while, so I wasn't immediately out of work, and my first project was to get the DC3 fixed so that it could eventually be sold to new owners. As part of this process I ended up bringing a replacement rudder across from St. Thomas in the USVI on the deck of the local ferry, Bomba Charger, and I was grateful to have the assistance of a number of US Navy personnel who happened to be on the same crossing. I was glad that I'd worn my uniform that day, with the four gold bars on each shoulder, as I'm sure the young sailors felt it was their duty to assist someone showing senior rank of any sort.

Once repaired the DC3 did some more flying, with the permission of the Receiver, for the local supermarket company, collecting their stock from San Juan but doing no work for other customers, but by late December I had been offered a temporary freelance position as a captain on Air BVI's last remaining DC3, which was still operating after the rest of the fleet had been replaced by HS748 50-seat turboprop aircraft. In January, I flew the ex-BCA DC3 for the last time, on its

An Air BVI DC3

Photo: TAHS

delivery flight to Fort Lauderdale, where it was to be sold, and as you can imagine it was not a happy trip. Although I had the temporary comfort of a freelance job with Air BVI it was unlikely to last more than a few months, so I knew I had to start looking for work yet again. However, in those pre-internet days there was very little I could do from the West Indies, so a return to the UK began to look like the most sensible option. By an odd coincidence, too, Larraine's job as PA to an accountant was also coming to an end as her boss and his family had decided to return to the UK, so all of a sudden everything was pointing towards our departure from the BVI.

We therefore gave notice to our landlords, started disposing of some of our household goods and chattels and began making firm plans for our return to the UK, so it was all rather ironic that Air BVI decided to offer me a permanent job, with a guarantee of training on the HS748, just a week or two before we were due to leave. However, by then the die was cast, and in any case we realised that having me working for Air BVI would not give us nearly as good a lifestyle as we'd had with BCA. Air BVI, as a passenger airline, did lots of flights at weekends, when most tourists would be travelling to and from Puerto Rico, and as a new joiner with low seniority I knew I would end up working most weekends during the year. As Larraine would almost certainly have to find another Monday to Friday job we knew we would have very little leisure time together, so although we still had our boat, which had needed only minor repairs after the storm, our little sailing trips would be much less frequent if I ended up working most Saturdays and Sundays.

Of course, we no longer had our little Cessna aircraft, which had been written off, and although we did get some insurance money back we couldn't really have afforded to buy and run a replacement even if we'd had the time to fly it. Therefore, despite the last-minute offer from Air BVI, we stuck to our plans for a return to Britain.

It was in April, 1985, that we finally set off on our journey back to England. We had left our much-loved boat with a broker, we'd sold both our cars (the ancient VW Beetle and a nearly-new hatchback), we'd packed up our belongings into large wooden boxes and sent them ahead by sea, and we'd had confirmation that our home in Haywards Heath had been vacated by our former tenants. There was no going back now.

We left Tortola aboard the last Air BVI DC3, the one I'd been flying for them, and at San Juan we boarded a British Caledonian flight to London. Larraine knew some of the crew, and soon after take-off the Purser came back to where we were sitting towards the rear of the economy section and asked us to follow her. We hoped we were being move into Business Class, but she took us right through to First, where the only passengers were a BCAL flight deck crew who were positioning back to London. Two of them were old colleagues of mine from British Eagle, so we had a wonderful trip back, chatting about old times and telling them about our three years in the Caribbean. It was great.

All good things come to an end, though, and in the early morning light we landed back at a drizzly Gatwick wondering yet again what on earth the future would hold. I suppose in many ways we were lucky; we had a roof over our heads and enough money in the bank to keep us going for a while, so things could have been far worse. And I have to admit that, in many ways, we were rather glad to be coming back to Britain.

We'd throroughly enjoyed our three years in the Caribbean, but despite our short flirtation with the idea of building a home there I think we both felt that before too long we might tire of looking at beautiful turquoise seas; of watching frigate birds and pelicans soaring overhead; of swimming in warm waters surrounded by spectacular corals and brightly coloured tropical fish; and of living in almost constant sunshine while being fanned by the trade winds.

Perhaps we were crazy, but we felt there was more to life than this.

Chapter 12

WE RETURNED TO THE UK and moved back into Larraine's house in Haywards Heath, West Sussex. Larraine quickly found herself a secretarial job, while I got back into full job-hunting mode, contacting any airline I could think of that might be interested in a 51-year-old pilot with nearly 19,000 hours of flight time while generally letting it be known amongst old flying friends that I was back from paradise and looking for gainful employment once more. I did not expect a quick response.

It was some weeks before my efforts brought any result, but in early June I had a phone call from a chap called Mark Whitby, whom I'd heard of vaguely during my IAS days at Gatwick and who was now looking after the operations of a company operating an African-registered DC8 based in Ostend, Belgium. He'd heard on the aviation grapevine that I was an experienced DC8 captain currently without a job, and he presented me with what was probably the most immediate job offer I'd ever received: would I be available to fly a DC8 cargo trip, as captain, to Luanda, Angola, less than 48 hours hence? I told him that as I hadn't flown a DC8 for nearly four years — and no jet aircraft at all for three — I simply could not accept the responsibility of commanding a DC8 flight without any refresher training, so I was sorry, but I had to say no. He then asked me if I would be prepared to fly as a co-pilot on the flight, but I was still hesitant; who exactly, I queried, would the captain be? Would he be current, competent and experienced on the DC8, and able not only to command the flight but also to give me any help I needed to get acquainted with the aircraft again? I was reassured that the captain was a very experienced British pilot called Mike Coram, who had been trained on the DC8 by Swissair, so after a few moments' consideration I agreed to do the flight.

Thus a couple of nights later I met up with Mike at Dover, ready to board the Ostend ferry, and on arrival we went straight to the airport. I had been to Ostend many times before on the old Bristol Freighter back in my Air Charter days, but I was interested to see how the airport had, over the years, developed into a fairly busy centre for cargo operations. Mike showed me around the DC8 so that I could start familiarising myself with it again, and I took checklists and operations manuals back to the hotel we were staying in so that I could spend an hour or two studying the most important bits before taking an afternoon nap in preparation for our departure that night. As I looked at the manuals it all started coming back to me, and I managed to operate as a reasonably competent co-pilot for the first six-hour sector to Lagos, Nigeria, by which time most of my technical knowledge of the aircraft was flooding back into the active parts of my brain from the memory banks where it had lain dormant for the past four years. After refuelling I did the take-off and landing on the next three-hour flight to Luanda, Angola, and the only criticism I got from Mike was that I had not raised the nose of the aircraft quite high enough on take-off. Of course, I could explain to him immediately why this was: for the past three years I'd been flying the DC3, which gets airborne in a level attitude once it's travelling at sufficient speed.

The DC8 was offloaded while the crew took a bit of rest, and then Mike suggested that I fly it back to Ostend as captain in the left-hand seat, with him operating as co-pilot. Everything went well, and on arrival we were met by the American co-owner of the aircraft, a guy called Duane Egli. He immediately checked with Mike as regards my ability, and when Mike confirmed that the trip had gone well he sent Mike home to the UK to take some leave — that's why I'd been offered a job so quickly — and asked me to stay on for a few days to operate more flights. I was in work again, though certainly not at the most glamorous end of the airline world.

My new employer was called Lukim Aviation and was operating mainly on behalf of Angola Airways, as most of that company's aircraft had been drafted into government service during the long civil war that still afflicted that country at that time. The Lukim DC8 was registered in Zaïre (as the Democratic Republic of Congo was known back then), and Duane was authorised by their Department of Civil Aviation to endorse my UK licence to allow me to command it, thus adding yet another licensing authority to the long list of those I'd flown under during my career.

For the rest of 1985, I operated out of Ostend, mainly to Angola, occasionally commuting back to Haywards Heath by ferry or, more often, staying in Ostend while Larraine visited me there. I bought an old left-hand drive Mercedes 300D that I kept in Ostend for getting about, and we gradually settled into this trans-Channel lifestyle, travelling back and forth on the hydrofoil when speed was of the essence or on the slower Sally Line ferry when we fancied a more leisurely trip with excellent food (their smorgasbord was absolutely wonderful).

As time went on, though, I realised that the cargo loads were becoming rather more military in nature, and it became clear that at some point we would probably be expected to operate into the war zone. I began to feel rather uncomfortable about the way things were going, particularly as the company was now bringing in some Icelandic pilots who had far fewer reservations about what, where and when they flew than I did. By November, 1985, I had decided that flying with Lukim was no longer right for me, so at the end of that month I did my last flight with them and came back home, complete with my Mercedes.

Again I was wondering where my next job would come from, but that question was very quickly solved, albeit temporarily, when I received a telephone call in early December, via Berne Radio in Switzerland, from a Zaire Air Cargo aircraft flying northwards towards Ostend. The Chief Pilot of that airline, an Englishman called Derek Wood, had been advised by his doctor to take a vacation, and he was in urgent need of a DC8 captain to replace him for a couple of weeks. I immediately agreed, so I took the ferry back to Ostend again and eventually flew back with Derek and his crew to Zaïre via a refuelling stop in Tunis.

We arrived in Zaire at President Mobuto's private airfield at Gbadolite, where we spent the night while the aircraft was offloaded, using guest accommodation near the incredibly ornate palace that the president had had built for himself in this remote part of that huge country. The following day Derek operated a flight with me to Kinshasa, Lubumbashi and back to Kinshasa, where I was installed in a hotel, and then he left on his much-needed holiday. For the next two weeks I flew all over Zaire to places such as Goma and Lubumbashi and did an occasional flight to Abidjan in the Ivory Coast. On several of the flights I was amazed to discover that the load consisted mainly of large bales of recycled clothing, which apparently would have arrived in Kinshasa by sea from Europe and then had to be distributed around the country to the marketplaces in towns and villages where the clothes would be sold to their new owners. In a land with few decent roads or other ground-based infrastructure the only way of achieving this kind of distribution was by air.

On 21 December I did a flight up to Ostend, where I handed the DC8 back to Derek Wood before catching the ferry home in time to spend Christmas in the UK. I was jobless again of course, so as soon as things were getting back to normal after the annual festivities I started the usual round of contacting anyone I thought might be interested to know that I was on the lookout for work. My strategy soon achieved a result, because in early January, 1986, I was contacted by Captain Roger Tolley, Operations Manager of a Khartoum-based cargo company called Trans Arabian Air Transport. They had just acquired a DC8 and needed a training captain, so I joined them on a one-year contract.

The flying was of two main types: longer flights from Sudan up to Europe (usually Gatwick or Amsterdam) or to other African destinations (such as Harare and Gaborone) to collect freight bound for Khartoum, and shorter flights within Sudan (mainly to Juba in the south) or to neighbouring countries across the Arabian Peninsula and North Africa.

One fairly frequent destination was Sana'a in Yemen, to which we often carried live cattle that had been bred and reared on fertile land near the Nile and would spend the rest of their lives on the rather poorer grasslands of Yemen. These were not the most pleasant of trips; the cattle would be accommodated in collapsible pens, and the aircraft floor was covered with straw in an attempt to absorb the inevitable effluent that the animals would produce during the flight. Because of the usually high temperatures at Khartoum, the cattle would be loaded very early in the morning, so our "passengers" would already be on board by the time we arrived on the aircraft. At Sana'a we would get off before they were offloaded and find somewhere cool — an air-conditioned office, for instance — where we would wait until our bovine friends had been offloaded and sent on their way. We would thus avoid the worst of the heat and muck, but even so it was always particularly good to get back to our crew accommodation — a large and fairly comfortable villa on the outskirts of Khartoum — and into a hot shower after we'd done a cattle flight.

Trans Arabian's first DC8
Photo: TAHS

One of these particular trips, in early February, 1986, has always stuck in my mind. I had been informed the previous evening by the owner of the airline that one of his young female relatives was on honeymoon in Sana'a with her new husband, a Khartoum policeman, and they had been unable find seats on a passenger flight back to Khartoum. On the TAAT DC8 we had a couple of very uncomfortable, rear-facing seats behind the flight deck, so I was asked to bring the couple back with us on the empty return leg of the next day's cattle flight. I did point out, of course, that conditions on the aircraft would not be pleasant for anyone sitting in the main cabin, as the mucky straw from the outbound trip would still be on the floor, exuding its strong aroma, but I was assured that there really was no other way of getting the couple back to Khartoum, so it was a case of "needs must".

Unfortunately, things started going wrong on our outward flight; after take-off form Khartoum we were advised that Sana'a Airport was temporarily closed to all movements because it was shrouded in low cloud, so we had to divert to Jeddah in Saudi Arabia until conditions improved. We were on the ground there for two hours as the heat of the day built up, so when we eventually got to Sana'a it was no huge surprise to discover that two of the cattle had not survived the journey. These were the only cattle we ever lost on any of the flights that I did for TAAT, and I assumed the Yemeni authorities would simply offload the carcases and send us on our way.

However, things were not going to be that simple. Because the actual cause of death could not be determined without some kind of veterinary enquiry, the Yemenis decided that the dead cattle must stay on the aircraft to return whence they came, so once the collapsible pens had been safely stowed at the back of the aircraft the two carcases were left lying on the floor. At this point our honeymoon couple arrived, and I was rather dismayed to realise that they clearly hadn't been told much about the conditions they could expect to find on board. They were happy, smiling and dressed in very smart clothes, so I had to explain to them that this flight would be much less comfortable than any passenger flight they'd ever done, and I apologised for the fact that they'd be looking at a couple of dead cattle for the duration of the trip. Fortunately, however, they were so pleased to be going back to Khartoum they were happy to put up with almost anything, so after they boarded the aircraft I briefed them on emergency procedures and use of the oxygen bottles stowed next to their not-very-comfortable fold-down seats, just in case of a decompression, and then off we went.

Everything was normal until we were on our initial descent into Khartoum, when we suddenly got a message from air traffic control that our company had arranged for us to do some crew training circuits on returning from this particular trip; I knew our first officer needed some take-offs and landings to complete his licence requirements, but I certainly hadn't planned to do them that particular day, as I knew we'd all be suffering from rather sore and watery eyes as a result of the polluted atmosphere that was a feature of all livestock flights. However, the company had decided that we must do the circuits on arrival back at Khartoum, so as we descended towards the airport I briefed the co-pilot that he would be doing an instrument approach to 200ft above the ground, then overshooting and coming back for another instrument approach and landing.

Fortunately, the flight engineer did find a free moment to slip back and tell our two passengers what to expect, otherwise they might have been rather alarmed when we suddenly put on full power again just as they were expecting the wheels to kiss the tarmac. I'm sure they didn't relish any extension of the two-hour journey from Sana'a, with the two deceased bovines lying just yards away from them on smelly, urine-soaked straw, but when they eventually left the aircraft they thanked all the crew profusely, such was their joy at being home. They did admit, though, that they'd got a bit worried when the two carcases started sliding towards them as we used reverse thrust after our final landing, and I'm sure that's an experience they eventually told their children about, though I hope they have much happier memories of their honeymoon in general.

A few days later I was positioned to Stockholm for a simulator check, during which my DC8 training credentials were endorsed so that I could train other pilots flying DC8's on the Sudanese register, and after that I went home to the UK for a few weeks. In early March I was back in Khartoum, and soon after my return I was rostered to do one of the regular internal trips to Juba, in southern Sudan, that we operated on behalf of the Sudanese army to keep their base supplied. In those days Sudan was all one country but with a huge religious divide between the mainly Muslim north and Christian south; South Sudan is now, of course, a separate national entity, though independence from the North has sadly allowed internal conflicts to erupt between various factions competing for power.

Anyway, even back in those days the southern part of Sudan was not exactly a safe area to fly into, and as a result we had to adopt a rather strange way of approaching Juba Airport. The area around it was reasonably secure because of the army base there, but farther out, in some of the wilder areas, it was not advisable to descend below 20,000ft in order to keep above the range of the surface-to-air missiles that some rebel elements were believed to possess. We therefore flew a rather unusual descent pattern to Juba, making sure we didn't stray below 20,000ft until we were in the safe zone overhead and then circling down to a landing.

These precautions worked, as I never saw any missiles heading my way on any of my many flights to Juba, including the one I did on 11 March, 1986, carrying a fairly normal thirty-ton load of military supplies. As we opened up the doors after landing, the military officer in charge of the airport told me that it would take about ninety minutes to offload the aircraft and then load it up again with about thirty tons of coffee beans. It was quite common for us to have back-loads of coffee from Juba; the sacks of beans would arrive overland from Rwanda and then would be flown up to Khartoum for eventual export via Port Sudan. The officer suggested that my crew and I should go to the nearby rest-house for a coffee and a bit of relaxation, and he gave us use of his Land Rover and a two-way radio so that he could call us when the aircraft was loaded and more or less ready to go. However, after a couple of hours we had heard nothing, so we decided to return to the airport to see what was happening.

A rather frightening scene greeted us as we pulled up: the officer-in-charge, plus a few more junior officers, were lined up against the perimeter fence under the watchful eye of a corporal wielding an automatic weapon. This corporal had apparently led a mutiny at the nearby army camp amongst his fellow soldiers, who had subsequently raided some of the local shops in Juba itself and had arrived at the airport complete with their spoils, mainly in the form of whisky packed in the usual cartons of twelve bottles. Initially, we were told to join the officers against the fence, an order with which we sensibly complied, and then the corporal told me his plans: he and his fellow mutineers — I reckon up to 200 people in total — were fed up with being in what was to them a hostile, Christian part of the country and were therefore determined to return to Khartoum. Our aircraft was to be their means of getting there.

I knew immediately that we would be grossly overloaded for take-off; the thirty tons of coffee already on board the aircraft plus the weight of the two hundred or so soldiers and their plunder would push our take-off weight well beyond the limit that we could officially lift from a fairly short runway such as Juba's, and I reckon now we would have been at least twelve tons overweight. I pointed out to the corporal that not only did we have no seats on board but also that we would be grossly overloaded unless we offloaded the coffee, but neither of these arguments seemed to interest him; he wanted to get to Khartoum with his men, and nothing, it seemed, would stand in his way.

This was definitely one of most frightening episodes of my whole flying career, and I knew there was no option but to do what we were told. As we climbed the aircraft steps I was thinking hard about what we should do to give us the best possible chance of *not* ending up in a nasty heap of twisted metal at the end of the runway, and as the mutineers climbed aboard and settled themselves on top of the sacks of coffee I briefed my copilot and flight engineer accordingly. As our estimated weight was way beyond the performance graphs, I'd decided to use a technique more appropriate to small, piston-engined aircraft than large four-engined jets: at the end of the runway we would apply full power whilst holding the aircraft on its brakes, but importantly we would *not* put the flaps down as we would have done for a normal take-off, because to gain maximum acceleration we needed the wings to be "clean". As we got near to the far end of the runway I would call for the flaps to be set to their normal take-off position, which would immediately create extra lift and — with luck — enable us to get airborne before crashing off the end of the tarmac and into the bush.

Well, it worked, otherwise I probably wouldn't be around to write about it now. As we climbed away, the corporal, who had stayed on the flight deck with his gun trained on us throughout our rather unusual take-off procedure, went back to join his friends in the cabin, and I believe they organised their own "in-flight service" using some of the bottles they'd taken from the shops in Juba.

Now that we were no longer being observed, I made a long-range (HF) radio call to Khartoum Air Traffic Control to report what had happened and give our expected time of arrival. I pointed out that as we were so heavy we were using more fuel than planned and might therefore need priority for landing, as by then we would be running rather short, and of course I also asked them to let TAAT know of our predicament.

Shortly afterwards I received a message from the company telling me we could expect army security to meet us, and after we'd landed safely at Khartoum, with not very much fuel left in the tanks, a "Follow-Me" van appeared and led us to the far end of the airfield away from the terminal buildings. Here the van driver stopped, got out of his van and signalled to us to stop engines; he then got back in his van and drove off at fairly high speed.

It's simply impossible to restart a DC8 without ground power, so although we could speak to the control tower on our VHF radio using the aircraft's batteries we were basically helpless. We stayed put on the flight deck, not wanting to interact any more than necessary with our unexpected and unpredictable passengers, and we had no steps up to the aircraft door so we couldn't get off anyway. Soon, however, our passengers decided that steps were surplus to requirements; they simply opened the front doors and overwing emergency exits and climbed down, using the emergency ropes fitted at each exit to lower themselves and their loot to the ground. It was then just a short walk to the perimeter fence, in which they quickly cut a large hole, and very soon all two hundred or so of them had left the airport and were walking towards the city, carrying their spoils with them.

We sat there for some time, waiting for a ground power unit to come out to us so we could start our engines again and taxi to the cargo shed, but then suddenly we were surrounded by a small fleet of armoured vehicles; a little late in the day, the army had arrived, so I went back to the open front door to tell them that the birds had flown and that there was nothing and no-one on board the aircraft now other than thirty tons of coffee and a rather relieved crew. They didn't seem too bothered, and as we watched them disappear again into the late afternoon heat the ground power unit finally arrived, and we were at last able to start our engines to get to where we were supposed to be. When I eventually got off the aircraft and checked with TAAT they told me that I'd be flying to Juba again the following day, and that was the end of that; no report needed, no interviews, no official enquiry, no time off to get over what had been a pretty stressful episode — it was as if nothing out of the ordinary had happened at all.

A month later, TAAT's DC8 was due to undergo a major maintenance check, and the company decided to send it to Spanair in Palma, Majorca, for the work to be done. The crew were to stay in Majorca with the aircraft, as the maintenance was expected to take no more than about five days, so I arranged for Larraine to fly down and join me for a short holiday in the Mediterranean sunshine. In fact, the maintenance went on a lot longer than expected, but as we'd been told we would be heading back to Gatwick at the end of it Larraine stayed on for a few more days, as she could obviously come back to London with us. We'd been there ten days when we finally had the good news from Spanair that the DC8 was virtually ready, so after breakfast the next morning we all packed our stuff and headed to the airport, thinking we would have a nice, easy flight to Gatwick.

We were in the midst of the usual preparations when I suddenly saw a chap on a little moped coming towards us across the tarmac. He stopped at the bottom of our steps and, having established that I was the captain, asked me to come over to the office of the handling agents that TAAT were using. Having no wheels of my own I had to walk over there, and when I arrived I was greeted with the news that TAAT had picked up a charter for the DC8, so we would not now be flying empty to London after all. In fact, our next movement would be to Cairo, where we were to collect forty tons of green beans that were bound for Rotterdam, whence we would eventually return to London after the cargo had been offloaded. Our quick flight to Gatwick had suddenly vanished into thin air.

We quickly arranged for some more fuel and filed a new flight plan to Cairo, but it was well into the afternoon before we got airborne, and it was late evening when we landed. We expected the beans to be ready for loading, but there was no sign of them, and we had no means of finding out where they were. We ourselves could not leave the aircraft as we had no Egyptian visas, so we all settled in to wait for as long as it took.

Now, at this point I need to explain one or two things about the TAAT DC8. It was in many ways a fine old aircraft that had given years of service, but it lacked one or two of the basic amenities that one might consider necessary. It had no galley, though it did have a "hot cup" for making tea, but perhaps more importantly it had no lavatory either. However, soon after I started with TAAT I had found a simple answer to this situation in the form of a glorious contraption called a Porta-Potti, available from all good camping and outdoor stores. If any crew member were taken short on the seven-hour flight between Gatwick and Khartoum he would make a trip to the back of the aircraft to use the Porta-Potti, and then, when we reached our destination, I would carry it off and arrange for the disposal of its contents and the cleaning of the Porta-Potti itself. I did get some rather incredulous looks from airport staff from time to time as I marched through, cradling the Porta-Potti in my arms, and I often wondered whether the Sudanese authorities thought I might be using it as a rather novel way of trying to smuggle whisky into Khartoum, which observed Sharia law and was therefore "dry". Had anyone asked me to prove my innocence I would have invited them to sample the Porta-Potti's contents, but no-one ever did.

Anyway, back to the story. One of the Cairo ground staff, who had come out to give us an update on what was happening and had realised that my wife was on board the aircraft, offered to take Larraine over to what he assured us were some rather better facilities near the terminal — well, better than the Porta-Potti — so I gave Larraine a few US dollars, knowing that she might need a bit of cash, and off she went. She wasn't gone very long, but when she came back she was able to tell us that the going rate for toilet paper in Egypt appeared to be a dollar a sheet, as after handing two dollars to the aged crone who was guarding the facilities she'd visited she was given just two sheets of paper. That would make the average roll of Andrex worth about $240 dollars in Cairo, so we wondered why we were still flying around in aeroplanes when our quickest route to riches would appear to involve toilet rolls and Egyptian airport lavatories.

Eventually the beans arrived and were duly loaded, but our total time on the ground had by now stretched to eight hours instead of the hour or so we'd expected when we landed. During this time we'd all managed to get a bit of shut-eye despite having to stay on the aircraft, but we were glad that dawn was breaking as we took off from Cairo and headed north towards Europe and our planned destination of Rotterdam.

All was well until, as we flew over the Alps, our flight engineer, Albert — who had been a flight engineer on the original BOAC Comets back in the 1950s and had twice completed trips on aircraft that had subsequently crashed on their very next flight — pointed out that the oil gauges on No. 2 engine were showing an increase in temperature and a drop in pressure. For a little while we kept a watchful eye on the situation, but as the readings gradually worsened we decided we would have to shut the engine down as a precaution. We also decided at this point that we should change our destination from Rotterdam to Amsterdam (Schiphol), as the latter had much longer runways and better facilities; when you have a problem, even a relatively benign one — in this case, one engine shut down but three perfectly good ones still operating normally — it makes sense to divert from a relatively small airport with limited facilities to a larger and better-equipped one. In this case, we decided that if we had to have an engine change it would certainly be much easier to arrange that at Amsterdam than at Rotterdam, so it was an easy decision to make.

I therefore made a radio call to air traffic control to let them know that we were now heading for Amsterdam, and then I called the company in Khartoum to tell them the glad news that our forty tons of beans would now be landing there instead of at their intended destination. This call involved contacting Berne Radio in Switzerland and asking them to set up a phone patch to the TAAT operations office in Khartoum, which they quickly did. Such connections are not always very clear, but we were able to hear the rather confused voice of the operations manager in Khartoum telling us that we were supposed to be going to Amsterdam anyway, so why on earth had we originally set course for Rotterdam?

I told him that the last instructions we'd received, way back in Palma, were to fly the beans from Cairo to Rotterdam, only to be told by him that he'd sent a message to the company's handling agents in Cairo to tell us about the change of destination. Clearly this last message had never got through to us, even though we'd sat on the ground for eight hours or more.

As we continued northwards across Europe we began thinking about what would happen after we'd landed and disgorged our cargo. We were in an interesting position, because although we'd done a precautionary shutdown on No. 2 engine, the engine had not actually failed, so if we needed it we could easily have started it again, and it probably would have worked OK, if only for a certain amount of time. We were under no obligation to report this situation to ATC or anyone else, and as the other three engines were functioning normally we came to the conclusion that the best course of action, after offloading, was to do a three-engine ferry back to Gatwick. This was a perfectly normal procedure — an empty DC8 can take off very easily on three — but it would mean quite a lot of extra paperwork to get a permit issued, so we decided to be slightly naughty: we'd do the flight on three engines but just not bother to mention it to the authorities at Schiphol. On a nice long runway the reduction in power would make very little difference in terms of safety margins, so we all agreed that this was what we would do.

By now we were all quite tired and rather mucky, having had no access to washing facilities for twenty-four hours or more, and when we eventually landed at Amsterdam we were also *very* hungry. Once the offloading was under way our first priority was to get something to eat, so we all trooped into the terminal and into the first food outlet we came to: a rather smart airport restaurant, with proper white table-cloths and waiters wearing immaculate white jackets and black bow-ties. We went to sit at a table near the centre of the room, but the head waiter, noticing our rather scruffy and less-than-squeaky-clean appearance, rushed over and ushered us to a table in the corner of the restaurant, clearly hoping that the other customers would be less likely to notice us there. We ordered our meals, and the waiter brought them to our table, with mine — a fillet steak in a mushroom sauce — being the last to arrive.

Unfortunately, though, as the waiter approached with my meal he failed to notice the co-pilot's briefcase on the floor in front of him until the moment he fell over it, at which point my steak, with its sauce and other accompaniments, became temporarily airborne before landing in my lap. My already quite mucky shirt was suddenly adorned with great splodges of sauce, and I was aware that the eyes of every customer in the restaurant had swivelled towards us to see what had happened. For a short while we were the centre of everyone's attention, and I can still remember the waiter's mortified expression as he realised that his plan to keep us out of sight and mind had gone so spectacularly wrong.

A replacement steak quickly arrived and was safely delivered, and I set about satisfying an appetite that had been sharpened even more by watching my table-mates tuck into their own meals while they were still hot. I can remember to this day how good that steak tasted, even though the option of washing it down with a nice glass of red wine was not open to me because I would soon be airborne once again.

After what we all agreed was a very good lunch we returned to the now empty DC8 and readied ourselves for departure. Our main concern was not that we would be taking off on three engines but that someone on the ground, perhaps in the control tower, might notice that one of them wasn't turning and report us, and we were therefore rather glad to be assigned to a relatively far-flung runway where the likelihood of being observed was not too great. We were indeed fortunate to be at a huge airport with multiple runways rather than at a smaller one where our three-engine condition could probably have generated rather more interest.

We were also fortunate that the dead engine was No. 2, the left inboard (i.e. closer to the fuselage), because that made the take-off easier than it would have been if No. 1 or No. 4 had been the one producing no power. A dead outboard engine would have created more swing to one side because of the asymmetric thrust resulting from having two good engines on one side of the aircraft and only one on the other, but with a dead inboard engine this tendency is greatly reduced and thus easily controlled. As we lined up at the end of the runway, having been cleared for take-off as normal, I pushed forward on the throttles of the two outboard engines, and as we gained speed along the runway I gradually brought up the power on No. 3 as well, countering any tendency to swing to the left by using nose-wheel steering initially and then applying right rudder. We used about the same length of runway to get airborne as we would have done with a full load and all four engines operating, and as we turned towards Gatwick I set the rudder trim to keep the aircraft straight and then engaged the autopilot. At last we were on our way home.

We landed safely at Gatwick and trundled over to the cargo zone, where our local TAAT representative was waiting to see us in. He had already arranged for No. 2 engine to be replaced with a new — or rather, newly-reconditioned — one, and he told us we would be flying back to Khartoum as soon as that was done, possibly in as little as ten hours' time. At this I very nearly used some rather rude words, but I somehow managed to control myself reasonably well as I explained to him that after such an epic flight we would definitely *not* be available for duty again for at least thirty-six hours.

He reluctantly accepted this and told us he would explain the situation to our bosses in Sudan, but in the event it was little more than thirty hours before my crew and I were airborne again on our way back to Khartoum. But at least we now had clean shirts, full tummies and four engines that were all working properly.

During the rest of 1986 I was kept busy with both normal flying and crew training duties, particularly when, at the end of June, TAAT acquired a second DC8. For a while I was reasonably satisfied, as I was getting back to Gatwick fairly often, but as time went on the number of UK flights decreased as the airline took on more work within Africa.

At the end of November I arranged to operate a flight to Gatwick so I'd be home for Larraine's birthday, and when she met me at the airport she was accompanied by a couple of aviation friends. Over dinner they told me they were planning to start a new, Bristol-based, passenger airline, catering to the inclusive-tour market and using McDonnell Douglas MD83 aircraft, a stretched and updated version of the DC9 short- to medium-haul airliner that had been one of the great workhorses of the US domestic airline system for many years. The MD83 was not yet on the UK register, but the new company had arranged to lease two of them and had signed contracts with various tour operators, so my friends asked whether I'd be interested in joining them, as my previous experience with IAS in getting the DC8 onto the British register would be particularly useful.

I needed little time to make a decision; it seemed unlikely that TAAT could offer me a long-term career, particularly as they were now employing some very good African pilots, and thus it came to pass that on 10 January, 1987, at the end of my one-year contract with TAAT, I flew what was to be my last ever DC8 commercial flight when I operated from Khartoum to Gatwick.

In fact, I thought this would be my last DC8 flight of any kind, though it later turned out that my long association with that aircraft was not *quite* at an end, and although I was very excited at the prospect of flying a brand new aircraft straight off the production line I couldn't help feeling sad; the DC8 was a wonderful aircraft that had given me some marvellous flying moments and will always, in my opinion, be one of the best airliners ever built.

Chapter 13

THE NEW COMPANY I was going to work for had decided to call itself
Paramount Airways, and its choice of a base at Bristol was a particularly happy one for us: Larraine had been brought up in Somerset and
had family there, so for her it was like going home. However, we still
had to sell the house in Haywards Heath and find somewhere to live
within reasonable distance of Bristol Airport and, as tends to be the
case in airline marriages, most of the work involved fell to Larraine. I,
of course, had to learn how to fly yet another different aircraft, which
this time meant a trip to Long Beach, California, where McDonnell
Douglas were based.

So as I was heading off to the warmth of California in late February
Larraine was heading down to Somerset to start looking for a new
home. While she was scouring estate agents' windows and viewing
houses I was doing my technical course, and as I was getting started
on my simulator training she was showing potential buyers around
our little place at Haywards Heath. I had a break of a couple of weeks
between my simulator sessions and the start of my flight training, so I
came back to the UK to look at a few of the properties Larraine had
picked out as possible new homes and to start the job of sorting out all
our possessions, deciding which would be going with us to Somerset
and which could be thrown out.

We put in an offer, which was accepted, on a little house in
Axbridge, which is near Cheddar, famous for its cheese and its gorge,
and only ten miles or so from Bristol Airport, while almost simultaneously we found a buyer for Haywards Heath, so by the time I left
again for California, around the middle of April, everything was
trundling along quite nicely. Of course, Larraine still had to finish off
the job of packing up our home into cardboard boxes, as well as
dealing with all the sundry matters that tend to arise when you're
moving house, but there was nothing much I could do to help her from
my temporary base in Long Beach, and as she had once organised a
move from Britain to the West Indies at just two weeks' notice I was
sure she'd manage better without me under her feet anyway.

Meanwhile, I was enjoying my flight training at Yuma, an airport in the Arizona desert with a lovely long runway and very little regular traffic and which was therefore ideal for training purposes. The MD83, with its long, narrow fuselage and rear-mounted engines (just two of them) was a very different beast from the DC8, and as I was the first one in our group of ten Paramount Airways trainees to actually fly the aircraft my colleagues were eager to know what it was like and how easy (or otherwise) it was to handle. The first thing I told them was that I'd had a rather alarming experience on take-off, but I wasn't trying to scare them, just warn them what to expect.

What I'd forgotten as I'd taxied the aircraft out to the runway, sitting in the left-hand seat with a McDonnell Douglas training captain in the right, was that, first, the engines were right down the back of the aircraft, a very long way from where I was sitting, and second, the aircraft had a rather noisy fan system to keep the instruments and radios cool on the ground. This system would automatically stop the fans as soon as the nose-wheel left the tarmac.

At the point of take-off, therefore, the flight deck suddenly became very quiet, and for a few hair-raising moments I thought we had lost power on at least one engine and possibly both. Then I suddenly realised what was wrong, which was, in fact, nothing at all. The fans had cut out as they were supposed to, and the engines were still working exactly as they should: it was just that they were so far away from the flight deck — farther away than any engines I'd ever flown on before — that I could barely hear them. I remembered that on engine start-up I'd had to look at the instruments to check that the engines were running OK, but that was while the cooling fans had been running, and it was only on take-off that I could experience for the first time exactly how quiet it could be on an MD83 flight deck whilst airborne.

As the Paramount aircraft was the first MD83 on the British register the CAA had decreed that the pilot due to command the ferry flight to the UK — and it was I who was to have this honour — had to complete a minimum of six sectors (i.e. trips from one airport to another, not just circuits or local flights landing back at the same place) before leaving Long Beach, so on the day after we had all completed our initial flight training we piled back onto the aircraft we'd been using (one kept by

McDonnell Douglas specifically for this purpose) and, with me in the captain's seat, a McDonnell Douglas training captain flying as co-pilot and the rest of the gang sitting in the passenger cabin, we set off on a little airborne tour of California, stopping first at Bakersfield, then at Fresno, then Stockton and Sacramento before landing once again at Bakersfield before returning to Long Beach. They were all short sectors of less than an hour, and all the landings, except the one at Long Beach, were just "touch-and-goes". As the shortest flights are usually the busiest ones, with little or no time to relax between top of climb and top of descent, I was rather glad to get off the aircraft at the end of the day, and the first beer I downed that evening barely touched the sides.

We then just had to wait for the go-ahead to pick up our own shiny new aeroplane, which was still undergoing its programme of production test-flying, and bring it back to the UK, but five days later, on 25 April, we were finally ready to set course for Bristol, with a planned

G-PATA, Paramount's first MD83 aircraft, taking off from Long Beach, Ca.

refuelling stop at Gander in Newfoundland. The weather forecast was good, and for the first time in my life I was at the controls of a brand new jet airliner. Things didn't get much better than this, I thought, and once again I dared to hope I was in a job that would last me for the rest of my flying career.

The ferry flight back to Bristol was really enjoyable, and although it involved two sectors of more than six hours I was able to get a bit of rest; of course, all of our newly qualified pilots were on board, so with the American training captain along as well we were able to give everyone a bit of time on the flight deck, where they would make the necessary radio calls and generally keep an eye on things while the autopilot kept the aircraft merrily flying along its planned route. As pilot-in-command, though, I was back on the flight deck well before we began our descent towards Bristol, ready for the rather special arrival we'd been told about before we left Long Beach. We had permission, confirmed by Bristol Approach as we made our descent, to do a fairly low "beat-up" of Brunel's Clifton Suspension Bridge, the city's most famous landmark, and then an even lower pass along Bristol Airport's runway before making our final landing. I knew I was going to enjoy this very rare opportunity to do something that would not normally be permitted.

I've often wondered since that day whether any of the good citizens of Bristol phoned up the police, or Bristol Airport, or even the BBC to report an aircraft flying up the Avon Gorge and over the famous bridge with what probably seemed like just a few feet to spare, but if anyone did I presume they were told that we had permission to do it. I never ever heard of any fuss, so I guess we didn't scare anyone too much.

At the end of the run over the bridge we turned towards Bristol Airport, ready for the next part of our little display: the fast, low-level run along the runway. I wanted to do this as quietly as possible, so that anyone expecting their eardrums to take a hammering would be pleasantly surprised, so I climbed the aircraft to about two thousand feet, then I set the speed to 250 knots and put the nose down so that we dived towards the airport; as we did this the power came back automatically so that when we levelled off at about a hundred feet above the runway we had very little power on and were thus making very little noise.

My plan worked beautifully; for our arrival, the airport had temporarily been closed to other traffic, and our Paramount Airways staff, along with a few other airport workers, had been allowed to stand on the grass along each side of the runway to watch us, though of course they had to withdraw to a safe distance before we actually came in to land. Many of them told me afterwards that they could hardly believe an aircraft could fly so quietly, and I have to admit I'd hoped, rather perversely, that someone had been checking our decibel level with the idea of complaining about the noise emitted by this new arrival. I don't think anyone did, though.

Mind you, the noise conditions outside the MD83 were rather different from those on the flight deck. On older aircraft, various methods, such as warning lights and horns, were employed to capture the pilots' attention if things were going wrong. On more modern machines, such as the MD83, these had generally been replaced by recorded voice warnings, so as we flew along the runway a cacophony of concerned voices suddenly began telling us to pull the nose up, to lower the undercarriage, to put down the flaps and to generally sort ourselves out, as it seemed we were in imminent danger of disaster. There's no "airport beat-up" mode on airliners, so we just put up with the racket until we raised the nose at the far end of the runway and climbed away, at which point the power automatically came up again, though by this time we were far enough away from the people who'd turned out to see us that no-one noticed.

It was great to be back in the UK with our lovely new aeroplane, but my delight was cut rather short when, after landing, I got to the Paramount office to discover that Larraine wasn't there and had missed it all. She had been staying with family about an hour away as we hadn't yet completed our move from West Sussex, but as a result of a silly misunderstanding she'd been told that I was not going to be on the delivery flight after all, so there was no point in her coming all the way to Bristol Airport. Had she known that an exciting arrival was planned, even without my own involvement, she would have come to see it anyway, but no-one mentioned that to her, so she missed one of the most exciting bits of flying I ever did in a large aircraft. She's still cross about it to this day.

The first commercial flight of Paramount Airways took place on 1 May, 1987, from Bristol to Tenerife and back; I was in command, and our 160 passengers boarded to the sound of a jazz band, who were standing on the tarmac playing for all they were worth in an attempt to drown out the sounds of other aircraft either taking off on the nearby runway or just taxying past. It was a bright, sunny day, and I felt that my future career prospects were looking bright as well. Surely this new job, working for an airline that could afford to invest in brand new aircraft, would see me through to my compulsory retirement from large jets at the age of sixty, now just seven years hence.

The day after that first flight Larraine and I moved into our new home in the very small town of Axbridge, a couple of miles from Cheddar and about ten miles from the airport. Larraine, of course, had made all the arrangements for the move and done all the packing-up of our previous home in West Sussex, but at least I was able to get the day off so I could meet up with her as she arrived from Haywards Heath in our large Mercedes, the one I'd brought back from Ostend, packed full of bits and pieces that she wanted to bring with her in the car. An hour or so later the removal lorry appeared with all the big stuff, and so by the end of the day we were established in our new home, albeit surrounded by cardboard boxes. I was back at work the next day, though, and as Paramount had managed to pick up lots of contracts to operate flights for various tour operators I, like all my fellow pilots, was kept pretty busy throughout the rest of the summer.

In many ways, Paramount was a pioneering airline because of one particular rule it enforced: *no-one* on board any of its aircraft was allowed to smoke at any time. These days, of course, we are all completely accustomed to the idea that people don't smoke whilst flying, but in the late 1980s it was a revolutionary idea. The vast majority of our passengers seemed very happy with the arrangement, and only rarely did smokers kick up a major fuss about being subjected to this restriction.

On one memorable occasion a Paramount Airways captain did land in Amsterdam to offload two passengers who absolutely insisted on lighting up during flight, but this was the only time that such drastic action was needed; as it turned out, the two passengers concerned had to find their own way home from Amsterdam and eventually had to pay damages for disrupting the flight, so their decision to break the rules cost them dear.

In fact, when Paramount was contracted by British Airways during 1988 to fly some of their Shuttle services, passenger reaction to our stance on the smoking issue was generally very favourable; BA still allowed smoking on its own Shuttle flights at that time, so I'm sure the good feedback they had from customers who flew on Paramount must have been useful. Of course, over a period of about ten years from the late 1980s smoking was gradually banned worldwide as airlines either took the initiative themselves or had the ban imposed on them by regulation, but Paramount was certainly way ahead of the game when it began its smoke-free operations in 1987.

During that first summer season Paramount operated flights to various European holiday destinations, not only from Bristol but from Cardiff and Gatwick as well. By late August I was cleared as a training captain, so as well as doing my share of normal flying I was now training new pilots, both on the aircraft and in the simulator in Long Beach, California, there being no MD83 simulators available in Europe at that time.

By now I'd assumed I would never get anywhere near a DC8 flight deck again, but then suddenly, in mid-September, I had a message from Paramount telling me they'd had a call from my former employers, Trans Arabian Airlines, asking whether I could be released for a day to do a check flight at Stansted on their sole remaining training captain so that he could continue to do his job. My own Sudanese training qualification for the DC8 was still valid, and Paramount were happy for me to do the flight, so on 18 September I found myself climbing aboard a DC8 once again to go flying. It was great to be back, even though we would be airborne for only an hour, and although I was by now accustomed to sitting in a much cleaner, neater and more modern flight deck I still relished every moment of being back in the old DC8 routine, with four engines instead of two, and with wingtips that I could actually see if I looked backwards from the cockpit window, unlike those of the MD83.

As I left the aircraft I thought that this must surely be my last ever flight on a DC8, but as it turned out I was wrong, because Trans Arabian called me up again early in 1988 to do check flights on both of their training captains, flying from Amsterdam to Stansted and then back to Amsterdam. This trip was fitted in just before my own Sudanese DC8 licence finally lapsed, so as I disembarked I knew I would almost certainly never set foot on a DC8 again, and this time I was right: I never did fly on another DC8, so that spring day in 1988 really *was*, for me, the end of an era.

Anyway, back to 1987, and in the autumn, as the volume of European holiday flights began to tail off, Paramount picked up some interesting charters working for other airlines. I even did one trip as far as Mombasa, Kenya, and I have to say that when I joined Paramount I hadn't imagined I'd be travelling as far away from base as East Africa in an aircraft such as the MD83 that was designed primarily for short- and medium-haul flying.

Over the winter we also operated the aforementioned Shuttle flights for British Airways, and then in the early spring of 1988 we did a series of internal French flights for a company called Air Liberté. Our commercial people were doing a good job of finding work for Paramount Airways, and things were looking good — so good, in fact, that the company decided to acquire two more MD83's, which arrived in May. With crews to be trained for these two new aircraft I had to make several more visits to Long Beach to do simulator training, and it was during this period that something from my past career caught up with me in a rather annoying way.

I would usually travel to Los Angeles on TWA, along with half-a-dozen trainees, but while the others would normally pass through US Customs and Immigration with no hindrance I was always stopped and searched, leaving the rest of my party hanging around until I was cleared to continue. After this had happened three or four times I finally asked for an explanation of why I was being targeted in this way, hoping that the officers I was speaking to wouldn't immediately clap me in irons for being awkward. It turned out that there was a simple but rather silly explanation: because I'd been in and out of San Juan, Puerto Rico, five days a week during the time I'd worked in the British Virgin Islands, my name had been flagged up on a computer watch-list as a possible drug smuggler! Despite my explanations and protestations of innocence, the airport officials were unable to remove the flag, so I had to write to the head of the US Customs Service asking to be cleared of this lingering suspicion that was based on nothing more than the normal flying routine that I'd followed whilst working for British Caribbean Airways.

Fortunately, I received a very polite letter in reply telling me that my name had now been taken off the watch-list and instructing me to show the letter to any US Customs officer who might attempt to stop me in the future. This did the trick; never again was I stopped and searched when trying to enter the USA, which was a great relief not only for me but also for all the pilots who subsequently flew with me to Los Angeles and thus no longer had to stand around waiting ages for me to emerge from the Customs Hall.

In any case, my trips to the USA became rather less frequent after Finnair's MD83 simulator in Helsinki was approved by the CAA for Paramount's use, from which point we would use whichever of the two was available when needed. Of course, everyone still preferred to go to Long Beach, particularly as winter set in, the lure of Californian sunshine being somewhat greater than the attractions of Scandinavian ice and snow. There was also the depressing fact that buying a "wind-down" beer or two in a Helsinki bar would deplete one's money reserves four or five times more quickly than it would in Long Beach.

During the summer of 1988, Paramount had set up two temporary bases, one at Newcastle and the other at Belfast, as well as a permanent base at Birmingham, all in addition to its original home at Bristol. I therefore found myself based for several days at a time at Newcastle or Belfast, staying in local hotels whilst doing a series of holiday flights to various destinations. In July, one of my flights, from Newcastle to Cyprus, was subject to a long delay after we'd boarded the passengers due to industrial action by Greek air traffic controllers. It was one of those awkward situations in which we could be given startup and taxi clearance at any moment, so we couldn't disembark the passengers because reboarding them all would take far too long if we were suddenly given a take-off slot within ten or fifteen minutes.

Fortunately, we had good ventilation and plenty of cold drinks to keep everyone happy — though I did allow a few small groups of smokers to pop back into the terminal for a quick cigarette, so long as they kept their eye on the aircraft and came back aboard as soon as they saw the anti-collision lights turned on — and eventually, after five hours of waiting, we were told to expect start-up clearance very shortly. Everyone was back on board anyway, so we were soon airborne, eventually arriving at Larnaca some five hours after our scheduled time.

At this point I had a decision to make: we were just about legal to do our return flight if we took off very soon, though by this time the crew would have been quite entitled to take a rest period before flying again. I think it says a great deal about the spirit and morale of Paramount's staff that all the crew were happy to carry on back to the UK, so we quickly boarded the passengers, who had been patiently waiting in the airport terminal, and set off for home. Fortunately, the Greek controllers' strike had finished earlier in the day, and as it was now late evening there wasn't too much traffic around anyway.

We eventually arrived at Newcastle at 1.15am and were obviously looking forward very much to getting back to our rooms in the nearby airport hotel for some well-earned sleep. However, something rather odd had occurred while we were away, something that in all my years of flying all over the world had never actually happened to me before. For some reason, the hotel had decided that our crew would not be returning to Newcastle at all that night, and although Paramount had paid for all the rooms in advance, someone at the hotel had decided they could put other guests in our rooms and thus sell them twice over.

I discovered this when I and other crew members had what you might call a "Baby Bear" moment: we opened our room doors and found strangers sleeping in our beds. We immediately summoned the Night Manager, who expressed his amazement that we were there at all and gave us the bad news that the hotel was completely full, so he had no alternative rooms to offer us. The hotel staff had apparently packed up all our belongings into our suitcases, so as soon as these were returned to us I organised a couple of taxis, and we all decamped to the much better and more expensive surroundings of the Hilton Hotel in the middle of Newcastle, where we eventually arrived around two-thirty in the morning and were at last able to get our heads down. Not surprisingly, Paramount immediately cancelled its contract with the hotel at Newcastle Airport and moved its crews to a different one that understood the strange and sometimes unexpected comings and goings of airline folk and could therefore be relied on *not* to resell rooms that were already bought and paid for.

In fact, within a month of that Newcastle experience, my crew and I had to be moved out of yet another hotel — the Europa in Belfast — but this time for safety reasons. I was just walking back into my room after lunch on a day when we weren't flying when suddenly the window imploded, scattering glass all over the floor; a bomb had been detonated outside, so I was very lucky I hadn't entered the room a few moments earlier and been closer to the window, otherwise the glass might have done me some damage. The rest of my crew had been out at the time, so none of us suffered any injury, and once I'd phoned the company and told them what had happened they quickly arranged to get us all out of the Europa and into another hotel out in the country. We were back flying the next day, but after that little experience Paramount made sure that all its crews were henceforth accommodated in this rather safer location when staying in Belfast.

As 1988 rolled on I was still thoroughly enjoying my job, particularly as I and other crew members had opportunities that sound quite incredible in this post-9/11 world; for instance, for the princely sum of just £10, we could invite a friend or relative to do a trip on the flight deck jump-seat, sitting right behind the captain, provided the flight concerned was not a training flight. I was therefore able to take individual friends and family members on round trips to various destinations around Europe, and it was particularly handy whenever we found ourselves running short of beers at home. I'd book Larraine into the jump-seat for a flight with me to Faro in southern Portugal, where the beers we liked to drink were particularly cheap, and she'd return with two or three cases of them as her "baggage". The Customs officers at Bristol were a bit puzzled at first and asked her where the rest of her bags were, but once they got to know that she was just the captain's wife doing a regular beer-run they just waved her through.

We could also get concession flights in the passenger cabin for family members, so Larraine used to come with me on trips where I'd be staying away for a few nights somewhere interesting. She spent one Christmas with me in Cyprus, as the company had worked out that the chances of weather disruption were much lower if our daily flight between Cyprus and the UK operated Larnaca-Bristol-Larnaca rather than Bristol-Larnaca-Bristol; by flying from Larnaca we would arrive in Bristol around lunchtime, when any early morning fog would have cleared. Anyway, on our way out to Cyprus for our Christmas trip Larraine was in the passenger cabin, and she got chatting to the lady sitting next to her. I was flying the aircraft, of course, so in my usual style I had been giving the passengers occasional updates on where we were and what they could see on each side of the aircraft;.

At one point, Larraine and her neighbour were chatting happily away when I pressed the PA once more to give everyone a further update, at which point Larraine's new friend said, slightly testily, "Gosh, doesn't this captain talk a lot?"

"Yes," said Larraine, "and I should know — I'm *married* to him!"

The other lady looked rather distraught for a moment, but Larraine soon assured her that she'd caused no offence and told her that in order to prepare my informative little speeches I always carried a school atlas in my flight briefcase so that I could look up the names of places that might not necessarily appear on the aviation charts. This was quite true, but I must explain here that the atlas I carried was *not* the one that I'd used in school myself because a great many changes had happened since my own schooldays — mainly, of course, the disappearance of the "pink bits" that had been the British Empire when I was a lad.

Paramount remained busy through the winter of 1988/89, and one of the MD83s did regular stints in Berlin, operating flights to the Mediterranean and Israel. Of course, this was before the fall of the Berlin Wall, so we were required to fly along one of the designated air corridors through East German airspace in order to get in and out of West Berlin's Tegel Airport. There were three of these corridors: the northern one went to Hamburg, the central one went to Hanover and the southern one went to Frankfurt, and if you strayed outside their ten-mile width you could expect some attention from East German or Russian fighters. Nothing much had changed since I'd been flying in and out of Berlin in the 1950s.

Fortunately, with modern radio aids it wasn't difficult to keep within the limits, so no Paramount aircraft ever had an awkward encounter with a Mig, but to this day I'm very grateful that I did several three-day trips to Berlin in the spring of 1989 when none of us had any idea that by the end of the year the famous Wall would have been breached. On two of these trips Larraine came along with me, and while I was doing flights from Berlin to Palma and back she did sightseeing tours around the divided city, first around West Berlin and then, on a subsequent trip, through Checkpoint Charlie to visit the East. We have since visited Berlin on another two occasions, seeing it during the 1990's, when it seemed the whole city was being rebuilt and the skyline was a forest of cranes, and again in more recent years, when the fact we had known the city as it was before and soon after the wall came down added hugely to the experience of seeing it as it is now. On one visit we had the rather chilling experience of visiting a vast, underground nuclear shelter built right under the city centre during the Cold War, something that convinced us both that had the worst happened we would have preferred to take our chances on the surface, thanks very much.

Anyway, during 1989 Paramount was still popular with tour operators, travel agents and passengers alike — with the exception, perhaps, of those heavy smokers who found themselves flying on a non-smoking airline when they hadn't expected to — but by now more of the larger travel companies were forming their own airlines, thus reducing the demand for stand-alone operators such as ourselves. Paramount had no "captive" tour company to support it, and perhaps this general tightening of market conditions in itself would have been enough to cause major problems. In the event, though, matters became rather more complicated than that because Paramount was linked to (but not actually part of) a group of companies called Eagle Trust, which had got itself into trouble with the Department of Trade and Industry following the apparent disappearance of some millions of pounds that the auditors were unable to trace.

To cut a long and complex story short, Paramount went out of business in the autumn of 1989, and I did my last flight with them — from Newcastle to Cyprus and then back to Bristol — on 31 October. It was the last day of the month and, quite possibly, the last time I would ever fly an MD-83, but on this occasion I had had time, during Paramount's dying days, to find myself a new job.

Thus the very next day, 1 November, I joined yet another new airline, a company called Birmingham European Airways, for whom I would be flying the BAC 1-11. This was a very much older aircraft type than the MD-83, though one that looked vaguely similar, with two rear-mounted jet engines but a much shorter fuselage.

Still, as I'd often found before, when it comes to flying jobs, particularly as you get older, beggars can't be choosers.

Chapter 14

BIRMINGHAM EUROPEAN AIRWAYS was a small, independent, scheduled airline that had been operating out of Birmingham Airport using Gulfstream I propjet aircraft, but at the end of 1989 they expanded by acquiring five BAC 1-11-400 jets, which they purchased from British Airways; in fact the company that owned Birmingham European, The Plimsoll Line, was a joint venture by British Airways and Maersk, the Danish shipping company. One of my pilot friends from IAS and Paramount Airways days had introduced me to the Operations Director of Birmingham European, and as a result I was recruited as a captain for the new airline, though I would have to do a British Airways course on the aircraft as I'd never flown it before.

One little irony was that I was starting my 1-11 course, held at Cranebank, BA's Training Centre, at the age of fifty-five, which was exactly when most BA pilots were being compulsorily put out to grass, so I imagine I was one of the oldest pilots they'd ever had through their doors as a trainee. Anyway, I'd completed my technical and simulator training by mid-December, and had finished my flight and line training by early March, 1990, ready to start flying in command on the company's routes around Europe to places such as Amsterdam, Belfast, Milan, Frankfurt, Stuttgart, Venice, Gothenburg, Copenhagen, Jersey and Stockholm.

A Birmingham European Airways BAC 1-11
Photo: MAP

Now although I was grateful to have gainful employment, I have to say that this was not the most enthralling phase of my flying career. The 1-11 is a strong, sturdy aircraft, but it was not particularly exciting to fly, and in any case I found myself spending quite a lot of time on standby in the bedsit I'd rented near the airport because the 120-mile trip back to Somerset was rather too much to do between flights. I also missed being a training captain, so by late summer I asked the company if they would be interested in promoting me to that position, as I knew they were considering applications.

I was invited to submit myself to the selection process that the company had set up, and I have to say it was not only extremely thorough but also unlike anything I'd undergone before. It was all very "British Airways" — in other words, very formal and precise — and it included intensive interviews designed not just to evaluate my aviation skills but also to explore my fundamental attitudes to training, and as part of it I even had to write a long essay. Apparently I did OK, but the company finally decided I was just a bit too old to be promoted, so I didn't get the job.

I was a bit disappointed, but at least this helped to convince me that I really didn't want to spend the rest of my aviation career flying in and out of Birmingham. I would carry on with Birmingham European as it would help pay the bills, but only until something more challenging came along, and we would certainly make no plans to move from Somerset.

Then one day in August I returned to my hotel room in Belfast, having completed a fairly typical Belfast-Birmingham-Amsterdam-Birmingham-Belfast trip, and turned on the TV. As I changed out of my uniform ready to go and meet my co-pilot for a beer in the hotel bar, I casually started watching the lunchtime business programme that used to be on BBC2 every day. As I was about to turn the TV off I suddenly heard the two magic words "new airline", and immediately I gave the set my undivided attention. Airtours, a well-known tour operator based near Manchester, was considering starting its own in-house airline, and I knew this could be the opportunity I was looking for. New airlines mean new jobs for pilots, even crusty old captains like myself, so I phoned Larraine at home in Somerset and asked her if she could find out any further information for me, such as whom I should contact for an application form.

By that same evening Larraine had arranged an appointment with an aviation consultant who was handling such matters, and on my next day off I had a meeting with him in Manchester. He told me the very welcome news that the airline was negotiating the likely purchase of five MD83's, which of course was perfect for me as I'd had so much experience on them, both as a line pilot and as a training captain. However, having so recently been declared too old to become a training captain with Birmingham European I decided to show him the recent assessment I'd done with them, and I was quickly reassured that if the new airline did indeed complete its acquisition of MD83's (as opposed to Boeing 737's, which it had also been considering), I would be a "shoo-in" for a training job.

In fact, had the final choice of aircraft gone the Boeing way I probably wouldn't have got a job at all, as there were already quite a number of 737 pilots available around the UK. That's the thing with aviation: no matter how good you may be at the actual job of flying, you're really only ever as good as the types on your licence, and if you're up against someone who has a type rating that you don't have you could well be out of luck when it comes to finding employment.

At this point, however, Larraine and I got involved in a little jaunt to the West Indies as part of Birmingham European's sailing team in an airline regatta held in St. Lucia. One of the company's captains on their smaller Gulfstream aircraft was our skipper, and as he was a really accomplished sailor we ended up winning a large silver cup as the best single-boat entry in the whole competition; some of the bigger airlines, particularly American ones, could support whole teams of boats, but we had just the one.

Anyway, before we'd left the UK I'd had confirmation of my new job with Airtours, so on returning to Birmingham I had a "good news, bad news" moment with BEA's Managing Director. First, I handed him the silver trophy that we'd won in the regatta, and then I gave him my resignation letter. He was delighted to receive the former but not quite so pleased about the latter, though I think he'd already realised that I might not be staying with the company forever, particularly when the Airtours opportunity came along.

In fact, I should have started with Airtours on 1 November, 1990, but because I didn't need to do a full technical course, just a very quick refresher, I was able to continue flying for Birmingham European until the end of December. Unfortunately, I then had to pay a fairly large sum of money to them before they would release me from the bond I'd had to sign when I joined the company to cover the costs of my training on the BAC 1-11. This document stipulated that if I left the company before I'd been with them for two years I'd have to pay back some of these training costs, the amount decreasing for each month I worked, and in the end it came to around three thousand pounds. I did try to get a tax rebate on this as it had been wholly necessary for my employment, but the Inland Revenue were having none of it. Still, even this couldn't detract from the pleasure I felt at getting back onto the MD83, especially as this one would have something even better than the Paramount ones; the brand new aircraft I'd be flying for Airtours came with EFIS (Electronic Flight Information System), and for someone who'd always flown with traditional dial-type aircraft instruments this was an enticing prospect.

Between my flights with BEA during December, 1990, I did a technical refresher course on the MD83 at the British Caledonian Flight Training centre at Gatwick (BCAL itself had been absorbed into British Airways in late 1987, but their training centre had not been part of the deal). BCAL Flight Training had bought a flight simulator for the MD83 in 1989, with the main intention of servicing the training needs of the two British airlines that flew this type at that time: Paramount Airways and BIA, the latter being a Gatwick-based charter airline. Of course, Paramount ceased operations during 1989, and BIA only lasted until early 1991, so I'm sure BCAL Flight Training must have been very pleased when Airtours decided to buy five MD83's for their new airline.

In fact, as soon as this new customer was confirmed, BCAL Flight Training converted their MD83 simulator from its original setup with dial-type instruments to state-of-the-art EFIS, otherwise known as the "glass cockpit", in which all the information the pilots need is shown together on colour video screens directly in front of them, thus saving them from having to keep scanning numerous dials and gauges. Of course, for safety's sake there are always backup instruments of the conventional kind in case some major electrical malfunction should happen, but the screens certainly made life much easier, not only from a flying point of view but also on account of their greater reliability and ease of servicing; if there were a problem, the engineers could simply remove the little electronic box that wasn't working right and slide a new one in.

Anyway, over the Christmas holiday period I was able to complete my refresher training on the Gatwick simulator, and by the end of the year I was cleared as a CAA Instrument and Type Rating Examiner so that I could start training the company's intake of pilots. Some of these pilots already had ratings on the MD83 because they had previously flown for Paramount or BIA, and I was able to do their training and renew their various ratings at Gatwick, which saved a great deal of cost and hassle.

However, we still had around fifty pilots who needed to be trained from scratch on the MD83, and all of these would be going to Long Beach, California, to do their technical course and simulator sessions with McDonnell Douglas. After all that, though, they would still have to undergo a CAA Instrument Rating test, so I had to go out to Long Beach as well to finish off the first set of eight crews. I eventually returned to Manchester via Las Vegas as a passenger on the delivery flight of Airtours' first aircraft, arriving on 25 February.

With a shiny new aeroplane parked on the Manchester tarmac, lots of new pilots doing their training courses and four more aircraft soon to come off the production line, the new Airtours airline was almost ready for action. However, there was still one more big hurdle to negotiate before commercial operations could start: our pilots still had to fly the aircraft itself.

Nowadays, some simulators reproduce handling characteristics so perfectly they can be used for what's called ZFT (Zero Flight Time) training; this means that an experienced pilot who is converting from one aircraft type to another does not have to fly the real aircraft at all until he or she does their first commercial flight on it. In other words, they don't have to do the circuits-and-bumps, emergency descents, go-arounds, stalls, practice engine failures and all the rest of what's generally involved in "base training" on the aircraft, because all of that can be done convincingly, more safely and much more cheaply on the simulator.

However, this was not the case for Airtours, and as it was a brand new airline we had an enormous amount to do in order to comply with CAA requirements. So from late February the company was involved in a hectic period of non-revenue training and proving flights, during which both pilots and cabin staff were able to get to grips with their new working environment.

All five of Airtours' MD83's plus all the staff at Manchester Airport were gathered together on the tarmac for this memorable photo taken a day or two before the company started operating flights. You can't see me, but I'm in the front row!

In fact, the travel industry in general was quite surprised that by late March Airtours had not only taken delivery of all five of its new MD83's but had also managed to train enough crews to start commercial operations. I did my first commercial flight for Airtours on 27 March, 1991, and this time I really *did* think that this would be my last airline job before retirement.

I was still based at Birmingham, where I had, of course, already been working for more than a year, and I was staying in the little bedsit in a large country house near Coleshill that I had used during my time with Birmingham European. Every so often I would be sent to Gatwick for a couple of days to train people on the simulator and to Manchester to do training on the aircraft, so 1991 was a very busy year, with a continuous intake of new pilots to be trained as well as regular licence renewals to be done for those who had joined us early on.

I've already mentioned that the Airtours MD83's had glass cockpits, but there was something else they had that was new to me as well: they were fitted with automatic landing equipment, so subject to certain regulations their pilots were permitted to do a complete approach and landing in the kind of extremely low visibility conditions that would normally force a diversion to another airport.

One of the conditions governing use of this equipment in genuinely bad weather conditions was that *both* pilots of the aircraft must have done at least six auto-lands in the past six months, and these could be done on either the aircraft or the simulator. Of course, in a normal six-month period it was rather unlikely that any pilot working in and around Europe would be faced with six instances of such poor visibility conditions that an automatic landing *had* to be made, so in order to keep all our pilots current on auto-land procedures we would often do these landings in good visibility on normal flights. This was very helpful for two reasons: first, both pilots could record it in their logbooks so they would be in compliance with the aforementioned regulations, and second, it enabled every pilot to see how well the automatic system actually worked and give them complete confidence about using it when it really was necessary to do so.

Of course, on these practice landings we would always be ready to take control and either do a manual landing or initiate an overshoot if we weren't happy about anything, and in any case we would always, in fair weather or foul, make a decision on whether to land or overshoot when we were down to fifty feet above the ground. This was measured on a gadget called a radio-altimeter, which bounced signals off the surface to give a very precise readout, and if you couldn't see anything, such as runway lights, from this height then you just had to give up the landing and go somewhere else. However, as the decision height for normal flights without auto-land capability was two hundred feet, the extra equipment was a very good thing to have on those occasions that demanded it.

During my time with Airtours I only did a few completely necessary auto-lands, including one at Birmingham on a very foggy January day, when lots of less well-equipped aircraft had already diverted elsewhere. I think my co-pilot that day had never actually been in the cockpit for a "proper" automatic landing in very low visibility conditions, and he was keen to make sure he got everything right as we descended towards the runway.

During our descent it was his job to look at the instrument panel and call out our height from the radio altimeter at 1,000ft, then 200ft then 50ft, while I would be looking ahead, with my hands resting gently on the throttles and the control column and my feet resting on the brakes, ready to put on the power if we needed to overshoot or to use the brakes and apply reverse thrust if we decided to land (applying brakes and reverse thrust were things that our auto-land equipment didn't actually do).

The co-pilot did his job well and, as required, called out "fifty feet" as we reached our decision height. Just a few moments before that, however, I'd caught sight of runway lights beneath me, so on his call I immediately responded, as required in these situations, by saying "Land" very clearly (had I not seen the lights I would have said "Go around"). This seemed to come as a huge surprise to my co-pilot, who had been expecting, given the conditions, that we'd have to divert as well, and he couldn't help but utter an amazed cry of "What?" as the aircraft continued lowering itself towards the runway and then settled onto the tarmac.

I applied full reverse thrust and braking in order to stop as quickly as possible — you're never quite sure how much tarmac is ahead of you when you're shrouded in fog, even if you're pretty sure you've touched down in the right place — and then we were told by ground control to stay where we were while they sent out a "Follow Me" truck to guide us to our stand. My co-pilot was still looking around as if he couldn't quite believe what we'd done, but I suppose it *is* quite amazing to think that with the aid of advanced electronics, aircraft can actually touch down safely in the kind of visibility conditions in which they still need the relatively low-tech assistance of a little van with an illuminated sign on it to guide them back to the terminal.

Anyway, we were soon parked up, having arrived on time and at our correct destination, a point which I hope all our passengers really appreciated, even if they later had a bit of a struggle driving home through the unrelenting fog. But perhaps the most impressed person on the flight was my co-pilot, having had what was clearly a new and quite remarkable experience that he probably remembers to this day.

In 1992, Airtours bought three more MD83's, so we needed even more pilots to fly them. I therefore spent time in Shannon during February and March with other training captains, helping to maintain an almost continuous sequence of take-offs and landings around the clock to get all our new pilots qualified before the summer season. There was simulator training to be done at Gatwick too, so it was actually quite relaxing when, after four or five days of solid training duties, I would go back to doing routine flights as a normal captain

My logbook records the fact that during 1992 I did more than sixty training sessions on the simulator at Gatwick, each of at least four hours' duration, and I estimate that when I add in extra time for briefing and debriefing trainees, I must have done three hundred hours on the simulator alone, not to mention the six hundred or so flying hours I totted up during that year. I certainly thought then that it would turn out to be just about the busiest year of my entire career, and as I was drawing ever closer to my expected retirement age of sixty — at that point less then eighteen months away — I thought I would probably never do so much work again in any twelve-month period. As it turned out I was wrong, but we'll come to that later.

Of course, the kind of simulator I was using at Gatwick was very different from the static DC8 ones I'd used in the past. This one was on hydraulic legs that moved the simulator cabin around in order to create the kind of G-forces one could expect in the aircraft itself — just like the much smaller and simpler machines you find in fairgrounds, amusement arcades and similar places nowadays — and the very clever audio-visual technology in each of the flight deck "windows" could be set up to give you exactly what you'd see from any one of many airports around the world. The instructor could set up all kinds of different weather conditions, including bad turbulence or difficult crosswinds, and could introduce mechanical problems such as engine failures or other malfunctions, so in a couple of hours in the simulator a pilot could be faced with more problems than he or she would probably encounter in several years of airline flying. Easy it was not.

Of course, such complex pieces of equipment needed regular maintenance of both mechanical and electronic varieties, and late one night, as my trainees were leaving the simulator to return to the hotel, a couple of engineers appeared and asked me if I'd like to stay on for a while to fly the simulator while they did a bit of routine maintenance; they normally did their work with the simulator turned off, but on this occasion they wanted to check something while it was working. They didn't need the hydraulics to be on, so the simulator wouldn't be moving, but the visuals were operating, so I set it up for Gatwick and lined up for take-off.

Once airborne I put the simulator into a fairly steep left turn but then heard a strange sound from behind me, as if something had fallen down. In fact, this was exactly what had happened, because as I'd gone into the turn both of the engineers had been looking out of the flight deck windows (i.e. the video screens showing the simulated outside view), and this had fooled their senses as regards which way was up. The result was an unscheduled meeting with the floor for both of them, but no lasting harm was done, and I'm sure that if they ever got into that kind of situation again they probably held on to the back of the pilots' seats or some other convenient equipment very tightly indeed.

Towards the end of 1992 I had an interesting opportunity to become involved in the world of executive flying. Of course, I'd done a bit of this before, when I'd been company pilot for the *Lawrence of Arabia* film unit in Jordan, and also later on in Tanzania, flying for Williamson Diamonds, but now I was to be working on a contract with one of the biggest companies in the world: the Ford Motor Company.

Ford had had an aviation division called Fordair, based at Stansted, Essex, for a number of years, and during 1992 they had decided to replace their ageing BAC 1-11 aircraft with MD87's, a slightly smaller but otherwise almost identical version of the MD83. Ford operated all their aircraft on the Bermuda register, which was ultimately under the authority of the British CAA, so they had asked the CAA for permission to use McDonnell Douglas's training facilities in

California. The CAA, however, wanted the training to be done in the UK if at all possible, and as Airtours was already operating MD83's Ford asked Airtours to do their training for them. As the summer season was over Airtours were delighted to oblige, so a contract was duly agreed and a couple of training captains were assigned to the Fordair job; one of them, of course, was me.

Thus in December I started instructing the Fordair pilots on the MD83 simulator at Crawley. The CAA had kindly decided to put the MD87 on my licence automatically, so once the simulator training was done I was able to instruct on the aircraft as well. In fact, over the next six months my duties alternated between doing initial and route training of Fordair crews and my normal duties as an Airtours training captain, which made for an interesting variety of work.

On one Fordair trip from Stansted to Valencia, where there is a large Ford factory, we were flying in excellent weather conditions with wonderful views of the Pyrenees stretching out on both sides of the aircraft as far as the eye could see. Almost instinctively I reached for the PA microphone, intending to make the kind of announcement I was accustomed to making on holiday flights, pointing out the great views that could be seen below.

Immediately, however, the Fordair captain whom I was line-checking grabbed the microphone from my hand and put it back in its holder, telling me in no uncertain terms that Fordair pilots *never* spoke to their passengers except in an emergency, as time spent in flight was nearly always put to good use for important meetings at which vital decisions were often made. I felt somewhat chastened, but I didn't make that mistake again.

However, some flights were a little more relaxed, such as the one I did from Stansted to Toulon in January, 1993, carrying a group of motoring journalists to the launch of Ford's latest new model, the Mondeo. We arrived in Toulon during the afternoon to find a whole fleet of Mondeos in various colours parked on the apron in a huge semicircle, and as the journalists disembarked they were each given a set of the keys along with directions to the hotel where they would all be staying. We watched them set off, but when they'd all gone there were still a couple of cars left, and I was delighted to discover that these were for the crew, to use as we liked during our two-day stopover. I was therefore able to boast, on my return to the UK, that I'd actually driven Ford's new car, so perhaps I can claim to be one of the first of that happy breed that came to be known in Britain as "Mondeo Man".

I finished my Fordair duties in June, 1993, so after that I went back to the normal round of Airtours holiday flights interspersed with training duties for the rest of that year. As summer became autumn I became increasingly aware that I was now within six months of having to give up this job, as on 1 March, 1994, I would be celebrating (though that's probably not the right word) my sixtieth birthday, the point at which the law decreed that I must stop flying large passenger jets. For the time being, though, I was determined to enjoy the last few months of my Airtours career.

It was during this winding-down period that I had one of those experiences that remind you that you can never take anything for granted in aviation. On 18 November I was in command of a normal Airtours flight from Birmingham to Malaga. We had left Birmingham at seven-thirty in the morning, and we had just reached our cruising altitude of 31,000ft over South Devon when the co-pilot and I suddenly heard a loud bang, the kind of noise that always causes worried looks on pilots' faces and an immediate surge of adrenalin in their blood.

It didn't take long, though, for us to see what was wrong: a series of cracks had appeared in my front cockpit window, radiating outwards from a point at the bottom of the glass. This was potentially a very dangerous situation, as the much higher pressure inside the aircraft could have put enough stress on the damaged window to blow it right out.

In fact, something a bit like this, but much more serious, had happened to a British Airways BAC 1-11 flight in 1990. On that occasion the whole window had come adrift because the wrong screws had been used to fix it in place, and the captain had ended up hanging out of the aircraft with the top half of his body wedged in the gap where the window had been. Amazingly he survived, thanks in large part to the efforts of a steward who hung on to his lower body to stop him going right out of the aircraft and also to the coolness of the co-pilot, who quickly got the aircraft down to a survivable altitude where the air was breathable and the pressure differential was much reduced. The co-pilot landed the aircraft safely, and although very battered the captain was not too seriously injured, so after a period of rest and recovery he returned to flying. A quite amazing story indeed.

I didn't immediately think of that incident when I saw what had happened to my own window, but I knew the first priority was to put the aircraft into an emergency descent to get us back down to around ten thousand feet, thereby reducing the load on the damaged glass and making its total disintegration less likely. While I controlled the aircraft my co-pilot contacted Air Traffic Control to let them know what was happening, and they immediately cleared us to return to Birmingham at low level. Once we were established at our safe altitude I made a PA announcement to explain the situation to our passengers and cabin crew, all of whom I'm sure must have been rather alarmed at our sudden descent, although as the aircraft had remained pressurised they wouldn't have had the shock of seeing oxygen masks dropping down in front of them.

Anyway, we eventually landed normally back to Birmingham at 8.45am, having been airborne for little more than an hour. Subsequent

A ground engineer took this photo of our damaged window after we landed back at Birmingham. The black rectangle beyond the control column is the very clever EFIS screen on which almost all the information a pilot needs is electronically displayed.

investigations revealed that the failure, which fortunately had only affected the outer layer of the glass, had been caused by a short circuit in the window heating system, so all that was needed was a quick replacement of the captain's window before the aircraft could carry on flying. I, of course, needed no physical repairs, but my co-pilot and I *were* given the rest of the day off.

Although I was, as I've said, fast approaching the age when I'd have to stop flying large passenger aircraft, I had no intention of giving up aviation completely. I knew the law would allow me to continue piloting smaller aircraft — the sort that could carry around thirty passengers rather than the 170 we could accommodate on the MD83 — until I was sixty-five, so I started putting out feelers in the hope of finding a job with a small commuter or cargo company to drop into once I'd finished my time with Airtours.

One such company, called Celtic Airlines, was operating from Bristol, so one day I popped up to Bristol Airport to see if I could talk to its chief executive, a chap called Mick O'Brien, whom I knew from Paramount Airways, where he'd been one of the Operations staff. Unfortunately, I arrived to find the office closed and a large van outside, into which furniture was being loaded by a couple of men. There was no sign of Mick, but one of the chaps told me that Celtic had gone into liquidation and that Mick had gone up to Blackpool to work for a company called Janes Aviation. How ironic, I thought: having worked for a number of airlines that had gone bust during my life, Celtic had packed up *before* I'd even joined it.

Anyway, the guy with the van was taking all the furniture up to Blackpool because Janes had acquired it, so I asked him to pass on my best wishes to Mick and to tell him I'd popped in to see him about a possible future job. Within a couple of days Mick got in touch with me, and as he still had his home in Somerset we arranged to meet up for a drink at a local pub next time he was down.

Mick didn't have anything for me himself, but he put me in touch with a couple of chaps who were trying to set up a new airline at Bristol called Community Express using Shorts 360 aircraft, which would carry thirty passengers. I'd never flown this particular type, so Mick suggested, and I agreed, that it would be a good idea to get it put on my licence so that I would already be qualified as and when the new airline got going.

I managed to get hold of all the relevant aircraft manuals and did a self-administered technical course (something that I doubt would be allowed these days) before successfully taking the type-rating written exam at Gatwick. At that point, Mick worked out an ingenious way of getting me the necessary flight training on the aircraft itself: he introduced me to a company called Streamline Aviation, who flew Shorts 330 aircraft (a type so similar to the 360 that the pilot rating covers both) and were in urgent need of an examiner who could do instrument rating renewals for all their pilots. I could do that even though I was not yet fully qualified on the Shorts, so I would be given the flight training to put the 330/360 on my licence in exchange for my services as an Instrument Rating Examiner.

Meanwhile, as my sixtieth birthday was rapidly approaching, Airtours realised that my departure from the company would leave them very short of training staff. Of course, I would not be able to instruct on the aircraft itself once I was over sixty, but there were no such age restrictions on the simulator, so Airtours offered me a one-year contract to continue working for them as a simulator instructor, which I happily accepted.

On 28 February, 1994, the day before my sixtieth birthday, I operated a routine holiday flight from Birmingham to Faro and back; Larraine was at the airport to meet me on my return, and the next evening we had a rather bittersweet celebration dinner to mark the fact that I would not be flying large jets again. However, we weren't *too* downhearted; for the next year or so I'd be staying in contact with the big jet world because I'd be spending eight to ten days a month at Gatwick doing simulator training for Airtours, which would still leave me plenty of time to pursue my involvement with Streamline Aviation and to see how things developed as regards Community Express. I still had five years to go before I'd have to give up commercial flying completely, so I felt I was looking at a fairly gentle let-down towards that inevitable day when I'd do my last ever flight as a professional pilot.

The end was in sight, but it wasn't *quite* within touching distance just yet.

Chapter 15

WHEN I STARTED DOING MY FLIGHT TRAINING on the Shorts 330 with Streamline Aviation on 14 June, 1994, it was the first time I had flown a propeller-driven aircraft since we'd returned from the British Virgin Islands in 1985, and the Shorts was certainly a quite different creature from the big jets I'd been flying for the past nine years. By the end of August I had completed all my training and was doing some night flights for Streamline as a freelance captain during most of the weeks when I wasn't needed for my Airtours simulator duties at Gatwick.

These night flights were mostly carrying small parcels, newspapers and mail around the UK — not the most glamorous of work, but the Shorts was an easy and pleasant aircraft to fly, even though it wouldn't win any beauty contests. I was therefore quite happy working for Streamline as one of my two "retirement" jobs, whilst still awaiting further news of Community Express. I even did some flights from Southend during this period, as Streamline had a second base there operating to points on the near Continent, and I would often remember the times when, at the other end of my career, I had flown such aircraft as Bristol Freighters, Vickers Vikings, Douglas DC4's and Canadair Argonauts from that same airport all those years before.

A Shorts 330 aircraft, similar to the one I flew with Streamline Aviation
Photo: MAP

By the autumn I was quite well settled into this new routine, and although it was rather frustrating that nothing much seemed to be happening as regards Community Express I just carried on with things as they were. A typical night's work with Streamline was one that I did on 27 October, flying a return trip to Plymouth from Exeter followed by a trip to East Midlands and back. However, what happened during the hours after that flight was far from typical, and it meant another unexpected change in my ever variable career.

It would have been around 3am before I got back to Axbridge, so I was still asleep when the phone rang sometime around eight-thirty. Larraine was already up and about, so she took the call and found herself talking to Colin Penney, the Director of Flight Operations at Airtours. She explained I was still in bed after flying overnight, so she offered to take a message and get me to call back.

"OK," said Colin, "but can you just ask him if he'd like to fly the MD83 again?"

"Hang on," said Larraine, "I'll get him to the phone."

I think I had been dimly aware of the phone ringing, so I was already clawing my way back to consciousness as Larraine shouted up to me. But as I stumbled down the stairs I wondered if I was still asleep and having some kind of dream. Had she really said something about flying the MD83 again? Surely not.

As I picked up the phone, however, I suddenly became wide awake. Colin was telling me that the CAA had decided to remove the aircraft weight restriction that prevented pilots over sixty from flying large aircraft, so he wanted to know whether I would like to return to flying instead of just doing simulator training. I believe I said something like, "Give me two seconds to think about that", but in the end I don't think I needed that long, and the answer was a definite "Yes, please".

By 4 November I had been requalified on the MD83 aircraft and restored to my position as an Airtours training captain, and the company had kindly agreed that I could continue doing some freelance flying for Streamline as long as it didn't conflict with my Airtours programme. So here I was, having retired once, but now with a full-time job *plus* a part-time one.

There was, however, one little problem that had to be overcome in regard to my work for Airtours. The regulatory change that had allowed me to fly MD83's again had precipitated a bit of a backlash in certain European countries, particularly where powerful pilots' unions had rejected the whole idea of loosening the age restrictions, fearing that older pilots would be blocking younger ones from promotion if they were allowed to continue flying large aircraft until they were sixty-five.

One of the countries that was robustly opposed to the CAA's unilateral decision was Spain, and as a great many of Airtours' Birmingham flights were either to Spanish destinations or routed through Spanish airspace it would have been well nigh impossible for me to continue flying from there. There was, however, a system whereby permission could be sought for individual pilots to operate to or over any countries that had different age restrictions, and this concession was successfully arranged by Airtours on my behalf for everywhere else in Europe; Spain, however, wouldn't budge.

Fortunately, though, the Airtours base at Gatwick was a lot busier than the one at Birmingham, with many more flights to southern and south-eastern Europe that went nowhere near Spain and which would thus be fine for me to operate as pilot-in-command. I therefore transferred my base from Birmingham to Gatwick, where I lodged with another Airtours pilot, who had a big house not far from the airport. In fact, I even did an occasional flight from Gatwick to Spain or Portugal as co-pilot because this *was* allowed, but most of my trips were to countries such as Malta, Greece, Turkey, Cyprus and Tunisia. Meanwhile, I was still doing occasional flights for Streamline, plus training sessions on the Gatwick simulator, so time passed very quickly as 1994 gave way to 1995.

I was able to continue combining my two jobs during the first half of 1995, but as the very busy school holiday season hove into view it was clear that Airtours would require all my available energies, so in June I did my last flight for Streamline. However, by this time I was already aware that Airtours were planning to buy some Boeing 757 and 767 aircraft, which would eventually replace their MD83's, and they'd actually started retraining some of their MD83 pilots onto the Boeings, both of which could be flown on the same type rating. At the same time, a few more European countries were expressing their doubts about allowing "old" pilots like me to fly in their airspace, so as far as my future career was concerned the writing was definitely on the wall.

Thus it came to pass that on 8 October, 1995, I did my last ever flight in command of an MD83, from Gatwick to Gothenburg, Sweden, and back. The weather was pretty awful in Gothenburg, with a 100ft cloud base and poor visibility, which meant we had to do an auto-land, but conditions back at Gatwick were fine, so I did a normal landing there, knowing it would almost certainly be my last on that type of aircraft. Thus, for the second time, I said a sad goodbye to the MD83, a lovely aircraft that I had greatly enjoyed flying, and as the company no longer needed me as a simulator instructor either this really was the end of my career with Airtours.

However, they treated me very well, and as a parting gift they gave me the use of the simulator and another training captain the very next day in order to renew my various certificates and ratings so that I would be released into the wild fully certificated for whatever future opportunities might arise, either in the UK or overseas. I was very grateful for that, as being "in check" is a very important string to a pilot's bow when he or she is looking for work.

Because I'd gone back to work for Airtours in the autumn of 1994 my prospective job with Community Express had also fallen by the wayside, as they had needed someone from the spring of 1995 who was able to commit lots of time and effort to completing all the work that needed to be done before the airline itself could start flying. In fact, it did start operations just a couple of weeks after my final Airtours flight, but it didn't worry me too much that I was no longer involved, as I was pretty sure Streamline would still be interested in using me. I wasn't wrong, because after I'd finished with Airtours Streamline actually offered me the post of Chief Pilot, and I was still considering this when another job offer came along.

My friend and former colleague Mick O'Brien, who had got me involved with Streamline in the first place, phoned me up one day and asked me if I would consider working for a Liverpool-based company called Emerald Airways, of which he was now Chief Executive Officer. In an age when it was common for people in their fifties to feel they were being consigned to the employment scrap-heap in order to make way for younger folk here I was, approaching the age of sixty-two, having to choose between two potential new employers.

Streamline had some clear advantages — the base at Exeter, only an hour or so from our home, was certainly attractive — but in the end I decided to go for the Liverpool job, even though it would require me to learn to fly yet another "new" aircraft: the HS748, a turboprop airliner that could accommodate around fifty people when in passenger configuration. In fact, I couldn't even have considered this job if the aircraft-weight/pilot-age regulations had not been eased, as it was over the maximum size that I could have flown at my age under the old rules, but as things were, and with most of Emerald's flights being within the UK, I was able to accept their offer.

Emerald Airways were operating twelve HS748's, and I had been offered the position of Flight Safety Officer, reporting to the Chief Pilot and to the CEO, my friend Mick. During November, 1995, I studied the technical manuals for the aircraft and passed the CAA exam, so when I presented myself at Liverpool in early December to take up my new post I was ready to start flight training. I also managed to find myself a house to rent in Frodsham, Cheshire, on the other side of the Mersey, so I was all ready for this new chapter in my career.

There are no simulators anywhere in the world for the ageing HS748, so I was immediately thrown into circuit training with Captain

G-BIUV, one of Emerald's HS 748 aircraft

Chris Alcock, who had flown the 748 for many years with Dan Air and was probably the world's most experienced pilot on this type. In two days and one night I had completed the necessary type and instrument ratings, so I made a quick trip to the CAA headquarters at Gatwick to get my licence stamped up. I did my en route (line) training — all of it at night — on a series of trips from Liverpool and Edinburgh to other points around the UK, mostly carrying mail, and by the end of December I was fully checked out on the 748 and flying in command.

I established a routine of spending most weekends at home in Somerset, as Emerald's contracts for mail, newspapers and small parcels were concentrated on weekday operations, so I would drive to Liverpool in the early hours of each Monday morning and then drive home on Friday evening. I would usually spend at least a couple of hours each day on office duties, and then most nights I'd be flying — *after* getting some sleep in the afternoon, of course.

At that time Emerald were in need of more training captains, so in late January, with only seventy hours of HS748 time in my logbook, I was to be checked out by the CAA as an authorised examiner on the type. This involved having a CAA check pilot sitting on the flight deck jump seat and watching as I carried out a check flight on another Emerald pilot, and on this occasion the CAA pilot was Captain "Ben" Gunn. He and I had met many times before; not only had he previously cleared me as an examiner on the MD83 with Airtours, but he had also flown with me as my navigator (with me as captain) on Bristol Britannias with British Eagle in the 1960s. It's a small world in aviation, and, as in so many other walks of life, it's worth being good to people when you're on the way up as you never know who you're going to meet on the way back down.

In fact, Ben is not the only person I have flown with who managed to remuster as a pilot after his original role became redundant due to the onward march of technology. Back in the very early days of my career, a long-range crew would often include a radio officer, a navigator and a flight engineer as well as a couple of pilots, and although I can't recall any of the radio officers I worked with who went on to fly aircraft themselves (though there could well have been some), I flew with several navigators and flight engineers who eventually became fully qualified pilots and thus managed to maintain their aviation careers. After radio officers, navigators were the next flight deck profession to be rendered obsolete, with the arrival in the 1970s of various electronic navigation systems, and then the next couple of decades saw the beginnings of the extinction of flight engineers, as complex computer systems replaced them on new aircraft types that were designed to have just the two pilots on the flight deck.

I don't think anything will ever replace loadmasters on cargo flights, and I'm sure there are still some older aircraft flying around with flight engineers, but I'm very glad that I did my long-haul flying in the days when every long-range aircraft had an engineer on board as well as two pilots in the front seats. When things go wrong there's something very reassuring about having a third mind to apply to the problem, particularly if that mind belongs to someone who has come via a different route to get into that seat on the flight deck, and I don't think I'm the only pilot who feels that way.

Anyway, Ben Gunn duly approved me as an examiner on the 748, and from then on I helped train an almost continuous intake of new pilots, some with quite low experience levels. Emerald Airways was the kind of company that young pilots could use as a stepping-stone into larger airlines, and the company therefore bonded them for two years (just as I had been similarly bonded in Birmingham European), during which time they would be required to repay an appropriate portion of their training costs if they left. In most cases they did work off their bond before going on to greater things, but some stayed on with Emerald, as by the end of their two years they were getting close to being eligible for command. Often they would be making the kind of decisions that I had had to make early on in my own career, so I understood the pressures they were under when trying to chart their future course, and I must admit I was rather glad to be in a job that looked very likely to see me through to the end of my own career.

In late April, 1996, Emerald launched a scheduled passenger service between Liverpool and Isle of Man, using one newly-acquired HS748 (G-OJEM) in permanent passenger configuration and, when needed, one of its original freight aircraft (G-BVOV) that could be converted fairly easily to carry passengers if for any reason G-OJEM wasn't available. Very few of our pilots had any passenger experience, so my background was very helpful in educating them in the subtleties of dealing with "walk-on freight", and as most of these flights were during the day I now had the luxury of doing far fewer trips in the dark and spending more of my nights in a comfortable hotel on the Isle of Man.

Having G-OJEM available meant that Emerald could offer passenger charters as well as its scheduled services, and as a result we did a number of flights around the UK for the MoD and for British Aerospace, who became regular customers. The company was still doing its "bread-and-butter" cargo flights, particularly carrying newspapers and mail, but the passenger side was developing nicely, so things were looking good. My own position improved as well; Emerald's Chief Training Captain moved onward and upward to take a job on KLM's MD-11 fleet, so I was promoted to his position, and then, not long afterwards, the Chief Pilot left to join another company, so I took over his job while another of our training captains took over mine.

My new position as Chief Pilot meant rather more office duties than before, but although this reduced my flying a little I still carried on with both normal line-flying and training duties, and I even got to do some interesting things such as evaluating potential new aircraft for the Emerald fleet. In July, 1997, a Cessna Caravan demonstrator aircraft arrived at Liverpool, and I was invited to try it out — under supervision, of course — on a forty-minute trip around the Mersey estuary, with Emerald staff filling all the passenger seats. It was a very impressive aircraft and great to fly, but it had one big problem: although it could carry up to fourteen people or three thousand pounds of cargo, the Caravan had just one engine, and although this engine was a turboprop rather than a piston engine, and thus extremely reliable, CAA regulations would simply not permit single-engine commercial flights of any sort at night. Emerald had hoped to use the Caravan for some of its smaller loads, and it did ask the CAA if it could have an exemption from the usual rules, but the CAA said no, so that idea had to be dropped. What a shame: if Emerald had bought a Caravan, that would have been another type I could have added to the long list of ratings on my licence.

The rest of 1997 passed with me in my usual routine of travelling up to Liverpool on a Monday morning and going home again on

Friday evening, with office work and flying in between. It was a busy life, and Larraine and I were spending more time apart than we liked (she came north occasionally, but with a horse to care for and her own small corporate publications business to run she spent most of her time in Somerset). However, as I was still earning a fairly good salary and thus not having to start diving into my pension savings we reckoned we really were very fortunate indeed.

In early 1998 Emerald won a freight contract out of Bournemouth, so the company based an aircraft there, and I spent some time down there setting up the operation before returning to Liverpool at the end of February and getting back in the usual routine. At the end of March I operated the usual Isle of Man passenger schedule of two return trips from Liverpool followed by a one-way trip back to the island in the evening for a night-stop. My co-pilot and I were then due to do the early-morning cargo flight back to Liverpool, so after dinner and a couple of drinks we retired to get a good sleep before our early call.

I'd been asleep for an hour or two when the phone rang, and for a moment I automatically assumed it was the front desk telling me it was time to get up. I was therefore surprised to find that it was not long after midnight and that the call was from Emerald's Operations Department, and I knew it was probably *not* good news; phone calls at that time of night rarely are.

"Captain Willmott", said the Ops officer, "we have Captain John Hackett on the phone from Stansted — he's on his mobile, so we'll put him through to you".

When John came on the line, he confirmed my expectations.

"Dave," he said, "I'm afraid we've written off your favourite 748".

I knew instantly which aircraft he was referring to: G-OJEM, Emerald's main passenger aircraft and the pride of their fleet. John then explained to me exactly what had happened, and as he talked I realised that although the news was bad it could have been very, very much worse.

He and his crew had been operating a charter flight for the Leeds United football team with forty passengers on board, including the team itself plus various other people connected to the club. They were returning to Leeds after playing a Premiership match at West Ham (which, unfortunately, they had lost), and everything was normal as the aircraft taxied out and rolled for take-off in cool, calm and clear conditions. However, just as they became airborne there had been a huge bang: the starboard (right-hand) engine had suffered a catastrophic failure and was on fire.

The co-pilot, who was flying the aircraft, had immediately handed over control to the captain, who had then made an instant decision that probably saved the lives of everyone on board. It is an almost universal rule in multi-engine aviation that if you suffer an engine failure just before or soon after lift-off you continue your take-off, fly a circuit on one engine and then land, but on this occasion Captain Hackett had decided *not* to do that. There was still lots of runway in front of the aircraft, and the wheels were still down and locked, so he'd just pulled back the power and landed the aircraft straight ahead rather than trying to keep it in the air.

Once safely back on the ground he'd applied full braking, but there was not quite enough runway left to bring the aircraft to a full stop so, as it slowed down, it had run off the end of the tarmac and onto the wet grass. It had then continued across the rain-softened ground and might have rolled to a fairly safe stop had there not been an obstacle in the way: an old concrete track that ran around the airport perimeter a few inches above the height of the grass. As it hit the edge of this track the nose-wheel had bounced upwards and come back down with a resounding thump, as a result of which the whole wheel assembly had collapsed and the aircraft had come to rest with its nose on the ground and its tail way up in the air.

The cabin staff had quickly swung into action to evacuate all the passengers, and very soon the airport fire-crew arrived and extinguished the flames. Fortunately, everyone had escaped from the aircraft with nothing more than minor injuries, but with the collapsed nose-wheel and the fire damage to her wing that G-OJEM had sustained it was already pretty certain that she had done her last flight.

Thus it was that Emerald Airways found itself very much in the news, and in some quarters certain comparisons were made between our Stansted accident and the Munich disaster that had killed and injured so many Manchester United players back in 1958. However, much of the publicity turned out to be very positive, because it highlighted what an excellent job all the crew had done. In fact, they were all invited to attend the next Leeds United home match the following weekend as honoured guests, and they went out onto the Elland Road pitch before the match to receive huge appreciation from everyone in the ground.

Anyway, as I lay there in my hotel room listening to John Hackett's quick summary of what had happened, I knew that as Chief Pilot I would be involved to some extent in the post-accident enquiry process, though I put that thought to one side before getting back to sleep. In fact, when I returned to Liverpool a few hours later I swapped to one of our two remaining passenger aircraft (we'd acquired a third one by this time) and flew a team of Manchester-based CAA investigators down to Stansted to start their enquiries, which I knew would not just be concerned with looking at the wrecked aircraft but would also delve into all sorts of background stuff, such as aircraft and aircrew certi-fication, company manuals and any other documentation that might be considered even vaguely relevant.

In the case of this accident, there was one factor that I feared could have caused us all a problem and could even have resulted in censure for the airline in general or Captain Hackett in particular. As I have already mentioned, the standard procedure on multi-engined aircraft that suffer loss of an engine just before or soon after take-off is to continue the climb-out, fly a circuit and then land, and this is certainly valid for large, powerful jets with high take-off speeds. In theory it applies to lower-powered aircraft such as the HS748 as well, but in the Emerald Airways Operations Manual, which had been approved by the CAA when the airline first started, the option of landing straight ahead in the event of an engine failure on take-off *had* been included, so in deciding to do that Captain Hackett had acted quite properly in going against the usual rule.

I have to say that this was quite a relief to all concerned, as at the

G-OJEM in a sorry state after its accident at Stansted

time of the accident I'd been work-ing on a revision of the airline's operations manual that the CAA had told the company to submit for their approval within a certain period. Had I already completed and published this revised manual before the accident, that option of landing straight ahead after an engine failure would have been removed because such ideas were no longer considered correct, so we had indeed been fortunate in more ways than one.

As it was, when the final accident report came out, not only were the captain's actions in landing straight ahead confirmed as appropriate, but it was also conceded that had he attempted to fly around the circuit the fire might well have burnt right through the wing, leading to a catastrophic crash and the loss of everyone on board, as had happened in a previous, somewhat similar 748 accident elsewhere in the world. In any case, I'm quite sure that even if John Hackett *had* been subject to official criticism for not following established procedures he would have considered that to be of virtually no importance against the fact that he, his crew and his passengers all lived to fly another day.

On 8 May, 1998, on a flight between the Isle of Man and Liverpoool, I recorded my twenty-five thousandth hour of flight in what was by then my sixth flying logbook. I'd also logged more than two thousand hours as an instructor in simulators, so if I hadn't done all that simulator time I would have had a lot more flying hours than the twenty-five thousand so far.

Emerald was still doing OK, though the scheduled passenger operation to the Isle of Man was not making a profit despite getting good loads; however, passenger charters were doing well and were helping to support the Isle of Man flights, thereby maintaining Emerald's status as a scheduled passenger carrier.

In the summer of 1998 the passenger charter side of the business was given a boost by the football World Cup, which was held in France that year. Unfortunately, I was no longer allowed to command flights into or over France and many other European countries, as many more of them had followed the example of Spain in banning older pilots (i.e. over sixty) from flying in command of large aircraft. However, I was OK to do trips to European destinations as co-pilot, and I was still flying in command within the British Isles, so there was still plenty for me to do.

In September, 1998, I did a very special flight indeed; it was a passenger charter, with a full load of forty-eight passengers, and the charterer was . . . ME! A few months previously Larraine and I had decided that the best way to mark my upcoming — and final — retirement from commercial flying would be to take some friends and family for a trip somewhere on the 748 with me in command, and we decided the best place for a jolly weekend would be Waterford, in Ireland. We'd done a reconnaissance trip by car and ferry and had found a great place where we could all stay — a motel that had lovely rooms and great food — so Larraine had set about organising the whole event, on the basis that we'd pay for the aircraft and a celebratory lunch on arrival if our guests paid for their accommodation and any other food and drink they consumed. We even arranged for a small coach to take the local contingent from the Axbridge area up to Liverpool, where they were joined by people from various other parts of the country for a night in a local motel before setting off for the airport early next morning.

Naturally, we were hoping that the weather would be kind to us, but as it turned out, the morning of Saturday, 19 September, 1998, was very foggy, particularly on the other side of the Irish Sea. We were delayed for more than an hour, and although things were meant to be

Guests boarding my pre-retirement celebration flight at Liverpool.

improving by the time we took off, the cloud-base as we approached Waterford was only *just* good enough for us to get in.

Larraine had organised a coach to come and meet us all and take us to our motel, and as we arrived it came and parked right next to the aircraft. Then all we had to do was offload the baggage and put it on the coach, a job which the men in the party accomplished with great speed, and once that was done we all got on the coach ourselves. This "do-it-yourself" system was the source of great excitement and amuse-ment; hardly anyone in the party had ever arrived at an airport without having to be processed through a terminal before, so this was a completely new experience for virtually all our guests.

On reaching the hotel we had our celebratory buffet lunch, and then we were off to do a tour of the Waterford Crystal factory, where Larraine had arranged to present me with a small, crystal globe of the world to mark the occasion. After that, everyone went their separate ways for the rest of the afternoon and evening until we were all due to meet up at the motel again for after-dinner drinks and a bit of late evening entertainment in the form of a local ceilidh band; they'd been expected to turn up around 10pm, but it was nearer midnight when they appeared, so everyone had a *very* late night. Of course, my crew and I (including our two stewardesses) made sure we didn't imbibe too much as we had to work the next day, but at least we could then feel a certain sense of superiority the next morning, when quite a few of our party looked distinctly bleary-eyed as they emerged from the hotel, blinking in the autumn sunshine.

The Sunday was an absolutely gorgeous day, and while some of the group went along to the local golf-course to send a few balls flying off in various directions others explored the local area, and one chap — a distant relative of ours who is absolutely addicted to aviation and had worn a leather flying helmet all the way across from Liverpool — even went in the sea, clad only in his underpants. Meanwhile, Larraine and my younger daughter, Gaynor, went horse-riding on a glorious sandy beach, which certainly blew away any cobwebs, while others went off to explore Waterford, all with strict instructions to be back at the hotel ready for a prompt departure for the airport at 2pm.

They all managed it, so after our coach delivered us straight to the airport apron again the men loaded the luggage back on the aircraft, and then we all climbed aboard and set off back to Liverpool. One of our guests was someone who hadn't expected to come along at all — the coach driver who'd brought Larraine and some other friends from Axbridge and whom we'd invited at the last minute to fill a spare seat on the aircraft — and we later heard that for months afterwards he kept telling his colleagues about the time he did a trip to Liverpool and ended up flying to Ireland for a big celebration. I have a feeling some of them got fed up hearing about it.

The Waterford trip had certainly been a fantastic way to mark the imminent end of my flying career, and Larraine and I are both, to this day, extremely glad we did it. Amongst our guests were my two daughters, my son-in-law and my two grand-daughters, plus my first wife, Pam, and her husband, John, along with all kinds of other people, from millionaires to labourers. If Emerald had still been a purely cargo airline, as it was when I first joined it, such a venture would have been impossible, so this was surely an occasion when I was in just the right place at the right time.

The end of 1998 came and went, and as 1999 arrived I was now into the last two months of my professional flying career. My last day of commercial flying for Emerald was scheduled for 28 February, the eve of my sixty-fifth birthday, but before that day came there was a development that meant I would not after all be saying goodbye to the company and the 748 immediately thereafter.

By sheer coincidence, two of Emerald's training captains — myself and Captain Chris Alcock, the chap who had originally checked me out on the 748 — would both be reaching our sixty-fifth birthdays in March, 1999, and losing the two of us at once was going to leave Emerald desperately short of training staff. In my capacity as Chief Pilot I had been in touch with the CAA to ask them if they could arrange for one of their check pilots to train and clear a candidate put forward by Emerald as a replacement, but unfortunately the CAA did not have anyone suitably qualified who could do the job within the necessary timescale.

It was essential to have another training captain available after Chris and I had left the company, so the CAA found an answer to the problem: they agreed to extend my training authority beyond my normal retirement age so that I could train up my replacement myself. This was an unusual step, but it was all quite legal: I wouldn't be operating the aircraft myself on commercial flights but just watching other people flying it, while on non-commercial training flights I would still be allowed to fly in command, sitting in either the captain's or co-pilot's seat depending on whom I was training.

Therefore by the time I operated my last commercial flights for
Emerald Airways — three return trips between Liverpool and the Isle
of Man during the afternoon and evening of 28 February, 1999 — I
knew that despite my enforced retirement this was not going to be the
end of my professional career. The HS748, and aviation in general, had
not seen the back of me just yet.

Chapter 16

THERE HAD BEEN A TIME, back in my forties and fifties, when I was
 t I'd be able to carry on flying until I reached sixty, let
 that age, and I'd more or less decided that once I'd
 g for a living I wanted to build my own small aircraft,
 the many very good kit designs available. Larraine and I
 visited the USA on several occasions in the 1980s and 90s
 shows where such aircraft were on display, both on the
 n the air, and we'd once driven down to a fairly remote
 nce where we'd had a demonstration flight in one parti-
 he Murphy Rebel, that we felt would be ideal for us.
 as time went on and my flying career continued to keep
 pied, even as I was supposed to be winding down
 ement, the time I would eventually have available to
 ilding project was shrinking day by day, week by week
 y month. Putting an aircraft together would also, of
 d a large investment in terms of money — some tens of
 ounds — and that, added to the estimated two to three
 st full-time construction work, during which I'd be
 ....r than flying, made the prospect even more daunting as
 olled by. There was also the practical matter of finding a
 orkshop or hangar where I could actually put the thing
 t yet more expense, of course).
 end it was Larraine, wise as she is on matters such as this,
 ll these "anti" arguments together and finally persuaded me
 nould drop the whole idea. Had I given up professional
 xty it might have been feasible, but now that I had managed
 e my very busy flying career right to its legally permitted
 – and even slightly beyond — there just wasn't enough time
 t an aircraft-building project, particularly if we wanted to
 asonable amount of leisure time together without having me
 dashing off to do a bit more to the aircraft because I'd just
 f a possible answer to some niggling construction problem. I

think Larraine was concerned that she'd see even less of me if I was *building* an aircraft than she had done when I was *flying* them.

In fact, I didn't need too much persuading because I could see she was right, but as my retirement from Emerald came ever closer I did feel it would be good to carry on doing some sort of flying afterwards, if only on a small, single-engined aircraft. I was therefore delighted to discover that just such an opportunity already existed at Bristol Airport, fifteen minutes from our home, in the shape of the Mendip Flying Group. This group, with a maximum membership of twenty people, owned a fairly old but very well maintained Piper PA28 Cherokee aircraft (G-BABG, otherwise known as either Bravo Golf or, more affectionately, "Cabbage"). The group itself was already recognised as being very well managed, so I contacted them and, as luck would have it, they had one vacancy for a new member. After paying a couple of thousand pounds for a share in the aircraft, I was in.

Me with G-BABG, the Cherokee that I flew privately for some years after my retirement.

Meanwhile, using my special CAA approval, I was still doing training sessions up at Liverpool on the 748, so I felt that before I had my official check-flight on Bravo Golf it would be a good idea to do a quick trip with an instructor on another Cherokee owned by the local flight school at Bristol, just to get used to how the aircraft handled. The flight went fine, but one unexpected result was yet another job offer: the flight school needed someone to work as a part-time instrument rating instructor, teaching people on a small and relatively simple simulator and then doing instrument tests on a light, twin-engined aircraft (a Piper P34 Seneca). I'd only be needed two or three days a week, so I decided to accept.

Thus during the rest of 1999 I was kept pretty busy with training flights for Emerald at Liverpool, simulator training and instrument rating check flights at Bristol and flying Bravo Golf for fun, usually on short trips to other airfields within an hour or so of home but sometimes a little farther afield. There was certainly no way I was going to get bored.

Christmas came again, and then the start of the brand new century. (Yes, I know there were arguments that 2000 was the last year of the twentieth and not the first of the twenty-first, but it was midnight on 31 December, 1999, when everybody celebrated the new millennium — including Her Majesty the Queen — so if it was good enough for her it was certainly good enough for me.)

As you may recall (if you're old enough), for many months or even years beforehand there had been dire predictions that electronic chaos would reign as 1999 ticked over into 2000, with all kinds of equipment — from electric kettles to mainframe computers — malfunctioning or even shutting down completely. Lots of companies, including airlines, spent large amounts of money on ensuring that all their equipment and systems were, in the jargon of the time, "Y2K compliant" — in other words, they would be immune to what became known as the "Millennium Bug" — but I'm sure that as the turn of the year came nearer there were probably more than a few people who avoided booking flights scheduled for 31 December or 1 January, just in case. I was due to do my last ever flight for Emerald — to renew the Certificate of Airworthiness for one of their 748's — on 8 January, but I reckoned that whatever mayhem might be unleashed on the world would probably be sorted out by then.

This meant, of course, that I was at home in Axbridge for the Millennium Eve celebrations, so after dinner Larraine and I duly sallied forth to have a drink or two in a couple of our local hostelries, after which we would join with the general throng in Axbridge Square to see in the New Year at midnight. Of course, this was a special New Year's Eve anyway, but to make it even more interesting Larraine decided to take with her, concealed in a suitably ventilated plastic box hidden inside her large handbag, a rather unusual pet that she just happened to have at the time: a Madagascan Hissing Cockroach called Sid.

Just to explain, Larraine is very interested in anything that creeps, crawls or slithers (with the possible exception of slugs), so having pet cockroaches was quite appropriate. (She has also had numerous pet rats in her time, though nowadays we're a little more conventional and have just one rather bossy black cat.) Anyway, on that special evening we went first to our favourite pub, where Larraine pulled out the transparent plastic box in which Sid was crawling around and shouted out, "Look, everyone, I've got the Millennium Bug." There were a few looks of horror and disbelief on people's faces, but some people were actually quite taken with Sid and asked if they could handle him, so Larraine took him out of his box for a bit of a run-around on various people's hands, during which he dutifully emitted the occasional hiss. After a few minutes of socialising he was returned safely to his travelling accommodation to await the next phase of his adventure, as it was now time for everyone to congregate in the town square.

As we walked down to the square there were quite a few families around, so Larraine took out Sid's box again and showed him to the first set of kids we met. They were thrilled, and soon Larraine was almost besieged by youngsters wanting to see the "Millennium Bug", even if some of their parents did not look quite so keen. It was great fun, and Larraine has always said how pleased she was to have Sid available on the only night in a thousand years when it could be considered appropriate to take your pet cockroach out in polite company!

As we all know, the electronic world didn't collapse into disarray as 1999 became 2000, and I duly completed my final flight for Emerald on 8 January. As I walked down the aircraft steps after landing back at Liverpool it looked certain that this would be my last ever flight on a 748, and although I'd never developed such a strong affection for the aircraft as I had for some other types — particularly the DC8 and the MD83 — I was still rather sad; after all, the 748 was considered a "large" aircraft, and I was pretty sure I'd never fly anything in that category again. Yet once again, in the fullness of time, my assumption was to be proved wrong, as had happened so often before in my life.

I carried on doing instrument training for the local flight school for a few months, but eventually it became clear that they needed a full-time instructor rather than a part-time one, and as I just didn't want to spend five days a week at work I packed it in to make way for someone else. I was glad, though, that the flight school job and my continuing duties with Emerald had eased my transition into retirement, and I was still doing plenty of flying on Bravo Golf, so I didn't feel I was out of aviation completely.

Larraine has always said that pilots are different from most other retirees because during their careers they've been given some of the best toys in the world to play with, only to have them snatched away when they reach an arbitrary age limit, at which point they usually have to be dragged kicking and screaming off the flight deck: a bit dramatic, perhaps, but I think her description does shed light on the sense of loss that many pilots feel when they are forced into retirement. Anyway, as 2000 wore on I was becoming more accustomed to being retired, and I was therefore feeling fairly settled when, in October, I had an unexpected phone call that got my aeronautical adrenalin flowing again.

The call was from Emerald Airways, to tell me that they had been contacted by a chap called Mike Hornblower, a former Fleet Air Arm pilot who had for years been involved with the "recycling" of old 748's, buying them up as they came on the market and then selling them on or leasing them out to various companies all over the world. One of his 748's was about to complete a lease contract in Tonga, and at some point in the next two or three months he would need it to be delivered from New Zealand back to the UK. Emerald didn't have any spare pilots, so they wondered if I might be interested in doing the trip. Yes, I certainly was, I told them, so long as all the necessary permissions and paperwork could be sorted out.

Although I couldn't be paid for my services because I would have to fly the aircraft as a private pilot, all my expenses for the whole trip would, of course, be covered by Mike Hornblower, and as far as I was concerned this was going to be my last big adventure before finally settling down into full retirement mode.

At this point, of course, you're probably expecting me to give you a full account of the whole trip, but for now I'm just going to say that I left the UK for New Zealand as a passenger on a United Airlines flight from Heathrow on 9 December and eventually returned home three days before Christmas. The flight from New Zealand had included stops in places such as Kathmandu, Bahrain and Luxor, so once Christmas was over I enlisted Larraine's help in writing up the story of my trip for the magazine of GAPAN (The Guild of Air Pilots and Navigators, now known as the Honourable Company of Air Pilots). Larraine had the clever idea of setting it out as an Adrian Mole-type diary, and it was duly published in GAPAN's Guild News in May, 2001. The whole article is reproduced in the Appendix to this book, and I do hope you'll find it amusing.

Refuelling the Royal Tongan 748 at Norfolk Island; see the Appendix for a full account of our ferry trip back from New Zealand.
Photo: Mike Hornblower

An account of the last sector of that journey also features in the Prologue to this book, as it brought me back to Southend Airport, where my commercial flying career had started all those years before. I'm sure you can understand the sense of "coming full circle" that I felt as we touched down at the end of that long journey from New Zealand, and to this day I feel extremely fortunate to have had the opportunity to round off my long-distance flying career in such a splendid way.

It wasn't quite the end of my flying days, though, and it wasn't even my last ever flight as a pilot on the 748. During January, 2001, I flew the same aircraft up to Blackpool, where it was to be stored pending possible sale, and some years later, in 2007, Mike Hornblower asked me and one of my former Emerald colleagues to deliver another 748 from Boscombe Down to Robin Hood Airport near Doncaster. This aircraft hadn't flown for more than three years, so I and my co-pilot (Bill Robinson, who'd flown with me on my retirement trip to Waterford) decided to leave the gear down all the way, a sensible precaution when you're flying an aircraft that hasn't been airborne for quite a while. Of course, we used a lot more fuel than we would have done with the gear up as normal, but at least we didn't have to worry about suffering major embarrassment if the wheels didn't descend when bidden. Anyway, everything went well, and we arrived safely at our destination.

This was indeed the last time I piloted a large aircraft; the end had come, but as I was by now getting close to my seventy-third birthday I felt I'd done pretty well. Of course, all through these later years I had still been flying Bravo Golf, and I was still flying it in 2007. In 2006 it had been fitted with some very swish satellite navigation equipment, and it was a matter of some amusement to me that in this little, four-seat, single-engined aircraft I had at my disposal the kind of electronics that we could scarcely dream of back in the days when I'd first started flying or even when I got my first command on DC6's. How the world had changed!

Indeed, my own world changed quite a lot in the second half of 2007, as in September I had to have a major operation for colon cancer. Before I went in for surgery I wondered whether I would be able to fly again afterwards, but once I came home from hospital I was surprised at how quickly I recovered, and by the end of January, 2008, I had had my medical certificate renewed and was flying again on Bravo Golf.

However, for various reasons I had always flown the Cherokee on my American pilot's licence rather than my British one, and this meant that the paperwork for my post-operation medical renewal had to be sent by my medical examiner here in the UK to the FAA office in

Oklahoma City. Eventually, a few months after I'd started flying again, someone there read my file and decided they needed a lot more information about my medical situation if I was to continue holding a licence. To give me time to organise the various tests and reports they required, the FAA said I could fly for another three months anyway, but when I looked at what they needed I knew my life as a pilot was nearly over. Even if I spent lots of time, money and effort getting all the stuff they wanted there was still no guarantee that they would let me carry on flying, and as switching back to my British licence would also be fraught with lots of difficult and expensive obstacles — again with no guarantee of success — I finally decided that the time had come to accept the inevitable and hang up my wings for good.

Fortunately, I had very little difficulty in finding a buyer for my share of Bravo Golf, and thus it was that on 14 August, 2008, at the age of seventy-four, I flew an aircraft for the very last time in my life. Larraine was with me, and after landing I handed the keys of Bravo Golf to the chap who'd bought my share for exactly what I'd paid for it: two thousand pounds. As we walked away I felt sad but also grateful to "Cabbage"; she had helped me make that difficult journey from being a pilot to being a former pilot, and I was so glad that she had come along just at the right time and in the right place.

Well, there's not much more to tell. As I write this, in the autumn of 2014, I'm now in my eighties, while Larraine is in her early sixties, and we're still living happily but fairly quietly here in Axbridge. I had to have some more major surgery back in 2012, but once again I made a good recovery, so we still do two or three cruises every year, and although I get around rather more slowly than I used to I have to say that life is still good.

Both my daughters have done very well in life — Allison lives in Scotland with her husband, Alan, and has two grown-up daughters, both of whom now have excellent professional careers of their own, while my younger daughter, Gaynor (otherwise known as Ron for reasons I won't bore you with), has lived in California for many years, where she works as an obstetric nurse (they don't call them midwives over there, but that's more or less what she does). I am very proud of them all.

For my eightieth birthday in March, 2014, the family bought me a wonderful gift: a session on the old Concorde simulator that used to be at Filton Airport, near Bristol — where the British Concordes were built — but which is now at the Brooklands Museum in Surrey. I was given a choice of various airport circuits around the world that could be set up for me to fly, and the one I chose was one that I'd flown many times in my life but which can no longer be flown by anybody, at least not for real: the Checkerboard Approach at the old Kai Tak Airport in Hong Kong. Though I'd never, of course, flown Concorde itself, flying the simulator brought back wonderful memories of times past, as the look and layout of the flight deck reminded me very much of the dear old Britannia that I'd flown for British Eagle on so many of those Hong Kong landings. Of course, both the Concorde and the Britannia had been built at Filton, so perhaps it's no great surprise that their flight decks looked somewhat alike, despite the enormous difference between them in terms of airspeed.

As I look back over the years, I feel tremendously glad that I was born when and where I was, because I know that being brought up near Southend Airport in the late 1940s and being put through National Service in the early 1950s were hugely important influences on my life and my choice of career. In fact, at least six of my contemporaries from my local area — four of them from my own school — went on to become airline pilots themselves and can therefore claim, like me, to have gone from Essex to just about Everywhere.

I am indeed a very fortunate man.

THE END

Appendix

Contents

The Round-the-World Diary of David Willmott, aged 66¾

The Story So Far: After 48 years and more than 25,000 hours of flying, I really thought that my days in command of "big" aeroplanes were over. Then, in August 2000, I had a phone call from Emerald Airways, the Liverpool-based freight operator of HS748 aircraft for whom I had worked as Chief Pilot in the final years of my flying career. They had been asked to provide a captain to ferry a 748 from New Zealand to the UK for Mike Hornblower, a former Royal Navy officer who has made a fascinating second career out of buying, selling and leasing as many 748s as he can get his hands on. The co-pilot for the trip would be Mike's son, Ross, who had just gained his New Zealand CPL and type/instrument ratings on the aircraft, hence the request for an experienced captain. Emerald, however, did not happen to have any spare captains sitting around doing nothing, so they phoned me to find out if I fancied a little jaunt to the other side of the world and back. Yes, I said, I most certainly did.

Plans for the flight were ultimately delayed until the autumn, and then it seemed likely that it would not happen until early 2001. Then suddenly, in November, I had an urgent call from Mike Hornblower. Maintenance on the aircraft had been completed, and if he could finalise all the other arrangements, like overflight permissions, he was hoping to get it back to the UK before Christmas. In other words, I was now on standby to go rushing off to the other side of the world at a moment's notice . . . and there was me thinking that retirement would be quiet, dignified and predictable. This is the story of what happened next.

21 November 2000: Phoned the CAA to gently broach the subject of licence coverage for my planned flight. "Would it be OK," I asked, "for me to ferry a Tongan-registered HS748 from New Zealand to the UK using the PPL privileges of my ATPL with a Class II Medical Certificate, bearing in mind that I still fly a Piper Cherokee every so often and I renewed my Instrument Rating on a Piper Seneca back in the spring." There was a brief pause, followed by the sound of rapid decision-making. "Hang on," said the CAA man, "we'll have a think about this and get back to you." I resisted the opportunity to say, "Would you like to ask the audience or phone a friend?" Didn't want to push my luck.

Later the same day: The CAA called me back. "To be honest, this is a bit unusual," said the man, "but let's just say it would make us *happy* if you would renew your Instrument and Type Ratings on the 748 and upgrade your medical to Class I."

Isn't it great to know you can make someone happy? Particularly the CAA.

24 November: Drove to Hampshire to present myself to Dr Ian Perry for the medical upgrade, then headed north to Liverpool , checked into a hotel and got ready to travel as supernumerary crew on an overnight cargo flight to Belfast. Returned just before 4am to find a notice on my door telling me I must vacate the room by 11am. Said something very rude then collapsed into bed.

25 November: Slept soundly through the morning (ignoring the 11am deadline) then got up, dressed, had lunch, and made my way to the airport. Weather was terrible – gales, rain, low cloud, gathering darkness, 30kts of wind across the runway – just great for a check flight. Learned from Emerald's training captain that I would be having an LPC. Wondered if that was a cross between an LP and a CD until he explained that it meant Licence Proficiency Check. Passed the check flight OK – great to discover I could still fly something big enough to have a toilet and galley in it. Drove home to loving wife, who was working out whether we would get any money back for the three-day Barcelona trip we had booked for early December (we wouldn't).

26 November: Phone call from Mike in New Zealand: the trip was definitely on, with planned departure from Christchurch on 14 December, routing via various points in Australia and the Far East with a stop in Kathmandu, where he would be doing some business. Now all I needed to do was get myself out to NZ, so began surfing the net and phoning travel agents. Not much luck – I should have booked earlier if I wanted to travel in the run-up to Christmas. Must dig out that crystal ball in case this happens again. Finally managed to get a seat (steerage class, of course) to Sydney via San Francisco on

9 December (Mike reckoned he could sort out the extra leg to Christchurch). Wife heaved a sigh of relief – our Barcelona trip was scheduled for 6 to 8 December, so we could fit it in after all.

27 November: Visas! I would need some. Wife surfed the net and find out what to do. Australian one was easy – one quick phone call and a credit card payment of £20 made me the proud possessor of an Australian ETA (Electronic Travel Authority). Decided only other visa I would need was for India, since I knew the lack of one might lead to an unscheduled night-stop in the airport lounge.

28 November: Drove to Birmingham, went to Indian consulate, paid £30, waited an hour and came out with a shiny new visa. Drove back to Bristol, collected air ticket, them came home. Piece of cake!

6 December: Wife and I rose brightly at 2.30am to drive to Heathrow for early morning Iberia flight to Barcelona – got there with time to spare so wife complained we could have had ten more minutes in bed. Spent next three days trundling round the Catalan capital on toast-rack tourist buses, leaping off whenever there was a bit of Gaudi architecture to gawp at (one of the wife's passions – she's funny like that).

8 December: Returned to Heathrow on evening Iberia flight and spent a happy twenty minutes or so in the holding pattern – great view of the Dome, though that was as much as I wanted to see of it. Spent night in Heathrow Comfort Inn, where a local firm was having its Christmas party, therefore not the most restful night we've ever had.

9 December: Said goodbye to wife as she returned to Somerset. Caught shuttle bus to Heathrow and checked in for United Airlines flight. Enquired politely about possibility of an upgrade, which seemed to amuse the ground staff. Couldn't even get an emergency exit seat, so settled in for a not-very-comfortable ten-hour haul on a completely full aircraft. Decided it's much more fun sitting up the front where all the switches, levers and dials are, even if you have to keep talking to strange people on the radio. Arrived at San Francisco feeling less than enthusiastic about the impending five-hour connection time and fourteen-hour onward flight to Sydney, and was even less thrilled with an extra hour's delay due to a faulty hydraulic pump. Still, managed to negotiate an emergency exit seat with bags of legroom for the sector to Sydney, which was much more comfortable. Arrived there too late for the morning flight to Christchurch, so decided to get myself horizontal for a few hours in the airport hotel before catching the evening one (Business Class this time). Felt almost human again by the time I met Mike Hornblower at the Airport Plaza Hotel around midnight local time. Everything was coming together well, so we should be on target for our departure on the 14th. Went to bed and slept like a log – or should that be plog? (Note for non-aviators: a "plog" or "Pilot's Log" is a term used in flight planning, although these days it also crops up in various non-aeronautical contexts as well).

13 December (as far as I recall, but when you've just travelled for the best part of two days and have crossed the dateline things can get very confusing): After a robust breakfast, started flight planning as far as Kathmandu, then did a very scenic acceptance/test flight in the 748 that I was to fly. Great appreciation from the group of engineers who came along for the ride. One of them told me that the aircraft had been built in 1973 and was then delivered straight to New Zealand, where it went into service as NZ-MCA with Mount Cook Airlines. It stayed with them until it was leased out to Royal Tongan Airlines in 1995, where it had continued in service until the summer of 2000. He knew all this because he'd been on the original delivery flight from the UK. Seems I'm not the only old codger who's still around.

14 December: This is it: D-Day (D as in Departure, of course). Had intended to launch at 7am, but with the usual last-minute niggles didn't actually get airborne until nine-thirty. Headed for Norfolk Island, a speck of land some 800nm north-west of Christchurch, which equates to about 4¾ hours of flying (the 748 is not renowned for its speed, but it's a very pleasant aircraft to fly – all good, solid, British stuff). Found Norfolk Island quite easily with the help of a hand-held Garmin GPS, and Ross, our newly-qualified F/O, made a great job of his first en-route approach and landing. Had a bit of fun trying to find the apron (it's hidden in a valley so can't be seen from the runway), then got stuck into what was to become our usual turn-round routine: I filed the onward flight plan while Ross checked the oils and kept an eye on the refuelling. Norfolk Island seemed like a nice place – perhaps I'll see more of it next time.

Took off again and headed west for Brisbane, where we were radar-positioned for a visual final among towering cumulus and rain showers. Got in with no problems, cleared Customs etc., and then looked round for an ATC office where we could check forward weather and file a flight plan. Found there wasn't one. This was clearly an airport for the big boys, the ones with fancy computer systems, efficient ground staff and all the paraphernalia that "proper" airlines provide for their crews. We were very much the poor relations of the aviation world, and it was only after hiring a car that we eventually discovered an off-airport Australian CAA office. It was shut, of course. Ah well, there's always tomorrow.

15 December: Returned to the CAA office, filed our flight plan and had a very good breakfast in their staff restaurant. Then departed for Mount Isa, but were in thick cloud most of the way. After picking up fuel in Mount Isa we went on to Darwin, where we did some cumulus-dodging before landing in the clear. Discovered that the place had changed completely since I was there in the 1960s with British Eagle, but then they *had* had a cyclone or two in the interim.

16 December: Had the same problem about filing a flight plan – in the end had to phone the office in Brisbane to do it. This lack of support for non-routine flights was to dog us for the whole of the trip and made me very cross – ferry-flying is tough enough without having to run around strange airports trying to find somewhere to file a flight plan. Eventually taxied out for our early morning departure, but had to give way to a large, frilled lizard that decided to cross the taxiway in front of us; he would have been less than frilled if we'd run over him, I'm sure. Stopped in Bali for fuel, then on to Singapore (Seletar). Hadn't been there for years either, and again much had changed. Didn't see anyone selling those funny little toy monks that used to be so popular here (sorry, I'm not saying any more on that score – if you don't know what I'm talking about, ask anyone who remembers Bugis Street in the old days).

17 December: Departed for Yangon (Rangoon) and soon ran into clear, calm weather that was to stay with us all the way to the Med. Completed our refuelling stop at Yangon without hitch and then headed for Kathmandu. Sun was setting as we started the VOR/DME step-down approach, so didn't get a chance to appreciate the spectacular view.

18 December: Wow, a whole day off! Except that I spent all the morning doing flight plans and all afternoon sorting out our impending Delhi transit with local agents. In between had a smashing lunch of chicken, rice and nan bread washed down with San Miguel beer (no, *I* couldn't' work out how the Spanish had got into Nepal either). The bill came to £1.50. Must bring the wife here on holiday.

19 December: Had planned to leave at 7am but found the airport shrouded in fog so had to wait until eleven. Took off and did the necessary spiral climb to around 7,500ft to clear the mountains before setting course. Great view of the Himalayas as we topped the haze layer – shame I was too busy to get the camera out, but I think the co-pilot got a few shots. Set course for Delhi, where we landed after 3¼ hours, then on to Karachi, thinking we would have to night-stop because of our late departure. The weather was so good, though, we decided to do the extra little five-hour hop to Bahrain, where we landed before midnight. A vague suggestion that we might get up at seven and set off again was quickly discarded in favour of a 24-hour stopover. Went off to the hotel and settled in for our little "holiday".

20 December: Another day off! Except that we would be leaving during the following night, so it would be a case of early to bed, *very* early to rise. Remembered that Christmas was coming and I still hadn't bought a thing for the missus, so walked all the way to the souk in the afternoon to get her something shiny, yellowish and metallic. Devastated to find that everything was shut because of Ramadan and wouldn't open again until long after I would be tucked up in beddy-byes. Oh dear, what a shame. She'll have to make do with chocs again.

21 December: Up before the lark for an early-hours departure for Luxor and thence to the Med. Was planning to land at Zakinthos until Athens told me there were men at work on the runway and I'd better go somewhere else if I fancied landing on hole-free tarmac. Diverted to Corfu, even though I had memories of difficult approaches there from my days with Paramount Airways and Airtours. No problems this time, though.

22 December: This was it – the last leg home. Just one more fuel stop in France (probably Troyes) and then on to our final destination: sunny Southend-on-Sea. Filled the tanks to the stopper and hauled ourselves into the air. All fine until we got to Nice, but then found everything at ground level obliterated by a layer of fog which stretched all the way to Le Touquet. How typical that our first major weather problem should come just as were getting close to home. Help was at hand, though: a thirty-knot tailwind at FL160 that sped us north. Arrived at top-of-descent for Southend with adequate juice in the tanks, a 400ft cloud-base, 4km visibility and two good funk-holes – Ostend and Le Touquet – within easy reach and in the clear. Took a slight tailwind down the ILS to Runway 24 and made the necessary "positive" landing, only to be ribbed by Mike because all the other landings had been silky smooth. You just can't win, can you?

My Round-the-World Trip in December, 2000

------▶Airline journey from London to Christchurch via San Francisco and Sydney
_____▶Delivery flight from Christchurch to Southend via thirteen intermediate stops
(each arrow indicates one sector of the trip)

Afterthoughts

Now that I've told you my story, I hope you won't mind my taking up a bit more of your time by giving you some of my own thoughts on how aviation has changed over the many years since I first became a pilot in the early 1950s. This will of necessity concern some technical matters, but once again I hope that it will be comprehensible to both aviators and non-aviators alike.

As far as the aircraft themselves are concerned, my long-haul career started on types such as the Avro Tudor, the Canadair Argonaut and the Doublas DC6, all powered by four relatively slow and noisy piston engines. Engine problems and even complete failures were a fairly common occurrence, and even well into the "jet age" — which actually began with the de Havilland Comet back in 1952, before I'd done my first Tiger Moth flight — aircraft flying on long transoceanic routes were required to have at least three engines in case one of them should fail. Nowadays, of course, jet engine technology and reliability have developed to the point where twin-engined aircraft operate on long-haul routes all over the world.

I've also seen great changes in the role of co-pilots during my career. When I first started flying on large aircraft back in the 1950s, occupants of the right-hand seat on the flight deck were seen as captains' helpers rather than true pilots, and as such they were not even required to have a rating on the aircraft if it was only carrying freight; if anything had gone wrong with the captain — a sudden heart attack, say — the chances that an inexperienced co-pilot could have saved the aircraft would have been remote, to say the least. In any case, aircraft captains were generally treated as if they were god-like, infallible creatures, with the result that lowly co-pilots would be very reluctant to question or object to their actions and decisions. These days, of course, co-pilots are trained to the same standard as captains, and great emphasis is placed on the concept of CRM (Crew Resource Management) in aircrew training. However, accidents in which poor crew co-ordination is judged to be significant do still happen, and I suspect that failures of the "human factor" will continue to feature in aircraft accident reports for the foreseeable future. To err is human, as they say.

There is also, of course, the vital matter of how pilots interact with the aircraft they fly, and I have certainly flown many types where the cockpit layout could have been thought out rather more carefully than it was. However, on every aircraft I've flown I did at least feel that it was *I* who was controlling the aircraft, both by manoeuvring its aerodynamic control surfaces (albeit with help from hydraulic systems where needed) and by setting engine throttles exactly as I wanted them.

Though I did learn to trust and appreciate developments such as "glass" cockpits and automatic landing systems, I have to admit I always had reservations about some of the very advanced "fly-by-wire" computer systems and strange new ways of linking pilot to aircraft that were developed during the last decade or two of my flying career, particularly in aircraft built by Airbus, now one of only two major manufacturers of commercial airliners in the world. (The other, of course, is Boeing, which swallowed up my "favourite" aircraft company, McDonnell Douglas, in 1997.)

As you may have noticed, of all the fifty or so aircraft types that I've flown over the years not a single one was built by Airbus. I shall therefore never know whether, had I ever flown an Airbus aircraft, I might have grown to appreciate their products, but to me there's something very odd about having a small, pistol-grip handle at the side of each pilot's seat rather than a proper control column that, when necessary, you can grasp with either hand (or both) whilst also being able to glance across and make sure that the other pilot has their hands clear so you know that *you* are the pilot doing the flying.

It also seems rather unhelpful that on Airbus aircraft (or some of them, at least) the throttle levers on the flight deck don't actually move when power is being increased or reduced by the autopilot. On the MD83 — the only aircraft I flew that also had an autothrottle system — the throttle levers would move forwards and backwards according to the demands of the autopilot, and I always liked having this easy visual confirmation of what was happening with the power settings without having to check the relevant engine gauge on the instrument panel. I don't want to sound like a right old dinosaur, but I really think that little things like this can make a difference, and there has been at least one major accident in recent years in which I feel that a more traditional flight deck design might have made a vital difference.

However, there is absolutely no denying that air travel is very much safer now than it was during the first few decades of my career, and for that I salute the aircraft companies, engine manufacturers, test pilots, licensing authorities, air traffic controllers, meteorologists and air crew who have made flying as safe and reliable as it is today.

I am very proud indeed to count myself a former member of this fantastic profession.

Summary of my aviation career		
Organisation/company	**Dates**	**Aircraft types flown**
Royal Air Force (National Service)	Early 1950s	DH Tiger Moth, DH Chipmunk, Airspeed Oxford
Channel Airways (East Anglian Flying Svcs)	Mid 1950s	**Auster Autocrat, DH Rapide**
Air Charter (London) Ltd	Mid 1950s	**Bristol 170**, Avro York, **Avro Tudor, Douglas DC4**
Overseas Aviation (C.I.) Ltd	Late 1950s	**Vickers Viking, Canadair Argonaut**
Continental Air Services Ltd	Late 1950s	**Vickers Viking, Douglas DC4**
Cunard Eagle Airways	Early 1960s	**Douglas DC6**
(1) Columbia Pictures and (2) Veens Air Service (both on secondment)	Early 1960s	**de Havilland Dove**
Aden Airways (on secondment)	Early 1960s	**Canadair Argonaut**
British Eagle International	Mid 1960s	**Bristol Britannia**
Williamson Diamonds (Tanzania)	Late 1960s	**Douglas D3 and DC4, DH Beaver, Beechcraft Baron**, Cessna 206
Zambia Airways Corporation	Early 1970s	**Douglas DC8**
Baron Air Charter, Southend, UK	Early 1970s	**Beechcraft Baron**
BIAS and Pomair (Belgium)	Early 1970s	**Douglas DC8**
Dan-Air Services, London	Mid 1970s	**de Havilland Comet 4c**
Air Malta	Mid 1970s	**Boeing 720B**
IAS Cargo Airlines (later British Cargo)	Late 1970s	**Douglas DC8***
United Air Carriers (Saudi Arabia)	Early 1980s	**Douglas DC8**
Saudia	Early 1980s	**Lockheed Tristar (L200)**
British Caribbean Airways (Br Virgin Is.)	1982-1984	**Douglas DC3, Beech 18**
Air BVI (British Virgin Islands)	1984-1985	**Douglas DC3**
Lukim Air Services (Ostend, Belgium)	1985-1986	**Douglas DC8**
Trans Arabian Air Transport (Sudan)	1986-1987	**Douglas DC8***
Paramount Airways, Bristol, UK	1987-1989	**McDonnell Douglas MD83***
Birmingham European Airways	1989-1990	**BAC (BAe) 1-11**
Airtours International Aviation, UK	1990-1995	**McDonnell Douglas MD83***
Fordair, UK (on loan from Airtours)	1992-1993	**McDonnell Douglas MD87***
Streamline Aviation (whilst with Airtours)	1994-1995	**Shorts 330**
Emerald Airways, Liverpool	1995-1999	**Hawker Siddeley (BAe) 748***
Bristol Flight Centre, UK	2000	Piper P34 Simulator

DH = de Havilland   **Bold type** indicates aircraft on which I was type-rated.
* indicates aircraft on which I was also a Type Rating Examiner (TRE).

In addition to the 27 different aircraft shown above, I also flew 23 other types, either commercially or privately, at various times; see next page for details.

Smaller aircraft that I've flown commercially on air taxi, charter or ferry operations:

Taylorcraft   Miles Messenger
Piper Apache   Piper Aztec   Piper Twin Comanche

Other aircraft I've flown:

Cessna 150   Cessna 310F
Cessna210   Cessna Caravan
Miles Gemini   Percival Prentice
Beechcraft 19 Sport   Beech Duchess
Beechcraft Queenair   Beech Kingair
Britten-Norman Islander
Piper Cub (on floats)   Piper Cherokee
Piper Comanche   Piper Seneca
de Havilland Heron   Partenavia P68
Douglas DC7c*

* This was while "hitching a lift" on an empty, US-based freight aircraft; as I already had lots of time on both the DC6 and the DC8, the captain kindly allowed me to fill the gap in my logbook by doing a take-off and landing on the DC7.

Total flying hours: 25,600
Simulator hours as instructor: 1,990
Aircraft types flown: 50
Aviation employers: 30 (plus the RAF)

Awarded GAPAN Master Pilot's Certificate in 1998
(see opposite)

THE GUILD OF AIR PILOTS AND AIR NAVIGATORS

MASTER AIR PILOT

Certificate number 794

AWARDED IN RECOGNITION OF SKILL, EXPERIENCE
AND SERVICE IN THE PROFESSION OF AVIATION

To *David Terence Willmott*

On the   3rd   of *September 1998*

BY ORDER OF THE COURT

GRAND MASTER